100% pleasure

D1303229

100% pleasure

from appetizers to desserts,
the low-fat cookbook
for people who
love to eat

by nancy baggett and ruth glick

 Rodale Press, Emmaus, Pennsylvania

Notice: This book is intended as a reference volume only, not as a medical manual. If you suspect that you have a medical problem, we urge you to seek competent medical help. Keep in mind that nutritional needs vary from person to person, depending on age, sex, health status and total diet. The foods discussed and recipes given here are designed to help you make informed decisions about your diet and health. They are not intended as a substitute for any treatment prescribed by your doctor.

Copyright © 1994 by Nancy Baggett and Ruth Glick

Photographs copyright © 1994 by Matthew Klein

All rights reserved. No part of this publication may be reproduced or transmitted in any form or by any means, electronic or mechanical, including photocopying, recording or any other information storage and retrieval system, without the written permission of the publisher.

Printed in the United States of America on acid-free ∞, recycled paper ♻

Cover design by Debra Sfetsios
Cover and interior photographs by Matthew Klein
Book design by Debra Sfetsios
Interior layout by Sandy Freeman
Front cover photograph recipes: Chocolate Layer Cake (page 324) with
    Chocolate Fudge Frosting (page 325)

Library of Congress Cataloging-in-Publication Data

Baggett, Nancy, 1943–
    100% pleasure : from appetizers to desserts, the low-fat cookbook
for people who love to eat / by Nancy Baggett and Ruth Glick.
      p.   cm.
    Includes index.
    ISBN 0–87596–191–6 hardcover
    ISBN 0–87596–368–4 paperback
    1. Cookery. 2. Low-fat diet—Recipes. I. Glick, Ruth, 1942–
II. Title.
TX714.B334 1994
641.5'638—dc20   93-28558
                                              CIP

Distributed in the book trade by St. Martin's Press

2 4 6 8 10 9 7 5 3   hardcover
2 4 6 8 10 9 7 5 3 1 paperback

Our Mission

We publish books that empower people's lives.

RODALE ❦ BOOKS

Nancy Baggett has authored or coauthored nine cookbooks, including *Dream Desserts: Luscious, Low-Fat Recipes, International Cookie Cookbook* and the award-winning *International Chocolate Cookbook*. She is a frequent contributor to *Eating Well* magazine, and her work has appeared in numerous other publications, including *Gourmet, Bon Appétit, Ladies' Home Journal, House Beautiful* and *First*.

Known for her reliable, carefully written recipes and especially for her desserts, Ms. Baggett holds a B.A. from Hood College in Frederick, Maryland, and an M.S. from American University in Washington, D.C. In addition, she's a graduate of the year-long Professional Pastry Program taught by White House Executive Pastry Chef Roland Mesnier. She lives with her husband in Ellicott City, Maryland.

Ruth Glick is the author or coauthor of seven cookbooks, including *Skinny Soups, Skinny One-Pot Meals, Eat Your Vegetables* and *Don't Tell 'Em It's Good for 'Em*. The former food editor of the *Columbia Flier,* she has written on food and nutrition for such publications as *Family Circle, Weight Watchers Magazine, Mademoiselle, Essence* and the *Washington Post*. In addition, Ms. Glick has written more than 35 novels.

She holds a B.A. from George Washington University in Washington, D.C., and an M.A. from the University of Maryland at College Park. She lives with her husband and cats in Columbia, Maryland.

Contents

Suppose your spouse loves creamy soups, cheese sauces and rich-tasting desserts. Further suppose he's suddenly told by his doctor that he has to eat a low-fat diet. You're the family cook. You would:

a) Lay down the law and tell him he has to eat brown rice forever.
b) Throw up your hands and refuse to cook another meal.
c) Sue for divorce.
d) Scurry to the library for a low-fat cookbook.

Years ago, when both of us faced this crisis, we selected option (d) and checked out the few cookbooks available. But we were disappointed with the vast majority of the recipes we found. Despite claims to the contrary, some were surprisingly high in fat. Others used weird ingredients, or they insisted on omitting flavor enhancers that had nothing to do with fat reduction, making the food so bland or odd-tasting that no one would enjoy it. They simply didn't deliver the pleasure that our families had grown to expect from our meals. Another problem was that some recipes made cooking dinner a two-day project.

Fortunately for us, we weren't limited to these alternatives. As food writers, we had years of experience developing recipes and writing cookbooks, and we'd also kept up with the latest nutritional information. So we were well equipped to devise delicious low-fat dishes of our own.

Our early successes included a creamy, full-flavored

lemon cheesecake with less than a third the fat of a conventional version. We made a great curried pineapple-chicken salad that cut the normal amount of mayonnaise by two-thirds, and then there was the split-pea soup everyone raved about.

That was only the beginning. We've been honing our skills ever since. And while we've been doing it, the importance of low-fat eating has become more and more widely recognized as a key to good health.

Eating for Pleasure and Good Health

At the heart of our philosophy is the seemingly obvious (but often overlooked) premise that food must taste good. So what if a recipe rates an A+ in nutrition? If no one will eat it, the dish has failed. Even if the food falls into the "tolerable" range, there's still a problem. The pleasure is sapped from meals, eating becomes a life sentence and all but the most dedicated give up trying to "eat right."

The strategies we've developed have served us well over the years. One key was avoiding the natural temptation to sweep every forbidden food off the pantry shelves. People hate being reminded of what they can't eat. We've found it's more constructive to play up what they can have and make sure it tastes so good they won't feel deprived.

Very few foods are banished from our tables. But the emphasis has changed. We still serve a wide range of poultry, fish, dairy products and meat (yes, meat!), but we're careful to choose those that are low in fat and to control portions, as necessary. Further, our meals are frequently built around the grains and legumes that are mainstays of many ethnic cuisines. And we employ every flavor enhancer in a good cook's repertoire—from herbs, spices, lemon zest, vinegars and wine to sugar and even salt in moderation when these are important to the success of a dish.

By the same token, we don't totally forbid fat. Instead, we use small amounts where it will provide the biggest flavor payoff. Sometimes it's a bit of extra-virgin olive oil to liven up a salad dressing or some oriental sesame oil to add flavor to a stir-fry. Sometimes it's a little margarine or butter to sauté vegetables or to pep up a sauce.

Desserts are not verboten either. We've found that if we don't occasionally offer something more sumptuous than a perfectly ripe pear, our husbands will sneak over to Sara Lee's house. Man really cannot live by bread alone. So we've carefully designed cinnamon buns, apricot bars, chocolate cake, lemon meringue pie and lots of other wonderful treats that can be enjoyed without guilt.

Over the years, our whole focus has been to make our food so appealing, tasty and satisfying that it's easy to stay with a sensible eating plan for life. Among our achievements are reduced-fat versions of macaroni and cheese, chicken gravy and fudgy brownies our families and friends love, along with a wealth of tempting main dishes, breads, salads, appetizers and snacks. In short, there's as much variety as is found in the typical American diet—if not *more*.

The Nutritional Bottom Line

While taste appeal is a vital consideration, we're very careful to make sure that our recipes are nutritionally sound. After all, our own and our family's health is at stake.

Upon reading the National Academy of Sciences groundbreaking nutrition report in 1982, we became convinced that fat was the chief villain in the American diet. Evidence of its detrimental effects has been mounting ever since. Clogging our arteries, adding unwanted pounds, increasing our risk of cancer and leaving us vulnerable to a whole host of other health problems, fat robs many of us of years of productive life.

The chief defensive measure the report advised was lowering fat consumption to *at most* 30 percent of total calories. And this is still the target number many researchers consider realistic.

In *100% Pleasure,* the overwhelming majority of recipes get fewer than 30 percent of their calories from fat. A large number of our appetizers, snacks, soups and main dishes, in fact, contain far less than 30 percent. And some dishes are completely fat free!

Surprisingly, some of our very light and healthful salads and vegetable dishes derive more than 30 percent of calories from fat. That's because they're so low in overall calories that even a smidgen of fat weighs heavily in the total count. Also, several desserts and sauces, like our reduced-fat Creamy Cheesecake with Raspberry Glaze and our Light Cheese Sauce are a little higher than the target number. But these are far leaner than traditional versions (which often get as much as 80 percent of calories from fat). If you combine these more sumptuous dishes with lower-fat foods, they can easily fit into a reduced-fat eating plan. It's important to remember that it's not the percent of fat for *each* individual dish that counts but the total percent of fat in your overall diet.

Because we want you to know exactly what you're getting, we've provided a nutritional analysis with each recipe. In addition to total fat and percentage of calories from fat, we've included figures for calories and cholesterol and the amount of saturated fat. You can use this information to select individual dishes or to plan entire daily menus featuring a whole host of dishes that won't bust your personal fat budget.

Most of our recipes also include shortcuts and streamlined techniques, since these days nobody has the time to make a career out of cooking dinner. And we won't send you off to Tahiti for exotic ingredients. On the rare occasion when we call for special ingredients or equipment, it's because they make a very useful contribution to cooking the low-fat way.

Not Just a Cookbook

This book is more than a recipe collection. It's a complete source book on low-fat cooking and the low-fat lifestyle. It pulls together everything each of us has learned about healthy cooking during our nearly 20 years of food-writing experience.

Knowing what to buy at the grocery store, for example, is a major step toward eating better. So we point out which cuts of meat and poultry are leanest, which dairy products are boons and which are busts to a low-fat diet, what to look for on food labels and which products can zip up your menus without adding fat.

When you get back home, we have a whole kitchenful of tricks for paring fat. For instance, we show you how to make light but delicious gravies and sauces and tell you how to pare the fat from your own favorite baked goods. And we introduce you to techniques, like low-fat sautéing, stir-frying, microwaving and steaming, that keep foods moist and tender but lean.

We've included numerous special features like a chapter on setting up a convenient low-fat pantry, a list of fat-free and very low fat snacks and treats, sample daily menus and a guide to making smart choices when you're eating out. We also point out that foods like nuts and avocados are surprisingly high in fat, although it is mostly monounsaturated. And we have loads of charts to help you get important information at a glance.

But best of all, we show you how to cook delicious meals that also happen to be very healthful. The truth of this was brought home to us recently when our families and friends got together to sample some of the recipes we were creating for this book.

After supper, one of our husbands pushed his chair away from the table and leaned back contentedly. "I didn't think I could stay on this diet forever, but the food is great. I never feel as if I'm missing a thing."

Not to be outdone, the other husband chimed in. "Lucky for me, I married a great cook."

We managed to look properly modest. But the truth is, we're pleased and proud that nobody who eats at our tables feels that anything is missing. Even though we're dedicated to healthy eating for ourselves and for our families, food is one of life's greatest pleasures. The recipes and tips in this book can be a pleasure for your family, too.

And the best part is that you can enjoy them without guilt.

LOW FAT: THE LIFESTYLE TO LIVE BY

Almost everyone agrees it's a good idea to eat less fat. Unfortunately, most people assume this means giving up good food. 100% Pleasure *proves this isn't true. The book is not about a restrictive diet that you go on for a few months to lose 10 to 15 pounds or to temporarily lower your cholesterol. It's about an easy-to-stay-with lifestyle, complete with delicious recipes, menu plans, shopping strategies and cooking techniques—all designed to significantly improve your health by lowering the amount of fat in your diet. It's about food so appealing, tasty and satisfying that it's effortless and enjoyable to eat the low-fat way for life.*

What's the Payoff?

Lowering fat is the *most important step Americans can take to improve our eating habits and, ultimately, to increase our chances for a healthy* life. The pluses include decreased risk of heart disease, lowered rates for colon cancer and lowered tendency toward obesity.

In studies of both people and animals, researchers have found that there is a link between diet and health. Animals whose calories are restricted live longer and show fewer signs of aging than those on more generous diets. And researchers have long recognized the relationship between eating habits in various countries and people's health.

The National Institutes of Health estimates, for example, that about 35 percent of the more than 500,000 annual cases of cancer in the United States are related to diet—most notably, high fat consumption.

The other major killer of Americans is heart disease. According to the American Heart Association, among the main contributors to this epidemic are high blood pressure, high blood cholesterol and smoking, along with obesity, diabetes, lack of exercise, poor diet and a family history of heart disease.

We have to accept our heredity, but we can control several of the other key factors—particularly our diets.

How Low Do You Have to Go?

The magic number is 30. You should get *no more than* 30 percent of your calories from fat. This number was recommended by the National Academy of Sciences in the landmark report *Diet, Nutrition and Cancer.* Relying on evidence from many sources, the report emphasized that this figure was a realistic target for the nation but noted that *even lower fat consumption should be encouraged.* This recommendation was echoed in 1985 by the National Institutes of Health Concensus Development Conference. Numerous doctors, researchers and organizations continue to endorse this guideline.

However, when health authorities first recommended lowering saturated fat in the diet to reduce the risk of heart disease, many people thought it was all right to simply replace animal fat with polyunsaturated vegetable oil and margarine and eat as much of these latter items as they wanted. Now we know that lowering total fat is the big priority.

Also, the fat picture is more complex than researchers initially thought. Dietary cholesterol was first identified as bad because it is a component of plaque—the waxy substance that builds up

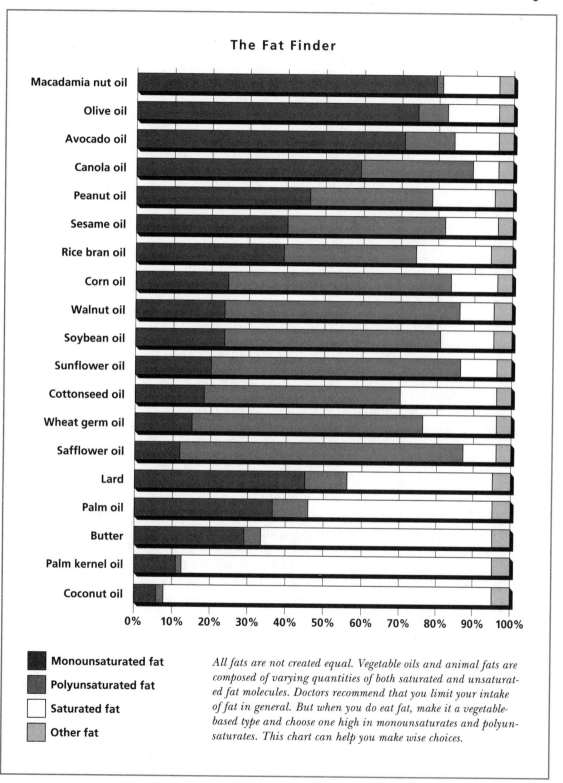

The Fat Finder

Macadamia nut oil
Olive oil
Avocado oil
Canola oil
Peanut oil
Sesame oil
Rice bran oil
Corn oil
Walnut oil
Soybean oil
Sunflower oil
Cottonseed oil
Wheat germ oil
Safflower oil
Lard
Palm oil
Butter
Palm kernel oil
Coconut oil

0% 10% 20% 30% 40% 50% 60% 70% 80% 90% 100%

- Monounsaturated fat
- Polyunsaturated fat
- Saturated fat
- Other fat

All fats are not created equal. Vegetable oils and animal fats are composed of varying quantities of both saturated and unsaturated fat molecules. Doctors recommend that you limit your intake of fat in general. But when you do eat fat, make it a vegetable-based type and choose one high in monounsaturates and polyunsaturates. This chart can help you make wise choices.

on the walls of blood vessels and contributes to atherosclerosis, hardening of the arteries. Then researchers found that one type of cholesterol—high-density lipoproteins (HDLs), sometimes called good cholesterol—has the ability to transport cholesterol molecules out of the arteries; they go to the liver and are subsequently eliminated from the body. Conversely, low-density lipoproteins (LDLs), "bad cholesterol", transport cholesterol *to* the artery walls. Because LDLs contribute to plaque buildup, they are considered a major risk factor in coronary artery disease.

The Plot Thickens

Researchers used to believe that all saturated fat contributed to the increase of LDLs in the body and that all monounsaturated fat helped decrease LDLs. Studies indicate things aren't that simple. Some monounsaturated fats act like saturated fat in the body and raise serum (blood) cholesterol. And some saturated fat—such as stearic acid, the main component of butter and also found in beef—does not raise LDLs. (This is why we sometimes call for butter as an alternative to margarine in our recipes.)

Moreover, trans-fatty acids, formed when polyunsaturates are hydrogenated (made solid, as in margarine), are implicated in raising bad cholesterol and lowering good cholesterol. Trans-fatty acids are also found in commercial baked goods, such as cakes, cookies and any other prepared foods made with partially hydrogenated oils.

Therefore, current guidelines recommend hedging your bets with regard to the fat you eat. In a diet where no more than 30 percent of the calories come from fat, the most recent advice is to get 7.5 percent from polyunsaturates (like safflower and peanut oil), 10 to 15 percent from monounsaturates (like olive oil and canola oil) and 7.5 to 10 percent from saturated fats.

So, what *should* you be eating? Start with complex carbohydrates. They are the stars in a low-fat diet and are the main component of pastas, grains, potatoes, bread and legumes, among other foods. They not only fill you up but also contribute lots of valuable dietary fiber. Vegetables, fruits and low-fat dairy products (which are a great source of calcium) play a strong supporting role, as do lean meats.

But why simply talk about what you should be eating? Let the wealth of wonderful recipes in *100% Pleasure* be your guide.

Chapter 2

THE FAT APTITUDE TEST

Here is a short, fun-to-take test to check whether you're already fat savvy or if you need a little help getting up to speed. A great score on the Fat Aptitude Test (we call it FAT for short) won't predict your success in college or a career, but it's a good indicator of how well you're prepared to plan, shop for and cook low-fat meals. It even suggests how well equipped you are to make fat-wise selections when you eat out.

If you keep abreast of health and consumer issues, you may know the answers to most of these questions. On the other hand, we've deliberately designed some of them to uncover common misconceptions and explain tricky concepts. So don't worry about a score that's less than perfect. The important thing is to pick up pointers that you can use in the future.

True or False

1. Fat is twice as fattening as starch, sugar or protein.

2. Switching to olive oil and other cholesterol-free oils is one of the best ways to lower intake of dietary fat.

3. Saturated fat is bad for you because it contains cholesterol.

4. A slice of regular deli-style cheesecake contains more than half the fat you should eat in a day.

5. Cutting back on cholesterol is the key to eating a low-fat diet.

6. Ground turkey is always a good choice for trimming dietary fat.

7. Eating more vegetables, fruits, grains and beans is one of the best ways to reduce your fat intake.

8. If a restaurant says all frying is done with pure vegetable oil, you're assured the oil has no cholesterol or saturated fat.

9. By choosing chicken instead of red meat, you're automatically eating leaner fare.

10. One-half cup walnuts has more fat than a three-ounce package of full-fat cream cheese.

11. A few simple cooking techniques—like trimming fat from meats and grilling or stewing instead of frying—can dramatically reduce the amount of fat in a meal or dish.

12. Choosing a salad bar lunch over a fast-food burger is a sure-fire fat trimmer.

Answers

1. True.
Fat is more than twice as fattening as starch, sugar or protein.
One gram of fat has nine calories, but one gram of starch, sugar or protein has only four calories. So trimming dietary fat is not only healthful but also the most effective way to cut back on calories.

2. False.
Switching to olive oil and other cholesterol-free oils does not *lower intake of dietary fat.*
All vegetable oils, from corn and olive to peanut and sunflower, have about the same amount of fat per tablespoon—13 to 14 grams. So the only way to lower intake is to eat less fat. The

advantage of switching to olive oil is that it is low in saturated fat and high in monounsaturated fat, which some studies suggest helps lower blood cholesterol. Peanut oil and canola oil are also high in monounsaturates. (Each type of cooking oil contains a different combination of monounsaturated, polyunsaturated and saturated fats as shown in the chart on page 3.)

3. False.

Saturated fat is bad for you, but not necessarily because it contains cholesterol.

Not all saturated fat comes from foods that contain cholesterol. Coconut oil, for instance, has lots of saturated fat but no cholesterol. The point is that saturated fat itself is unhealthy. This is because most types of saturated fat *raise* your blood cholesterol, and elevated blood cholesterol is a key risk factor for heart disease.

4. True.

A slice of regular deli-style cheesecake can indeed contain more than half the fat you should eat in a day.

A single slice of cheesecake made with regular cream cheese and whole eggs averages a whopping 35 grams per slice. If you eat 2,000 calories daily, you shouldn't consume more than 65 grams of fat. As a result, that cheesecake leaves you with only 30 grams for the rest of the day. Fortunately, you cheesecake lovers don't have to give up this creamy treat completely—just switch to a reduced-fat version such as Creamy Cheesecake with Raspberry Glaze. It has less than 10 grams of fat per slice.

5. False.

Cutting back on cholesterol is helpful, but it's not the key to eating a low-fat diet.

Fat and cholesterol are not the same thing. Consuming less of all fats, but especially saturated fats, is the most important step you can take when adopting a healthful diet. Reducing intake of dietary cholesterol—which is found *only* in animal products—is just one part of an effective fat-reduction plan.

6. False.

Ground turkey isn't always a good choice for trimming dietary fat.

Whether or not ground turkey is low in fat depends on which cuts were used to make the ground product. Ground turkey made from skinless breast is an excellent choice. Ground turkey prepared with the skin and dark meat can have as much fat as some types of ground beef.

7. True.

Eating more vegetables, fruits, grains and beans is *one of the best ways to reduce your fat intake.*

With a few exceptions, these foods are all low in fat (as long as fat isn't added during preparation or at the table). Plus, beans, grains and grain-based foods such as pasta and bread are so filling and satisfying that eating the recommended daily amounts of them leaves less room for super-fatty items. Current recommendations call for 6 to 11 servings of these foods each day.

8. False.

Frying with pure vegetable oil doesn't ensure that the oil has no saturated fat.

You can be certain that there is no cholesterol, but you can't tell about saturated fat. As we said, only foods of animal origin contain cholesterol. And vegetable oil obviously does not come from animals. However, the oil may contain a large amount of saturated fat. So it's not enough to know the restaurant is using a vegetable-based oil; you need to be assured it's a *low-saturated-fat oil* such as canola, safflower or corn.

But that's not all. Even if a restaurant cooks with an oil low in saturated fat, the food might not be particularly healthful. Fried foods—especially deep-fried items—are excessively fatty no matter what type of oil is used.

9. False.

Choosing chicken instead of red meat does not guarantee *that you're eating leaner fare.*

Batter-dipped fried chicken is not a better choice than well-trimmed roasted eye of beef round, for instance. Two fried drumsticks (about four ounces of meat) have more than 20 grams of fat; four ounces of the round roast has 6.4 grams.

On the other hand, if your choice is braised skinless chicken breast rather than some beef ribs, you are making a smart move. Generally, chicken *is* leaner than beef, but some cuts of red meat are low in fat. Beef top round and eye of round are fairly lean. So is pork tenderloin. Chicken isn't really healthful if eaten with the skin on or with lots of added fat.

10. True.

A half-cup of walnuts does *have more fat than a three-ounce package of full-fat cream cheese.*

The walnuts have about 35 grams of fat and the cream cheese has 30. Although most people assume all plant-based foods are much leaner than foods of animal origin, there are some important exceptions. Nuts are one. So are avocados, olives and coconut.

11. True.

A few simple cooking techniques can *dramatically reduce the amount of fat in a meal or dish.*

Simply taking care to trim all visible fat from meat before cooking can lower its fat content considerably—sometimes by 50 percent or more. A well-trimmed three-ounce serving of roasted pork loin has 11.1 grams of fat; an equal amount of untrimmed meat has almost *double* that amount, 18.4 grams.

Choosing braising or stewing instead of frying also yields impressive savings: A braised chicken leg has about 7 grams of fat, compared with about 11 grams for one that is batter-dipped and fried.

12. False.

Choosing a salad bar lunch over a fast-food burger is not *a sure-fire fat trimmer at all.*

A salad bar has plenty of pitfalls. Regular dressings, heavily dressed salads and fatty garnishes like cheese, meat, eggs, olives, avocados and fried croutons are just loaded with fat. A mere three tablespoons of ranch or other mayonnaise-based dressing can add about 25 grams of fat to an otherwise lean salad. Throw in several tablespoons of any of the toppings mentioned and you can easily bring the total to 35 grams (the same as a slice of regular cheesecake!). While the vegetables and fruits in the salad are low-fat and healthful, all the extras are not.

What Your Score Means

Give yourself one point for each correct answer.

11–12: Congratulations! You know a lot about eating a low-fat diet. Even the trickier questions didn't trip you up.

10: You have a very good grasp of the basics and just need a little help with some of the finer points.

8–9: Your knowledge is a bit sketchy. Use this book to help fill in the blanks.

0–7: Sit down and read the first eight chapters of *100% Pleasure* before you make another trip to the grocery store or go out for a meal.

SHOP TO YOUR HEART'S CONTENT

Your first line of defense in the war on dietary fat is your shopping know-how. The products you bring home from the grocery store determine what you eat week in and week out. So get into the habit of reading the nutritional panel on labels so you'll know exactly what you're buying. And consider your choices carefully as you stop your cart by the dairy case and meat counter—since there is an astonishing difference in the fat content of choices available at these two locations.

Savvy Shoppers Read Labels

Just as you can't judge a book by its cover, you can't necessarily guess the fat content of a particular food by its appearance. Or even by its taste or texture. Consider plain pasta and egg noodles, for example. They look similar, taste similar and are cooked in similar ways. But egg noodles can have twice as much fat as dry pasta. To further confuse the issue, *fresh* pasta in the dairy case can have more fat than egg noodles.

Or take crackers. All of them are dry, crisp and crunchy, but they vary widely in the kind and amount of fat used—everything from none or a little bit of canola oil to a lot of highly saturated coconut oil or even lard. You can't tell which are which by the taste or texture. Even the name isn't a tipoff, since some of the ones that sound wholesome are actually quite high in fat.

Unfortunately, until recently you couldn't even be sure of what you were getting by reading the label on the package, since some manufacturing claims were confusing, if not downright misleading. For example, statements like "97 percent fat free" and "no cholesterol" were likely to describe foods that were actually quite high in fat. Another tactic was making the serving size so small that only a Munchkin would be satisfied with that amount—but the label could advertise a minimal amount of fat and calories per serving.

Now that the U.S. Department of Agriculture and the Food and Drug Administration (FDA) have agreed on standards for food labeling, a lot of the confusion and misinformation has been swept off the supermarket shelves. Today, reading the label really is a good way to make healthful choices.

To begin with, almost all foods (except fresh meat and poultry) must have nutritional labels. Some of the exemptions include products from companies with sales of less than $50,000 a year, restaurant food, plain coffee and tea, some spices that contain no significant amount of any nutrients and packages too small for a nutritional panel. Labeling information on raw foods is voluntary.

Most labels are laid out in a new standard format and contain information on the amount per serving of saturated fat, cholesterol, dietary fiber and other important nutrients. Total calories are at the top of the list, followed by calories from fat. (To compute the percent of calories from fat, you must divide the calories from fat by the total calories and multiply the result by 100.)

Serving sizes are no longer up to the discretion of the manufacturer but are standardized for all products of the same type. This means that serving sizes represent amounts people actually eat. It also means you can look at several products of the same type and easily compare them.

A major feature of the new label is the inclusion of Daily Reference Values (DRVs) for such things as fat, cholesterol, sodium, carbohydrates, protein and dietary fiber. The DRVs are intended to give consumers an idea of how the food fits into an overall daily diet and to make comparisons clear. All values are based on a 2,000-calorie-a-day diet.

DRVs for 2,000 calories are calculated as follows:

Fat. 30 percent of calories; less than 65 grams.

Saturated fat. 10 percent of calories; less than 20 grams.

Cholesterol. Less than 300 milligrams.

Carbohydrates. 60 percent of calories; 300 grams.

Protein. 10 percent of calories; 50 grams.

Dietary fiber. 23 grams.

Sodium. Less than 2,400 milligrams.

The DRVs can help make label claims clear. Where once a food with 5 grams of saturated fat per serving could appear to be low in fat, today it would be apparent that it contains one-quarter the total allotment of 20 grams.

While these guidelines are very helpful, there *is* one problem with DRVs to keep in mind. The FDA has adopted 2,000 calories a day as the reference value and gives you the recommended amounts based on that figure. But not everyone eats that many calories—or that few. If you're shooting for 1,500 calories a day, for example, your total fat intake would be only 50 grams, and your saturated fat intake would be just 17 grams. The bottom line is that if you don't fit the 2,000-calorie mold, you'll need to do some basic calculations on your own before you can really evaluate how foods fit into your personal allotments.

One of the most beneficial features of the new labels is the standardization of terms:

Low fat. Refers to foods that contain three grams or less per serving.

Low saturated fat. Contains one gram or less per serving.

Lean. Contains less than 10 grams of total fat, less than 4 grams of saturated fat and less than 95 milligrams of cholesterol per 100 grams (3½ ounces).

Extra lean. Contains less than 5 grams of total fat, less than 2 grams of saturated fat and less than 95 milligrams of cholesterol per 100-gram serving.

Reduced. The product contains 25 percent less calories, fat, sodium or whatever than the regular form of the product. A "reduced" claim can't be made on a product if the regular version already meets the requirements for a "low" claim.

Less. The food contains 25 percent less of a nutrient or calories than a comparable food. For example, pretzels that have 25 percent less fat than potato chips can carry a "less" claim. "Fewer" is an acceptable synonym.

Light. This can mean one of two things. First, that a product contains one-third fewer calories or one-half the fat of the regular product. (If the food normally derives 50 percent or more of its calories from fat, the reduction must be in fat.) The second definition is that the sodium content of a low-calorie, low-fat food has been reduced by 50 percent.

Also, the term "light" still can be used to describe such properties as texture and color, as long as the label explains the intent. Examples would include "light brown sugar" and "light and fluffy."

The new label regulations also address a few other claims. A product selling itself as a certain percent "fat free" must be a low-fat or fat-free product. In addition, the claim must accurately reflect the amount of fat present in 100 grams of the food. Thus if a food contains 5 grams of fat per 100 grams, the claim must be "95 percent fat free."

Claims that a main dish or complete meal is "free" of a nutrient such as sodium or cholesterol must meet the same requirements as those for individual foods. However, other claims can be used under special circumstances. For example, "low calorie" means the meal or main dish contains 120 calories or less per 100 grams. "Low cholesterol" means the food contains 20 milligrams or less of cholesterol per 100 grams and no more than 2 grams of saturated fat. "Low sodium" means 140 milligrams or less of sodium in 100 grams of food. "Light" means the meal or main dish is low in fat or calories.

In the Dairy Case

There's no doubt that the food industry is responding to consumer demand for more healthful choices. All you have to do is walk through the dairy section of your supermarket to see the wealth of low-fat and nonfat products now available. Throughout *100% Pleasure,* our recipes take full advantage of these options. A few nonfat and reduced-fat alternatives can simply be substituted for their full-fat counterparts in most recipes. The majority, however, work well in some types of dishes but not others. Here's a rundown of what's available—along with guidelines and suggestions for using them.

Butter. Because it is high in saturated fat, butter's gotten a bad reputation. But newer studies have shown that the stearic acid in butter may actually be less harmful than the polyunsaturates in most margarines. So we often give you the option of using margarine or butter, as desired.

Buttermilk. Although the texture is thick and creamy, buttermilk is almost always made from low-fat or skim milk. (Check the label for details; some brands do contain more fat than others.) Buttermilk adds richness and flavor to many baked goods. It also makes them more tender. And a carton of buttermilk keeps in the refrigerator for several weeks.

Cottage cheese. A number of reduced-fat and fat-free brands are available. You can use them in place of ricotta in some casseroles, cheesecakes or other dishes. Some people also like to use low- or reduced-fat cottage cheese for dips and spreads, but we prefer the smoother texture of nonfat ricotta.

Cream cheese. You'll want to try various reduced-fat and fat-free brands, since they do vary in taste. Nonfat cream cheese is a bit bland by itself, but it can be an excellent base for cheese balls and tangy spreads. It works best in recipes that do not require cooking, although we have successfully used it in our Creamy Cheesecake with Raspberry Glaze. A few of our recipes call for reduced-fat cream cheese, which has one-third less fat than the regular variety.

Hard cheese. Most hard cheese (such as Cheddar, Monterey Jack, Parmesan and mozzarella) is very high in fat—around 9 grams per ounce. However, there are now many reduced-fat and nonfat substitutes on the market. We've tried most and find we like some varieties better than others.

All nonfat Cheddar and mozzarella is fairly bland but can be used successfully when combined with herbs, spices and other seasonings. Reduced-fat Cheddar (five grams of fat per ounce) and part-skim mozzarella are other alternatives. We use these alone in some recipes and combine them with the nonfat varieties in others.

Feta cheese is naturally lower in fat than many other cheeses. Also, because the flavor is distinctive, a little goes a long way.

Fat Exposé

Most people have gotten the message that fried foods like potato chips, doughnuts and french fries are loaded with fat. And they realize that such dairy products as butter and regular cream cheese are also fat repositories.

They've also absorbed the message that fruits, vegetables and grain-based foods are healthy. What they don't always realize is that certain members of the "healthy" vegetable kingdom can blow their fat budget sky high.

Consider: Ten medium black olives have 8 or 9 grams of fat. And an avocado has 27 to 31 grams of fat (as opposed to virtually none in apples, bananas, peaches and blueberries).

Nuts of all sorts (except chestnuts), nut butters, seeds and coconut are likewise well-endowed with fat. Think about that the next time you absentmindedly nosh on any of them. Some, like avocados and many types of nuts, contain beneficial monounsaturated fat. But eating these in quantity can lead to weight gain and make it impossible to get only 30 percent of your calories from fat.

You probably know that such baked goods as croissants and Danish pastry are diet busters, with few, if any, redeeming qualities. But it may come as a surprise that crackers, granolas and trail mixes are sometimes extremely fatty, too. Read labels carefully to ferret out the lowest-fat brands.

In some recipes, we use a little full-fat cheese. Again, because the taste is so rich, you can add a great deal of flavor with just a little cheese. Cheese substitutes, which replace natural fat with oil, are also available. If you use these, check labels for the amount of fat. It's often higher than in reduced-fat cheese.

Margarine. Because it's made by hydrogenating oil, margarine contains trans-fatty acids, which can raise blood cholesterol, so we minimize margarine use.

Although stick and nondiet tub-style margarines have about the same amount of fat (11 to 12 grams per tablespoon), we normally prefer the tub-style because it is less hydrogenated. We find that diet tub-style margarine (around 6 grams of fat per tablespoon) works well as a table spread or for adding to vegetables. However, because of its high moisture content, it is a poor choice for most baking or cooking. Note that different manufacturers have different names for their diet margarine—some use the term "light," while others call essentially the same product "extra-light." The only way to know for sure is to compare nutritional data on packages.

To confuse things further, ultra-light margarines, which have four grams of fat or less per tablespoon, also go by several different names, from "ultra-light" to "super-light" to "extra-light." Here again, check nutritional panels to be sure. We find ultra-light margarine a bit bland, but have jazzed it up and used it successfully in our Herb Bread recipe.

When solid shortening is called for in baked goods, we most often substitute nondiet tub-style margarine. It has enough body for good texture and is lower in trans-fatty acids than stick margarine.

Mayonnaise. For salads and other recipes in this book, we use reduced-fat mayonnaise (five grams of fat per tablespoon). There are several brands on the market; try them and see which you prefer. While nonfat mayonnaise is also available, we don't find that it passes for the real thing. You may feel differently.

Milk. When milk is called for in our recipes, we generally use skim milk or low-fat milk. (However, a few of our dishes do need whole milk for appealing creaminess and richness.) A few dishes also make judicious use of nonfat dry milk.

Ricotta cheese. Nonfat ricotta is very useful for making creamy, rich-tasting salad dressings, dips and spreads. For some other dishes, such as casseroles, we sometimes use reduced-fat ricotta.

Sour cream. There are several brands of nonfat sour cream on the market. As with other nonfat products, you'll want to experiment to find out which you like best. Try using nonfat sour cream, zipped up with picante sauce or chives, as a topping for baked potatoes. It also works well in Tex-Mex dishes.

Yogurt. Nonfat yogurt adds tangy flavor and moistness to baked goods as well as sauces and dips.

At the Meat, Poultry and Seafood Counters

Traditional cookbooks taught us to build our menus around meat—often a roast, steak, pork chops or whole chicken. Now it's time to rewrite the book on menu planning and make meat just one of the ingredients in a pleasurable dining experience.

Start by doing your homework at the meat counter. It's not just a matter of how much meat, poultry and fish you buy but which selections you make. All cuts are not created equal. In fact, high-fat ones have two or three times as much fat as the leaner selections. (For all the details, see the tables starting on page 351.)

Beef. Consider these figures: An untrimmed rib roast has 27 grams of fat in a three-ounce portion. The same amount of well-trimmed lean top round has only 4.9 grams. Three ounces of ground chuck has more than 20 grams of fat, while three ounces of ground round has only 7.4 grams. Simply by buying the ground round, you can trim more than 12 grams of fat per serving. Other lower-fat beef cuts you'll want to select are eye of round, bottom round and chuck arm roast.

Some markets carry lean grass-fed beef, sometimes called diet lean beef. Grass-fed beef is tougher than grain-fed, but since it has less fat, you may want to give it a try. It tastes best after long, slow cooking.

Pork. In response to consumer concerns, the pork industry has developed meat with less fat. Loin is the leanest part. Three ounces of cooked pork tenderloin has only 4.1 grams of fat, which makes it a very good choice for low-fat recipes. Other cuts that fit well into a low-fat diet include well-trimmed ham, Canadian bacon (which is smoked loin) and sirloin.

Certain cuts, of course, are best avoided or used only on rare occasion. Regular bacon, for instance, has an astronomical 41.9 grams of fat in three ounces. That's about two-thirds of an average-size woman's daily allowance.

Poultry. Some cuts of poultry are outstanding fat bargains. Your top choice is turkey breast. Without the skin, a three-ounce portion has a minuscule 0.6 gram of fat. Next best is skinless chicken breast—a three-ounce portion has only 3 grams of fat.

However, in both cases, removing the skin is a big part of trimming the fat. Three ounces of skin-on turkey breast has 6.3 grams of fat—a tenfold increase. The same amount of chicken breast with skin has 6.6 grams of fat.

Don't assume that because white meat is low in fat that dark meat has a similar composition. Actually, dark meat is relatively high in fat. A three-ounce portion of turkey leg with skin, for example, has almost as much fat (8.3 grams) as the same amount of porterhouse steak.

Then there's ground turkey. Because skin and dark meat may be included in this product, it can be as fatty as ground beef. Check the label or quiz your butcher before buying. Alternatively, purchase a boneless, skinless turkey breast and have your butcher grind it.

Two fowl to go light on are duck and goose. Three ounces of duck meat with skin has 24 grams of fat. The same portion of goose has 18 grams. Reserve either for a special treat.

Fish. Although most fish is leaner than red meat, it does vary considerably in fat content. All shellfish is low in fat. A three-ounce portion of cooked clams, crab or lobster meat has less than two grams of fat. The same portion of shrimp has less than one gram of fat. All of these are good choices.

Cod, flounder, grouper, red snapper, sole and yellowfin tuna are also very low in fat—with 0.5 to 1.5 grams of fat for a three-ounce cooked portion. These fish are such excellent fat bargains that you should consider serving them two or three times a week. Other good choices include haddock, hake, mahimahi and monkfish.

On the other hand, bluefish, catfish, mackerel and salmon are higher. In fact, three ounces of cooked sockeye salmon has over nine grams of fat, more than twice as much as skinless chicken breast. Nevertheless, these fatty fish do contain beneficial omega-3 fatty acids, which have been shown to help lower blood cholesterol and triglyceride levels. So, don't automatically dismiss them because they contain more fat.

Chapter 4

THE LOW-FAT PANTRY

When preparing the recipes in this book and planning low-fat menus, you'll find it a big help to have certain staples on hand. The following inventory is taken from our own refrigerators, pantries and cupboards and includes items that make it possible for us to turn out a wide assortment of delicious low-fat meals with no extra fuss or bother.

Your own needs will determine what you stock. If you bake frequently, for instance, you'll want dried fruit, a variety of sweeteners and several kinds of flour and flavorings on hand. No matter what your specialty, you'll find low-fat meals more enjoyable if you have a good supply of spices, condiments and other seasonings to draw on. You might even want to grow some of your own herbs, since there's nothing else like the taste of herbs such as chives, basil and cilantro fresh from the garden.

In the Refrigerator

Dairy products. Unopened, most of the following items keep up to a week—depending on the grocery store "pull date." Once the container is opened, the contents must be used fairly quickly. Unlike other cheeses, grated Parmesan will keep for several months. Since we are not heavy mayonnaise users, we buy small jars of reduced-fat mayonnaise. Our indispensables:

- buttermilk
- nonfat and reduced-fat Cheddar cheese
- nonfat and reduced-fat cream cheese
- liquid egg substitute
- stick and tub-style margarines (preferably with canola or safflower oil)
- reduced-fat mayonnaise
- nonfat and reduced-fat mozzarella cheese
- grated Parmesan cheese
- nonfat ricotta cheese
- nonfat sour cream
- nonfat yogurt (plain and fruit)

Vegetables and fruits. We rely heavily on aromatics such as carrots and celery as part of the flavoring in many of our soups, stews and other one-dish meals. We find that celery must be replenished weekly. Carrots, citrus fruit and some other fruits last longer. We value citrus fruit not only for the juice but also for the zest (the colored part of the peel), which we use in many baked goods. Frequently on hand:

- apples
- carrots
- celery
- lemons
- limes
- oranges
- pears

Seasonings and sweeteners. The wider the selection of seasonings you have available, the wider the variety of dishes you can produce. Since we love all types of ethnic cooking, we stock everything from picante sauce to hoisin sauce, which is used in Chinese cookery. We stock:

- apple butter
- Dijon mustard
- ginger root
- hoisin sauce
- jams and jellies
- ketchup
- maple syrup
- picante sauce
- pickle relish
- commercial salsa

In the Freezer

Vegetables. Although we prefer fresh to frozen vegetables, there are several kinds we do use on a regular basis:

- black-eyed peas
- corn (yellow and white)
- green beans
- green peas
- lima beans
- spinach

Meat. For convenience or to take advantage of sale items, we sometimes buy larger quantities of meat or poultry than we need and freeze the remainder. We keep a supply of:

- bone-in chicken breasts
- boneless, skinless chicken breasts
- plain (not breaded) fish fillets
- ground round of beef
- shrimp
- lean stew beef
- turkey breast cutlets

Fruit. Fruit frozen in syrup is handy for making sauces and simple desserts. Dry-packed berries are convenient for adding to fruit salads and compotes as well as to baked goods. We like to keep:

- blackberries
- blueberries
- cranberries
- raspberries
- strawberries

In the Pantry

Meat and seafood products. Because broth is both flavorful and low in fat, we use it extensively in soups, one-pot meals and a wide selection of other dishes. It's even valuable as a partial replacement for oil in salad dressings. Canned clams and clam juice are both useful for seafood chowders and other seafood dishes. We keep these items on hand:

- beef broth
- chicken broth
- bottled clam juice
- minced or chopped clams
- water-packed tuna

Tomato products. Canned tomato products are rich in flavor, almost fat free and long lasting—which makes them an extremely useful base for many of our main and side dishes. Our pantries include:

- reduced-fat spaghetti sauce
- Italian (plum) tomatoes
- stewed tomatoes
- whole tomatoes
- tomato paste
- tomato sauce

Vinegars. They're indispensable in everything from salad dressings to main dishes and are a great fat-free way to bring out flavor without adding a lot of sodium. Because these keep so well and have so many uses, we make sure that we always have a selection on hand.

- apple cider vinegar
- balsamic vinegar
- red wine vinegar
- rice vinegar
- white wine vinegar (plain and tarragon)

Oils. Since oils are at their best for only a few months after opening and because we tend to use small quantities, we buy small bottles and limit our selection to these:

- canola oil
- olive oil
- peanut oil
- safflower oil
- oriental sesame oil

Canned beans. We like canned beans because they're such a time-saver. Since they're salty, we rinse and drain them well before using. These are a few of our favorites:

- black beans
- cannellini or Great Northern beans
- garbanzo beans
- kidney beans
- pinto beans

Dry beans. Although canned beans are super-convenient, we also like to keep a good selection of dry varieties on hand. They don't take up much room, and they last a long time. Some types, such as lentils and split peas, don't need presoaking and cook fairly quickly. We particularly like legumes because they're an inexpensive, low-fat source of protein. A good assortment includes:

- black beans
- black-eyed peas
- Great Northern beans
- kidney beans
- red and green lentils
- lima beans
- navy beans
- split peas

Canned vegetables and fruits. Given a choice, of course, we'd prefer our fruits and vegetables fresh. But there are certain things that are really convenient to have in canned form. And they let us whip up dinner or dessert in no time at all, so we stock these:

- unsweetened applesauce
- water-packed artichoke hearts
- chopped green chili peppers
- mandarin oranges
- juice-packed crushed pineapple
- juice-packed pineapple chunks
- solid-pack pumpkin
- water chestnuts

Long-lasting vegetables. It would be very difficult for us to cook without onions and garlic, since they add such depth of flavor to many of our main and side dishes. Potatoes, too, play an important part in our kitchens. If we're stuck for a quick dinner idea, we often turn to baked potatoes with several toppings. We always have onions, garlic and potatoes in the kitchen.

Pasta, grains and baking supplies. A comprehensive selection of these products is invaluable for turning out tasty, filling, low-fat dishes. Consider these the basics:

- baking powder
- baking soda
- pearl barley
- bulgur
- Chinese rice noodles
- cornmeal
- cornstarch
- couscous
- nonfat and reduced-fat crackers
- graham crackers
- no-yolk egg noodles
- cake flour
- flour (white and whole wheat)
- instant nonfat dry milk
- rolled oats
- pasta shapes in a variety of sizes
- brown rice
- instant rice
- white rice
- spaghetti

Sweeteners. Many low-fat baked goods rely on the taste of their sweetener—molasses, honey or brown sugar—for part of their flavoring. Light corn syrup is an invaluable aid to reducing the fat in graham cracker crusts and some cookies since it lends crispness without adding fat. In fine-textured baked goods, sometimes only granulated sugar will do, so we keep that on hand, too. Our inventory:

- dark brown sugar
- light brown sugar
- light corn syrup
- granulated sugar
- honey
- molasses

Dried fruit. Dried fruits are featured prominently in a number of our baked goods as well as some of our main dishes and salads. They also make a good snack when you want a bit of sweetness with no fat. This is a good basic selection:

- apricots
- currants
- dates
- figs
- prunes
- raisins

Flavoring ingredients. These add a big flavor boost with little or no fat:

- almond extract
- brandy or brandy extract
- unsweetened cocoa powder
- hot-pepper sauce
- liqueurs
- sherry or sherry extract (not cooking sherry)
- reduced-sodium soy sauce
- vanilla extract
- red and white wine (you may use alcohol-free wine if you prefer)
- Worcestershire sauce

Spices. We stock so many herbs and spices that we each have three spice cabinets. Here's a "starter kit" of what we use most often. Since herbs add wonderful flavor without fat, you'll probably want to include others as you work through this book.

- basil leaves
- bay leaves
- black pepper (ground, crushed and whole)
- chili powder
- ground cinnamon
- ground cloves
- ground cumin
- curry powder
- ground ginger
- dry mustard
- paprika
- saffron threads
- thyme leaves

In the Garden

We're lucky that we have space to grow fresh herbs. Chives are our favorite because of their delicate flavor, which complements all sorts of dishes from salads to casseroles to side dishes. But we love to use sprigs of fresh thyme in our stews and tarragon in our salads. We also add tarragon sprigs to white wine vinegar to make our own tarragon vinegar. And there's no comparison between fresh and dried dill or fresh and dried basil.

If you can't have a garden, it's worth seeking out a market that sells fresh herbs. Here are a few herbs that we like to grow. Use this as a starting point for your own herb patch.

- basil
- chives
- dill
- mint
- parsley
- tarragon
- thyme

Chapter 5

P L A N N I N G
L O W - F A T
M E A L S

Do you cook every day for a family of five? How about for just a two-some? Or do you eat the majority of your meals away from home? No matter what your lifestyle, you need an overall strategy for putting together or select-ing low-fat menus. Knowing what dishes to emphasize and which to play down can mean the difference between easily following a diet that gets no more than 30 percent of its calories from fat and routinely exceeding this rec-ommended target.

Even if many of your meals are eaten out, the following general guide-lines can steer you toward the more healthful choices. The number of changes you need to consider making will, of course, depend on whether your current diet is long on burgers and fries or slanted more toward greens and grains.

If fatty meals are now your norm, you'll need to be realistic about setting goals. Instead of trying to completely give up your favorite high-fat foods, start by cutting back portion sizes and by eating those foods less frequently. Or try switching to lower-fat versions of the same items. You might, for example, substitute our recipes for lean chicken gravy, cheese sauce and chocolate cake for your usual recipes when cravings for those foods hit.

Bye-Bye American Pie Chart

You probably remember the Basic Four Food Groups pie chart. It divided all foods into four categories and told you to eat from each group every day. Well, it's time to pitch out that pie and start thinking pyramid. In 1992, the U.S. Department of Agriculture issued updated nutritional guidelines in the form of the Food Guide Pyramid.

The pyramid divides foods into five major groups and suggests how many servings you should eat from each group every day. It emphasizes the same kinds of food choices that we do throughout this book: generous quantities of grains, pastas, breads, fruits and vegetables along with moderate amounts of reduced-fat dairy foods and meats. It recommends only very limited amounts of fats and oils. In short, the focus is on foods that are hearty, satisfying and full of vitamins, minerals and fiber.

At the base of the pyramid is the grains group. Positioning it there clearly suggests that grain foods should form the foundation of your diet. This group covers a wide range of foods—including yeast breads, quick breads, rice, barley, bulgur and other grains, pasta, cereal and all low-fat, low-sugar flour products (from pancakes and pretzels to lean crackers and dumplings). Depending on your body size and calorie needs, you should consume from 6 to 11 servings from this group each day.

Above the grains are the vegetable and fruit groups. You should eat three to five servings of vegetables a day and two to four of fruit.

Higher still are the milk and meat groups. The meat group includes not just red meat but also poultry, fish, eggs and, surprisingly, dry beans and nuts. Even eating reduced-fat forms of these foods, you should limit yourself to two to three servings from each of these two groups.

At the tiny tip of the pyramid are fats, oils and sweets. There are no recommended servings of these foods. We generally get all we need of them from other foods.

The real beauty of the Food Pyramid is that following its recommendations almost automatically means eating a healthful, leaner diet. Here are some tips on putting the pyramid to work:

■ Start thinking about menus in a brand-new way. Stop focusing on meat and then adding accompaniments to it. Think instead of grain-based foods as your main dishes and use meat or dairy products as enhancements for the starches served. Dishes like pasta with cheese or rice with shrimp curry are good examples of this principle.

■ Start from the bottom of the pyramid and work up. Meals based on lots of tasty grain, vegetable and fruit dishes—with modest amounts of lean meat and dairy products—are so satisfying that there is little room left for other foods.

Putting Pyramid Power to Work

Here's a rundown of the food groups into which the new Food Guide Pyramid is divided, along with how many daily servings you should get from each group and some examples of what serving sizes are. Naturally, you'll want to choose low-fat versions of all foods.

While most of the serving sizes are straightforward, there are some things you need to know about the meat-group listings. The recommendation is for two to three servings. If you're eating lean meat, poultry or fish, count two to three ounces as a serving.

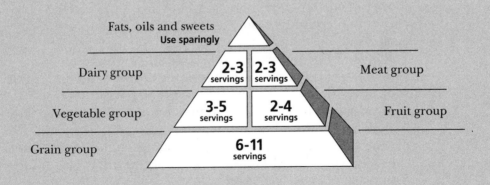

Fats, oils and sweets — Use sparingly

Dairy group — 2-3 servings — Meat group — 2-3 servings

Vegetable group — 3-5 servings — Fruit group — 2-4 servings

Grain group — 6-11 servings

Group	Recommended Servings	Sample Servings
Grains (includes breads, cereals, rice, pasta)	6–11	1 slice bread 1 tortilla ½ cup cooked rice, pasta or cereal 1 ounce ready-to-eat cereal 3–4 small plain crackers
Vegetables	3–5	1 cup raw leafy vegetables ½ cup cooked or raw other vegetables ¾ cup juice
Fruit	2–4	1 medium piece fruit (such as apple, banana or orange) 1 melon wedge ¾ cup juice ½ cup chopped fresh, cooked or canned fruit ¼ cup dried fruit
Dairy	2–3	1 cup milk 1 cup yogurt ½ cup ricotta cheese 1½ ounces cheese
Meat (includes poultry, fish, dry beans, eggs, nuts)	2–3	2–3 ounces cooked lean meat, fish or poultry ½ cup cooked beans* 1 egg* 2 tablespoons peanut butter* ⅓ cup nuts*

Equivalent to 1 ounce of meat

■ Keep in mind that seemingly insignificant "add ons," such as salad dressings, sauces, gravies, toppings, dips, butter and spreads, are major sources of excess fat in meals. To make the pyramid really work, limit those foods. Better yet, switch to low-fat versions such as the ones we've included in this book.

■ Choose foods from the meat and milk groups carefully. Even though the Food Pyramid recommends several servings from each of these groups daily, some milk and meat products contain lots of fat, so make an effort to select the leanest items. Remember that nuts, which are in the meat group, are fatty. Eat them sparingly.

■ When counting servings from the food groups, keep in mind that many dishes combine foods from more than one group. Lasagna, for example, contains pasta from the grain group, beef from the meat group, cheese from the milk group and tomato sauce from the vegetable group. And quantities do count. If the lasagna is heavy on meat and full-fat cheese, you may end up eating more than you realize of those foods.

■ Watch out for hidden fat. Depending on the particular recipe and preparation method, some usually healthful foods may be fatty. For example, delicious muffins and breads *can* be prepared with relatively little fat, but they are often very fatty. The same is true of granolas, trail mixes and myriad other foods. Read labels and select recipes carefully.

■ If you have a sweet tooth, indulge it—but wisely. While desserts are often fatty and sugary, they don't have to be. In fact, we've devised a whole chapter of sumptuous desserts that are low in fat but include generous amounts of lean dairy foods, fruits and grain products (especially wheat flour and oats). Best of all, they deliver the sense of indulgence and eating pleasure that almost everybody occasionally needs.

■ Make the pyramid the starting point for all your food choices. Few people actually eat "three squares" these days. Snacks and light meals are a major portion of what we consume, so select them with the same care you'd give full meals.

Figuring Your Fat Budget

While following the overall recommendations of the Food Pyramid is an excellent way to moderate your food intake without actually counting fat grams or calories, it's a good idea to

29 Lean Snacks and Treats

When you're snacking, it's so easy to reach for something high in fat—and to eat lots more of it than you intend. So when you really *need* a snack or feel entitled to a treat, pick an item from this list. You'll satisfy your craving and still maintain your resolve to eat smart. Items marked with an asterisk refer to recipes in this book.

angel food cake
Applesauce-Streusel Muffins*
baked potato with Curry Sauce*
bread with apple butter
celery stuffed with Blue Cheese Spread*
crab or shrimp cocktail
fat-free corn chips with picante sauce
fat-free crackers with Chutney Dip* or Hot Artichoke Spread*
fig bars or other very low fat cookies
French bread with jam
nonfat frozen yogurt
dried fruit
fresh fruit
fruit compote with Creamy Vanilla Sauce for Fruit*
nonfat fruit yogurt with fresh or cooked berries
fruit-flavored ice pops
nonfat ice milk
Meringues and Sour Cherry Topping*
Mulled Cider*, lemonade or cranberry juice
orange segments drizzled with Grand Marnier
Marinated Mussels*
pear or peach halves with low-fat cottage cheese
peppermint or cinnamon hard candy
plain bagels with nonfat cream cheese and chives or Fruit
    Spread*
plain popcorn
pretzels
sherbet or sorbet
snowballs and slushes
watermelon, cantaloupe or honeydew wedge

know how much fat you can eat and still comply with the 30 percent guideline.

There is a quick means of figuring your daily fat budget if a very rough estimate is all you want. Simply divide your normal weight (or your *realistic* preferred weight if you're slightly overweight) in half. For example, if you weigh 120 pounds, your *maximum* daily fat allowance would be about 60 grams. This rough guide method won't work if you are extremely underweight or overweight. Otherwise, it gives you a number to shoot for.

To more accurately figure a fat budget, it's best to know how many calories you consume each day. Obviously, the most precise way to determine this is to keep track of exactly what you eat during a day and then tally up the calories. However, if this task is too daunting, simply use this general guide: Most women consume between 1,500 and 2,000 calories daily; most men between 2,000 and 2,500. Naturally, your size, level of physical activity and age all affect how many calories you need each day to maintain your weight. If you are a small older female office worker, for example, you'll need fewer calories than a tall younger female exercise instructor. If you're a burly 30-year-old lumberjack, you'll need far more calories than a thin 45-year-old male computer programmer.

Once you have estimated your calorie intake, coming up with a fat budget is easy. Find your level on the table in "How Much Fat?" on the opposite page and read across to the proper column. In addition to providing fat allowances for a diet that gets 30 percent of its calories from fat, we've also included figures for a 25 percent diet and an even lower one—20 percent. Although 30 percent is often given as the target, more and more evidence suggests that getting even fewer of our total calories from fat is more healthful for most American adults. And it's easy to do using the recipes in this book.

Menus: More Pleasure, Less Fat

Frankly, the task of coming up with a week's worth of great-tasting, varied and satisfying low-fat menus was easier than we expected. Moreover, these meals deliver so much eating pleasure that it was hard for even us to believe they were healthful, too. However, the nutritional data provided along with them

How Much Fat?

If you know approximately how many calories you eat a day, you can easily determine the upper limit of your fat intake. This table gives you gram amounts of fat for three different levels of fat consumption.

Calories	30% Calories from Fat (g.)	25% Calories from Fat (g.)	20% Calories from Fat (g.)
1,500	50	42	33
1,600	53	44	36
1,700	57	47	38
1,800	60	50	40
1,900	63	53	42
2,000	67	56	44
2,100	70	58	47
2,200	73	61	49
2,300	77	64	51
2,400	80	67	53
2,500	83	69	56

proves it! For each menu item, we give the number of calories and the grams of fat. At the bottom of each menu (beginning on page 35), we tally the numbers and also provide the percentage of total calories from fat.

What kind of food can you eat on a low-fat diet? Look at Menu Four: It has Canadian bacon, Beef Burgundy, Asparagus Salad and ice cream with Chocolate Sauce. The day's totals come to about 2,300 calories and 60 grams of fat (24 percent of calories). Menu Six includes French Toast, Bean Burritos, crab cakes, potato casserole and Lemon Meringue Pie. Without the optional snacks, the figures come to about 2,100 calories and 48 grams of fat (21 percent of calories).

All dishes whose recipes are contained in this book are marked with an asterisk. The figures given are for one serving. Each of our menus includes optional snacks. Depending on your appetite and your target calorie intake, you may want to omit these selections.

Also note that our menus have the customary accompaniments like margarine or butter for bread and muffins and salad dressings for greens. We've included these because most people are in the habit of using them. However, it's an excellent idea to eat these sparingly or skip them. The additional calorie and fat savings will be considerable.

Although our menus can certainly be followed to a tee, feel free to customize them by substituting other comparable dishes. Use different recipes from this book or select commercially prepared reduced-fat foods. We hope our daily plans will also serve as inspiration for many more meals of your own.

Keep in mind as you draw up your own menu plans that it's not necessary for *each* dish to get less than 30 percent of its calories from fat. It's the whole meal and, ultimately, the whole day's menu that matters.

Start Your Day the Low-Fat Way

Traditional breakfast fare tends to be heavy on fat. But you don't have to scarf up fried eggs, strips of bacon and hash browns to gratify your appetite and your soul. Instead, look over these tasty low-fat suggestions. They'll get the day off to a good start, whether you have the time to indulge in a big hearty breakfast or just grab one that's light and quick.

■ Switch from rich sweet rolls and doughnuts to bagels, English muffins, raisin bread, cinnamon toast made with extra-light spread or low-fat frozen waffles. Or, try our recipes for Cinnamon Buns or French Toast.

■ Serve toast with jam or fruit spread only. If you can't break the butter habit, use a small amount of tub-style margarine or a super-low-fat diet spread.

■ Similarly, serve pancakes and waffles with syrup or a fruit sauce only.

■ Liquid egg substitute works well when making French toast. It even makes respectable scrambled eggs and omelets.

■ For a hot, filling breakfast, have an old-fashioned cooked cereal, such as quick-cooking oatmeal or cream of wheat. Preparation can be super-fast, and many are available in packets with low-fat flavorings like cinnamon or brown sugar.

■ Instead of fried hash browns or other potatoes, switch to

(continued on page 42)

Menu One

	Calories	Fat (g.)
Breakfast		
¾ cup banana and orange slices	71	0.2
1 cup nonfat fruit yogurt	200	0
1 Raisin-Oat Muffin*	203	4.8
Lunch		
Carrot and Sweet Pepper Salad with Garbanzo Beans*	183	6.6
Baked Ziti Casserole with Spinach and Cheese*	281	9.3
1 piece Italian bread with 2 teaspoons diet tub-style margarine or 1½ teaspoons butter	119	5.7
Molasses-Honey Gingerbread*	259	6.3
Snack (optional)		
1 Raisin-Oat Muffin*	203	4.8
1½ cups plain popcorn	25	0.5
Dinner		
Marinated Tomatoes with Oregano*	44	2.3
Marinated Thin-Sliced Steak*	220	6.4
Baked Stuffed Zucchini*	72	2.5
Easy Eggplant-Vegetable Skillet*	43	1.6
No-Bake Light Pineapple Chiffon Cheesecake*	160	4.3
Total (*with* optional snack) (24% calories from fat)	**2,083**	**55.3**
Total (*without* optional snack) (24% calories from fat)	**1,855**	**50.0**

*See recipe

Menu Two

	Calories	Fat (g.)
Breakfast		
¾ cup orange juice	83	0.1
Spanish-Style Scrambled Eggs*	54	0.6
1 English muffin with 2 teaspoons diet tub-style margarine or 1½ teaspoons butter	180	5.7
Snack (optional)		
1 Blueberry Muffin*	152	3.7
Lunch		
Microwaved Vegetables and Cheese*	124	3.3
White Bean and Pasta Soup*	239	4.5
1 dinner roll with 2 teaspoons diet tub-style margarine or 1½ teaspoons butter	132	6.6
1 Chewy Brownie*	167	4.3
1 cup 2% fat milk	121	4.7
Snack (optional)		
1 Blueberry Muffin*	152	3.7
Dinner		
Grilled Fresh Salmon with Dill*	114	5.0
Leek-and-Carrot Sauce*	81	3.5
2 Stuffed Potatoes*	286	7.0
1½ cups mixed greens salad with 3 tablespoons reduced-fat dressing	80	2.8
Banana Cream Pie*	285	6.7
Total (*with* optional snacks) **(25% calories from fat)**	**2,250**	**62.2**
Total (*without* optional snacks) **(25% calories from fat)**	**1,946**	**54.8**

*See recipe

Menu Three

	Calories	Fat (g.)
Breakfast		
¾ cup orange juice	83	0.1
Sautéed Apples*	143	1.3
1 cup oatmeal with ½ cup 2% milk and 2 teaspoons sugar	235	4.6
Snack (optional)		
1 Blueberry Muffin*	152	3.7
Lunch		
Curried Chicken Salad*	236	4.7
½ cup mixed berries with Vanilla Custard Pudding*	205	4.5
1 dinner roll with 2 teaspoons diet tub-style margarine or 1½ teaspoons butter	132	6.6
1 cup 2% milk	121	4.7
Snack (optional)		
1 Blueberry Muffin*	152	3.7
Dinner		
Roasted Sweet Pepper and Eggplant Salad*	61	3.0
Lamb Shanks with Couscous*	224	4.9
1 dinner roll with 2 teaspoons diet tub-style margarine or 1½ teaspoons butter	132	6.6
Creamy Cheesecake with Raspberry Glaze*	284	9.0
Total (*with* optional snack) (24% calories from fat)	**2,160**	**57.4**
Total (*without* optional snack) (24% calories from fat)	**1,856**	**50.0**

*See recipe

Menu Four

	Calories	Fat (g.)
Breakfast		
1 grapefruit half	37	0.1
3 Mixed-Grain Pancakes* with	570	15.2
2 teaspoons diet tub-style margarine		
or 1½ teaspoons butter		
and 3 tablespoons maple syrup		
2 slices Canadian bacon	86	3.9
Lunch		
Vegetable Minestrone*	200	3.0
1 grilled cheese sandwich made with	346	16.5
2 ounces reduced-fat Cheddar or		
American cheese and 2 teaspoons		
diet tub-style margarine or 1½ teaspoons butter		
Snack (optional)		
1 Oatmeal-Raisin Cookie*	85	2.0
1 medium peach or plum	37	0.1
Dinner		
Beef Burgundy*	493	8.1
Asparagus Salad*	61	3.2
Chinese Pea Pods with Sesame Seeds*	64	1.6
¾ cup light ice cream or ice milk with	292	6.5
Chocolate Sauce*		
Total (*with* optional snack)	**2,271**	**60.2**
(24% calories from fat)		
Total (*without* optional snack)	**2,149**	**58.1**
(24% calories from fat)		

*See recipe

Menu Five

	Calories	Fat (g.)
Breakfast		
¾ cup vegetable-cocktail juice	35	0.2
Sautéed Apples*	143	1.3
Potato, Pepper and Ham Frittata*	255	7.6
1 English muffin with 2 teaspoons diet tub-style margarine or 1½ teaspoons butter	180	5.7
Lunch		
Pasta-Turkey Salad with Tarragon*	232	8.7
Salad made with romaine lettuce, tomatoes, radishes, carrots, cucumbers and 2 tablespoons reduced-fat dressing	70	2.2
¾ cup chocolate ripple light ice cream	150	3.0
1 Oatmeal-Raisin Cookie*	85	2.0
Snack (optional)		
1 Apricot-Orange Muffin*	153	4.4
Dinner		
Pork Loin, Caribbean-Style*	432	8.3
1½ cups mixed greens salad with 3 tablespoons reduced-fat dressing	80	2.8
Broccoli and Sweet Red Pepper Stir-Fry*	64	1.9
Brown Sugar Bundt Cake with Caramel Glaze*	331	8.5
Total (*with* optional snack) (23% calories from fat)	**2,210**	**56.6**
Total (*without* optional snack) (23% calories from fat)	**2,057**	**52.2**

*See recipe

Menu Six

	Calories	Fat (g.)
Breakfast		
¾ cup orange juice	83	0.1
2 servings French Toast*	388	8.6
½ cup frozen fruit in syrup	94	0.1
Snack (optional)		
1 bagel with 1 ounce reduced-fat cream cheese	246	6.4
Lunch		
Bean Burrito*	295	6.1
1½ cups mixed greens salad with 3 tablespoons reduced-fat dressing	80	2.8
½ cup frozen fruit in syrup with Creamy Vanilla Sauce for Fruit*	145	0.1
1 cup 2% fat milk	121	4.7
Snack (optional)		
1 Apricot-Orange Muffin*	153	4.4
Dinner		
2 Spicy Crab Cakes*	146	4.6
Sliced tomatoes and cucumbers with 2 tablespoons reduced-fat dressing	67	2.1
Potato and Parmesan Casserole*	163	2.6
1 dinner roll with 2 teaspoons diet tub-style margarine or 1½ teaspoons butter	132	6.6
Lemon Meringue Pie*	364	9.8
Total (*with* optional snack) **(21% calories from fat)**	**2,477**	**59.0**
Total (*without* optional snack) **(21% calories from fat)**	**2,078**	**48.2**

*See recipe

Menu Seven

	Calories	Fat (g.)
Breakfast		
½ cup blueberries	41	0.2
Honey-Spice Granola*	372	8.4
¾ cup 2% fat milk	91	3.5
Lunch		
Old-Fashioned Turkey-Vegetable Soup*	289	7.1
1 slice bread with 2 teaspoons diet tub-style margarine or 1½ teaspoons butter	114	5.6
1 Chewy Brownie*	167	4.3
1 cup nonfat fruit yogurt	200	0
Snack (optional)		
1 Gingerbread People* cookie	175	3.6
Dinner		
Red Snapper and Shrimp Étouffée*	345	5.5
Pan-Grilled Summer Squash*	57	1.9
1½ cups mixed greens salad with 3 tablespoons reduced-fat dressing	80	2.8
Apple Crisp*	336	6.1
Total (*with* optional snack) (19% calories from fat)	**2,267**	**49.0**
Total (*without* optional snack) (20% calories from fat)	**2,092**	**45.4**

*See recipe

our oven-broiled Potato Slices.

■ Serve regular bacon only as an occasional treat. When you do, cook it in the microwave to drain off as much fat as possible. Better yet, substitute Canadian bacon (made from lean pork loin).

■ If you can't give up sausage, switch from regular varieties to lower-fat ones. Turkey sausage is often the leanest, but check labels to be sure.

Eat Well When Eating Out

It's not so difficult to stay in control of the fat you're eating when you're dining at home. The going gets rougher when you're at a restaurant where someone else did the shopping and prepared the food. But there *are* a number of strategies to help you stay within your fat budget even when you're enjoying a meal away from home.

■ If you're in a large group, order first so you won't be tempted by other diners' high-fat selections.

■ Most restaurants serve complimentary bread—which is a good nonfattening way to start your meal *if* you don't slather on butter or margarine.

■ Don't order garlic bread or cheese bread. Both are loaded with fat.

■ Go easy on the high-fat munchies that come with many meals, such as the tortilla chips in Mexican restaurants, the fried noodles served with Chinese soups, the potato chips that garnish sandwich plates and the peanuts available in cocktail lounges.

■ Many appetizers are high in fat. Be wary of fritters, fried dumplings, *anything* that's deep-fried, savory pastries and tidbits or pâtés laced with cream or cheese. Choose instead shrimp cocktail, steamed clams (without butter), smoked fish and crudités with a dip served on the side (use the dip sparingly).

■ Steer clear of cream soups. Better choices are clear soups, vegetable soups, tomato-based chowders and bean soups.

■ Don't order deep-fried side dishes like french fries, onion rings, tempura or fried zucchini, mushrooms or other vegetables. Baked potatoes and steamed vegetables are much healthier alternatives.

■ Ask for sauces and dressings on the side. Then use them

sparingly. The fat savings can be enormous.

■ Don't be afraid to make other special requests. The kitchen may be perfectly willing to broil your fish or chicken or to omit a rich sauce. Make it clear that you do not want your broiled entrée brushed with a lot of butter during cooking.

■ At the salad bar, emphasize undressed greens and vegetables. Skip high-fat items such as olives, cheese, sunflower seeds, avocados, meats and oily or mayonnaise-laden salads. If you want to indulge in a dressed salad, such as potato salad or macaroni salad, let it act as the dressing for the rest of your salad.

■ Bring a packet or small container of your own low-fat salad dressing.

■ Look for dishes that combine a small amount of meat with pasta, rice or other grains. If the two components are served separately, use the grain as the base of your meal and go easy on the meat portion. Then, take the extra home for another meal.

■ When ordering pasta, select tomato-based sauces rather than creamy types. Avoid dishes like lasagna, manicotti or stuffed shells that are loaded with high-fat cheese.

■ For dessert, select sherbet, sorbet, ices, meringues or simple fruit desserts—without whipped cream, custard sauce or other fatty embellishments. A little liqueur or brandy, on the other hand, can dress up fruit without adding fat.

■ Ask for milk or low-fat milk instead of cream with your coffee.

Chapter 6

FAT-TRIMMING TECHNIQUES

Using the right kitchen techniques is just as important as savvy shopping when paring fat from your diet. Fortunately, these procedures are really quite easy. For example, simply pulling the skin off chicken before cooking will remove three to four grams of fat per three-ounce serving. Limiting the amount of meat you eat is another easy fat-busting strategy. One way to do that is to combine small portions of meat with lots of vegetables in stir-fries, stews and other dishes. Complete your filling, low-fat meal by serving the meat and vegetables over pasta, rice or other grain, such as bulgur.

Because vegetables and low-fat cuts of meat and poultry can dry out during cooking, special care should be taken to keep the food moist. One way is to stew or braise vegetables and bite-size portions of meat in flavorful liquids, sauces and gravies. Another is to marinate the food before cooking.

This is especially helpful for food that will be broiled, grilled or lightly sautéed. Marinating infuses lean meat and poultry with extra flavor and also helps keep them moist. To slim down conventional marinades, replace some of the oil with defatted chicken broth or other liquid.

We've discovered that pureed and ground vegetables can have a number of important uses in low-fat cooking. Not only do they add texture and flavor, but they also contribute to the volume of many dishes—thus helping to make higher-fat ingredients go further. Pureed potatoes, corn and other vegetables, for example, can thicken and add rich taste to creamy soups—without using any cream. Simply remove some of the vegetables and broth from the soup pot after cooking and puree them in a blender. (You can also use a food processor, but the texture will not be as creamy.)

When making stews and other one-pot meals, add ground or grated vegetables like carrots, peeled broccoli stems, cabbage and celery stalks to the pot early in the cooking process. These vegetables contribute subtle flavor to the dishes and give them a more substantial texture. In recipes featuring ground round of beef, such as our Spaghetti and Sauce, ground carrots and green vegetables have another advantage: They masquerade as additional meat—thus making the dish seem more sumptuous.

You can also add grated or ground vegetables (along with grains) to meatballs and meat loaves. But don't go overboard or the texture and meaty taste will be affected.

Here are additional fat-cutting suggestions that are easy to fit into your kitchen routine. They cover both cooking methods and a few pieces of our favorite equipment. And we've even included a section on how to slim down your own baked goods.

Reduced-Fat Cooking Methods

The cooking method you use can have a big impact on the fat content of a dish. These are some of our favorite low-fat techniques.

Sautéing. In many instances, sautéing chopped vegetables, such as onions, celery and carrots, is a step that shouldn't be skipped, because the cooked vegetables lend rich flavor and pleasing texture to the finished dish. But while traditional recipes often call for a great deal of fat for this procedure, we've discovered that it's easy to use far less. Instead of the usual two to four tablespoons of fat, we make do with a tablespoon or less of oil or margarine and stir frequently.

This technique works best in a nonstick pan. Also, use a slightly lower temperature than usual and allow a little more time than with the conventional method. To further prevent the vegetables from sticking to the pan and burning, you may need to add two to three tablespoons of broth to them as they cook.

A second way to "sauté" vegetables is in the microwave. This method doesn't yield quite the same flavor as pan sautéing, but it has the advantage of needing *no* fat. It's also faster and easier than stove-top sautéing. Simply chop the vegetables, place them in a small microwave-safe glass container, cover with wax paper and microwave on high power until the vegetables are tender. That will probably take from 4 to 12 minutes, depending on the type of vegetables, their volume, the size of the container and the wattage of the oven. To ensure even cooking, especially with a larger amount of vegetables, you may need to stir them once or twice and give the container a quarter turn after stirring.

While we don't recommend the microwave method in all recipes, it works quite well in a number of them, such as our White Pizza. If you really miss the full-bodied flavor of pan-sautéed vegetables, you may add one to two teaspoons of oil or margarine to the vegetables before microwaving them.

Browning. Many cuts of meat and poultry have more eye appeal if they've been browned before cooking. Ordinarily, that means using a lot of fat. But you can easily substitute the following fat-reducing techniques.

For chicken: Remove the skin and trim all visible fat. Brown boneless, skinless breasts in a nonstick pan coated with nonstick spray. Cook the pieces on one side until they begin to color, then turn them and do the second side. The method works well with either bite-size pieces or larger ones. As with sautéing, this type of browning may take a bit longer than cooking in oil. When preparing stir-fries and other dishes where the chicken will receive further cooking, sauté the pieces only until the chicken has changed color or begins to brown. For salads and other recipes that call for cooked chicken meat, add a little water and continue until the pieces are completely done.

For beef or other meat cubes: Use the broiler. Coat the cubes with a dusting of flour or leave them plain. Place them in a shallow pan with a little space between the pieces. Adjust the oven rack so the meat is two to three inches from the broiler. Brown for seven to eight minutes, turning once or twice, until all sides are nicely browned. Use the same method for bones when making stock or such dishes as lamb shanks.

For meatballs: Place the meatballs in a shallow nonstick baking pan that you've coated with nonstick spray. As with the meat cubes, make sure the pieces are not touching. Bake at 350° for 10 to 15 minutes, until nicely browned on all sides. There's no need to turn the meatballs; they will brown on the bottom as well as the top. Remove them from the pan with a slotted spoon and continue with your recipe.

For ground beef: After browning the beef in a skillet in the usual fashion, turn the meat out onto a plate covered with a few layers of paper towels. The towels will absorb all the excess fat. Wipe out the skillet with more paper towels, then return the meat to the pan and continue with your recipe.

Roasting. When roasting meat or poultry, place it on a rack so that the fat can drip off and be discarded. Baste the meat with broth, wine or fruit juice instead of drippings. We also find that roasting works beautifully with vegetables. When roasting skinless turkey breast, use a plastic oven roasting bag or a tightly closed foil tent to help seal in the juices (add several onion and celery slices to enrich the flavor). This will keep the meat moist even though the fatty skin has been removed.

Poaching. In this method, food is cooked on top of the stove in water or another hot liquid that is kept just below the boiling point. Bubbles should form on the bottom of the pan but not break the surface. Poaching is a good fat-free technique to use when a recipe calls for cooked chicken breast meat. Cut boneless, skinless breasts into large pieces and poach for 10 to 13 minutes. The procedure is also an excellent way to cook firm-fleshed fish.

Steaming. In steaming, food is cooked in a closed pot using just enough water to generate steam. You can do this in an ordinary covered saucepan. Place the food in a sieve, colander, metal steamer basket or raised perforated tray—anything that will fit inside the pan and keep the food above the level of the water. Steaming preserves the crisp texture and bright color of vegetables such as broccoli and carrots. Cooking time is about

Secrets of the Rich and Thin

Here's how we slim some traditionally fatty dishes and still keep their rich flavor.

Soups, stews and stock simmered with meat or bones can contain a lot of fat. But since oil and water don't mix, fat released during cooking always floats to the top of the pot. Almost all of it can then be removed by skimming the surface with a large, shallow spoon. Don't worry if you remove some herbs as well; their essence will have already flavored the dish.

You can also use a gravy skimmer to remove fat. Strain the liquid from your soup, stew or stock into this special plastic cup that has a spout placed low on the body. The fat will rise to the top. You can then pour the nonfat portion through the spout and back into your soup, stew or clean stock pot. As the liquid level in the cup falls, the fat will eventually come through the spout, so be careful as you near the bottom of the container.

A third way to defat these dishes is to chill them overnight. The fat will form a solid layer on the top. You can easily lift it away. Since most soups and stews taste richer and more full-bodied if you make them a day ahead, this method does double-duty.

When there's no time to prepare homemade chicken or beef stock, we suggest using commercial broths. Although these products do contain fat, it can easily be eliminated using one of the methods above.

Sauces and gravies tend to be problematic because they often start with a roux, which combines equal parts of fat and flour. We use a smaller portion of fat than flour. If the mixture lumps a little, we whir the finished sauce or gravy in a blender or food processor. In some recipes that would ordinarily start with a classic, fatty white sauce, we start with a combination of milk and cornstarch to produce a thick, creamy base that can be flavored in any number of ways. We produce other sauces by braising grated vegetables until they become thick and savory. Or we reduce broth and pan juices until they thicken slightly.

Custards are traditionally made with whole eggs, whole milk and butter. You can imagine how high in fat they are! Fortunately, you can produce surprisingly creamy, flavorful custards using low-fat milk, egg substitute and just a little margarine.

the same as when boiling the vegetables. Steaming is also a good way to cook fish.

Stir-frying. In addition to requiring very little fat, stir-frying is a great way to stretch a small portion of meat or poultry by combining it with lots of vegetables. It's an excellent alternative to conventional frying. For best results, cut the food into small, thin, uniform pieces. (Or use vegetables such as snow pea pods and sprouts that are naturally thin and very quick-cooking.)

Use a wok or skillet, preferably nonstick, with a very small amount of oil added. We also add some liquid such as soy sauce, broth or wine to keep the food from sticking as it cooks. For even doneness, gently toss and stir the food constantly during cooking.

From a practical point of view, main-dish stir-fries have the added bonus of saving cooking and clean-up time because most of the meal's components cook in one pan.

Indispensable Equipment

Basically, we use the same kitchen equipment for low-fat cooking that we've always used for preparing meals. But we've found that three additions to our kitchens have been very useful. These are nonstick skillets, a Crockpot or other slow cooker and a microwave oven. Because the microwave is so useful and microwave cooking techniques differ somewhat from conventional methods, we'll discuss it in its own chapter (see page 56).

Nonstick skillets. Pans with a nonstick coating are invaluable for sautéing and stir-frying using minimal amounts of oil or margarine. We find it convenient to have several sizes to accommodate both small and large cooking jobs. Metal utensils damage most types of nonstick surfaces, so be sure to use wooden or plastic spoons and spatulas with these pans. Follow the manufacturer's instructions for seasoning and cleaning nonstick skillets.

Crockpot or other slow cooker. Many ingredients can be put into a slow cooker without sautéing them first, so there's really no need to use extra fat. Onions, garlic, other vegetables and some cuts of meat are among those foods. Ground meat is an exception; it must be browned in a pot on the stove first. Drain off all the fat before adding the meat to the slow cooker.

There are a number of special techniques important when using a slow cooker. For example, you should cut vegetables into small, uniform pieces for even cooking. Layer them at the bottom of the pot because they actually take longer to cook than meat.

Try not to remove the cover during cooking, because that results in a significant loss of heat. To have a peek at the cooking food, shake the lid back and forth without actually lifting it. This will knock off the droplets of condensed moisture that would otherwise obscure your view.

One prime attraction of the slow cooker is that you can have a meal cooking while you're at work or out of the house. On the high setting, many dishes take 3½ to 4½ hours. On the low setting, the time stretches to 6 to 9 hours. In either case, you don't have to worry about the food, since it's almost impossible to overcook anything in a slow cooker. You should be aware that the long, slow cooking process does change the taste of some herbs and spices—so the seasonings of conventional recipes may need to be adjusted.

If you don't already have a slow cooker, we recommend buying the largest size—five quarts—because it's very convenient for the preparation of family meals. Also, look for one with a removable ceramic well, since this makes cleanup a snap.

Fat-Bust Your Baked Goods

In all the baked goods in this book, we've already done the fat-busting for you. While it might not be obvious, we've taken a number of steps to remove excess fat and at the same time made important adjustments to preserve appealing texture and taste.

Below are the details of some of the techniques we used. Follow them to slim down your own favorite recipes. In most cases, nutritionally improving baked goods will involve a little trial and error. Try our suggestions, check the results and then make further changes as needed.

Keep in mind that your slimmed-down recipes are much more likely to have a pleasing taste and texture if you avoid making radical changes. Creating truly tempting *reduced-fat* versions of dishes is a realistic goal; creating tasty *no-fat* versions at home usually is not. Moreover, it isn't even necessary to eliminate all fat from your recipes for them to be healthful, as the nutritional analyses provided with all the baked goods and desserts in this book prove.

We should emphasize that simply replacing all fatty ingredients with nonfat versions of themselves isn't the best way to approach slimming your recipes. With some ingredients, this might work. But in many cases, a better idea—with better results—is to use less of something fatty rather than none at all. Here are some of the ingredients that fatten up cakes and other baked goods, along with our guidelines for cutting back on them.

Chocolate. Replace *some* of the unsweetened chocolate called for with unsweetened cocoa powder. Although chocolate and cocoa are both "chocolatey," a one-ounce block of unsweetened chocolate has 15 grams of fat, while a comparable amount of unsweetened cocoa powder has about 3 grams. So, in recipes that call for all unsweetened chocolate, replace an ounce or two of it with cocoa. Use 2 to 2½ tablespoons of cocoa for every ounce of unsweetened chocolate removed. If this substitution is successful, you might try replacing an even larger portion of chocolate with cocoa the next time you prepare the recipe.

It is risky to replace *all* the chocolate with cocoa, because the two don't taste exactly the same. Let's face it, the chocolate has a more full-bodied flavor. Also, in some recipes, removing all the chocolate may leave the dough or batter so lean that it lacks tenderness.

Substituting cocoa for *sweetened* chocolate is complicated by the fact that some sugar usually has to be added along with the cocoa to compensate for the sugar in the chocolate. Moreover, semisweet chocolate is often milder than either unsweetened chocolate or cocoa powder, so the substitution may alter the taste of the end product.

Milk chocolate is an even more complicated proposition. It is milder *and* it contains milk solids, which are not that easy to replace with something else. Still, if you enjoy experimenting, you can achieve significant fat savings.

Eggs. You'll want to trim back on egg yolks in baked goods. The yolks have all of the fat and cholesterol in an egg (about five grams of fat and around 215 milligrams of cholesterol per large yolk). So, limiting or omitting yolks can be an effective means of reducing fat.

There are two basic ways to avoid using yolks: Use only egg whites or switch to liquid egg substitute. In *most* baked goods, either of these approaches will work, and both have advantages.

It's really a matter of which you prefer. Recipes that are not good candidates for eliminating all egg yolks include cakes, cookies and breads that depend on yolks for either a very tender crumb or a distinctive custardy flavor. In such recipes, you may be able to *reduce* the number of yolks used and still have good results.

Liquid egg substitute is formulated to look and taste like slightly beaten whole eggs. The effort is only partially successful; it does look like regular eggs, but it does not have the characteristic egg taste. Egg substitute is, however, quite convenient. Using it, you're spared the bother of separating whole eggs and discarding the yolks. All you do is measure out the product from a carton. Egg substitute is composed of egg whites, which the manufacturer combines with a bit of vegetable-based coloring, gums, flavorings and sometimes salt.

Some brands taste better than others, and some have considerably more salt and fat than others, so read labels and try different brands to decide which you like best. To replace whole eggs with liquid egg substitute in your favorite recipes, use 3½ to 4 tablespoons of the product for every large whole egg omitted.

Unlike liquid substitute, egg whites are always the same—fat free and with no salt, gums, flavorings or additions of any kind. To substitute egg whites for whole eggs in baked goods, use one large white plus one teaspoon of water for every whole egg omitted. Note that, contrary to many recommendations, it is not usually necessary to use *two* large whites to replace a whole large egg. In fact, adding extra whites can sometimes make baked goods tough and dry. That is because the white of the egg contains most of the proteins that hold dough together, and too much binding produces toughness.

Fat. You're generally safe using a little less fat than the recipe specifies. For example, if the recipe calls for one-half cup vegetable oil, experiment with one-third cup. Just this simple step will trim more than 30 grams of fat! If the recipe is still fine with the reduced amount of fat, either keep making it that way or try removing a little more the next time you prepare it. If you like, keep trimming until the quality of the baked good is affected and then retreat to the last reduction that yielded appealing results.

To determine whether a recipe has already undergone defatting during development (and thus can't be successfully

Low-Fat Baking: Making Adjustments

Fat plays an important role in the baking process. It helps keep dough tender, prevents dryness in various types of baked goods and boosts flavor. When you cut back on fat, you need to make adjustments in both your techniques and other recipe ingredients. Here are some tips for doing that.

Tenderizing. Fat helps tenderize baked goods by waterproofing flour particles. That prevents the flour from forming tough protein strands (called gluten) that otherwise naturally develop when flour gets wet and is then stirred.

There are two easy ways to help minimize gluten development in lean baked goods: One is to mix the batter or dough as little as possible after wetting it. The second is to use a low-gluten flour, such as cake flour or soft wheat pastry flour, instead of all-purpose flour. This substitution is particularly helpful in cakes but can also be beneficial if you're striving for very tender muffins and quick breads.

Moisturizing. Fat has a moisturizing effect in baked goods. It helps keep the flour from soaking up all the liquid (thus freeing up some to add moistness to the finished product). And due to its unique oily consistency, it provides a smooth, almost slippery feeling to a cake or quick bread crumb.

Fortunately, a number of other ingredients can help prevent dryness in lean doughs. In quick breads, muffins and some cakes, try adding pureed or shredded fruits or vegetables. Ripe bananas, applesauce, apple butter, pureed prunes, pumpkin puree, shredded zucchini and grated carrots are all good choices. Nonfat yogurt works very well in cakes. When making cookies, try corn syrup or honey (most of the other ingredients we just suggested would give your cookies a cakelike texture that you might not find desirable).

Flavoring. Fat carries and amplifies flavors and aromas. When you cut back the fat, you need to increase the amount of flavorings you use. You might, for example, try doubling the amount of vanilla. Or you could use half again as much spice, citrus zest or almond extract. Other flavor enhancers include brandy, brandy extract, various types of liqueur, coffee, molasses and dark brown sugar.

trimmed much more), use this rough guide: Muffin and quick bread batters containing more than two tablespoons of oil or margarine per one cup of flour, cornmeal or rolled oats may be candidates for further fat reduction. Likewise, cake batters and cookies containing more than three tablespoons of oil or margarine per cup of flour *may* be suitable candidates. (The *exact* minimum amount of fat needed varies considerably depending on the type of cake or cookie.)

Besides simply trimming fat, you may also want to try switching to a less saturated or less hydrogenated type than the one originally specified. That's because saturated and hydrogenated fats tend to raise cholesterol more than other fats. You might, for example, use canola margarine or oil to replace some of the butter. Or substitute regular tub-style margarine for stick margarine.

When making cookies, proceed with care. Substituting tub-style margarine for a more solid fat may cause the dough to be softer than desired. The cookies will spread or run more than usual during baking. A better approach is to experiment by replacing just a small part of the specified fat. It's best not to attempt to substitute *diet* tub-style margarine in any baked goods, as this product contains a large amount of moisture and can radically alter the results.

Milk. You can generally substitute skim milk for whole milk in cakes, muffins, quick breads and other baked goods. In most cases, there will be no detectable difference in the taste or texture. This simple replacement can save you about eight grams of fat per cup used.

Nuts. You can reduce the number of nuts in recipes or omit them altogether. While nuts don't have a lot of *saturated fat,* they are nevertheless extremely fatty. One cup of most kinds has about 70 grams of fat.

To make a reduced quantity of nuts go further, intensify their flavor by briefly toasting them: Spread them in a rimmed baking sheet and toast at 350°, stirring occasionally, just until fragrant and lightly browned. Let cool completely before using.

Sour cream. Try using plain nonfat yogurt or fat-free sour cream to replace regular sour cream in cakes, coffee cakes, muffins, breads and such. While both of these lean alternatives work well, they produce slightly different results, so you might want to try each to decide which you prefer in various recipes.

Although yogurt can impart a strong taste to fillings and sauces, in baked goods it lends a pleasant flavor as well as moistness and tenderness. In fact, it works much as sour cream does. The key difference is that nonfat yogurt contributes no fat, and regular sour cream contributes about 48 grams per cup.

When you choose fat-free sour cream to replace regular sour cream, be aware that your results will vary somewhat depending on which brand you use. In general, nonfat sour cream usually yields a slightly lighter, fluffier texture and a creamier, richer taste than nonfat yogurt. On the other hand, it contributes a little less moistness to baked goods. (This can be partially offset by adding a tablespoon or two of water.)

Chapter 7

WAVE GOOD-BYE TO FAT

The microwave oven is a very effective tool for minimizing fat. For one thing, food can be cooked absolutely fat free, without any chance of burning or sticking. Also, some low-fat dishes cook much more quickly or conveniently in a microwave than in a conventional oven or on the stove top.

The microwave is particularly useful for "sautéing" vegetables using little or no fat and for getting low-fat foods like baked potatoes on the table in a hurry. It's also helpful for defrosting foods quickly. (Use the defrost setting and follow the directions that came with your unit.) There are a number of other quick and easy applications for which the microwave is well suited, and we cover them later in this chapter.

But first, let's review a few of the variables that make microwaving a slightly trickier method of cooking than conventional means.

Getting Up to Speed

Keep in mind that there is a huge difference in the speed at which microwave ovens operate. That makes it difficult for us to give cooking times that will work for all models.

Our recipes were designed using microwave ovens with 650 watts of power. But because microwaves of the same power might differ in cooking times, we do give a range of times in our recipes. If your microwave has more or less power than ours, you may need to decrease or increase cooking time accordingly.

Besides the wattage, several other factors affect the length of cooking time:

Efficiency. Some ovens are better designed than others and thus cook faster.

The amount of food being cooked. The more food, the longer it takes to heat it. That's because microwave ovens generate the same number of waves no matter how much food is placed inside.

The size and shape of the dish. A container that is too large for the amount of food will increase the cooking time, so follow dish and casserole specifications carefully. Also, a round or rounded container cooks more efficiently than an elongated one, which tends to overcook food in the squared-off corners.

The type and condition of the covering being used. Wax paper, paper towels, plastic wrap and glass or plastic casserole lids can all be used to cover food being microwaved. Paper towels work best for bread. We prefer wax paper or casserole lids for most other microwaving jobs. While plastic wrap holds in more steam than wax paper, the plastic could adhere to the food. Therefore, you should not use plastic wrap if the wrap will touch the food.

Getting Even

Uneven cooking is a problem with microwave ovens, including those with turntables. The problem is that the waves produced simply do not hit all interior areas of the oven equally. In general, food in the center of a dish cooks more slowly than that at the sides. This is why we are so specific about the placement of the food or the dish in some recipes.

Stirring the contents of a dish during the microwaving period helps ensure uniform doneness. To make it easier to do this without removing the container from the microwave, you may want to purchase special utensils with bent handles. Naturally, stirring is appropriate for only some types of dishes. For microwave ovens without a turntable, rotating the container several times during the cooking period helps ensure that foods that can't be stirred will cook more evenly.

Micro Tips

Here are some tips for cooking or reheating various dishes in the microwave. The directions are all designed for microwave ovens with a turntable. If your oven does not have one, stop and give the dish a quarter turn every few minutes.

Acorn squash. Prepare a tasty, healthful side dish in a jiffy as follows: Select squash that are ¾ to 1 pound each. Cut each in half lengthwise and scoop out the seeds. Arrange the halves, cut side down, around the perimeter of a microwave-safe plate. Make sure they're evenly spaced and that the pointed (stem) ends face toward the center. Microwave two halves on high for three to four minutes; allow six to seven minutes for four halves.

Turn the halves so the cut sides face up. To each cavity, add one-quarter teaspoon tub-style margarine or one-half teaspoon maple syrup (or both). Prick the flesh several times with a fork so the flavorings can permeate the squash (but don't pierce the skin or the flavorings will drip out). Lay a large sheet of wax paper over the squash halves. Microwave on high power until the halves are tender when pierced with a fork at the thickest end—that would be about three to four minutes for two halves and six to seven minutes for four. Season lightly with salt and pepper before serving, if desired.

Apples. Here's how to prepare a fast, fat-free side dish or dessert: Core an apple and cut it crosswise into half-inch-thick slices. Arrange the slices in a circle around the perimeter of a microwave-safe plate. Sprinkle with cinnamon (and a little sugar, if desired). Cover loosely with wax paper and microwave on high power until tender, two to four minutes, depending on the amount prepared.

Bacon. If you *must* treat yourself to bacon occasionally, you can eliminate an amazing amount of fat by microwaving the slices. Place them between double or triple thickness of paper towels and place on a microwave-safe plate. Two slices will take anywhere from 1½ to 2½ minutes. Give the plate a quarter turn after 45 seconds. Check after another 45 seconds and microwave longer, if necessary.

Chicken or turkey breast. To cook breast meat for use in salads, sandwiches, casseroles and such, place 1 to 1¼ pounds of boneless, skinless chicken breast halves or turkey breast slices on a microwave-safe plate. If the pieces are not evenly thick, arrange them so the thickest parts are toward the outside of the plate. Sprinkle the poultry with one tablespoon defatted chicken broth, water or wine. Loosely cover the plate with wax paper. Microwave on high power for four to eight minutes, or until the meat is opaque at the thickest part; be careful not to overcook.

Eggplant. This vegetable has always been a challenge for those hoping to cut back on fat because eggplant soaks up oil like a sponge. But you can decrease considerably the amount needed to sauté eggplant cubes if you partially cook them in the microwave first. Spread the cubes in an even layer on a microwave-safe plate, leaving the center of the plate open. Sprinkle with two tablespoons water and cover loosely with wax paper.

Microwave on high power until the eggplant is just slightly softened but not mushy, two to four minutes, depending on the amount. Stir once or twice during microwaving and test for doneness with the tines of a fork. Drain the eggplant well; pat dry with paper towels. Then proceed with sautéing, using only a teaspoon or two of fat.

Grilled cheese. Have a craving for an occasional grilled cheese sandwich? You can make one that's much lower in fat than usual with the microwave. Start by toasting two slices of bread. Slip a slice of reduced-fat cheese between them. Place the sandwich on a paper towel in the microwave. Cook on high power for 20 to 30 seconds. Add interest—but not fat—by topping the melted cheese with thin slices of tomato and microwaving about 10 seconds longer. For even more flavor, garnish with alfalfa sprouts or a little picante sauce just before serving.

Mixed-vegetable casserole. For a quick side dish, combine about two cups peeled potato cubes and a small chopped onion in a 2½-quart microwave-safe casserole. Cover with the casserole lid and microwave on high power for six to eight minutes, stopping and stirring once, until the potatoes are partially cooked. Add three cups mixed quick-cooking vegetables such as zucchini slices, yellow squash slices, strips of sweet red or green peppers and broccoli or cauliflower florets. Cover and microwave for an additional six or seven minutes, stopping and stirring once, until the vegetables are tender. Serve with a sprinkling of herb seasoning. Or stir in two teaspoons of diet margarine.

Potatoes. The microwave oven makes it possible to serve baked potatoes with virtually no advance planning. Instead of taking the usual hour or more, they can be ready in a few minutes. Use the potatoes as a filling low-fat side dish or as a healthful entrée with a lean topping. Before cooking, pierce each potato several times. Line a microwave-safe plate with a paper towel. Arrange the potatoes on the towel in a spókelike pattern,

Potato Power

A few years ago, *the* fad food in shopping malls across the country was the baked potato—decked out with a variety of tempting, although often fattening, toppings.

Since a baked potato is one of the most satisfying low-fat foods you can eat, bringing this concept home from the mall is an excellent idea. The best part is that you don't need any fattening accompaniments to create a tasty, filling meal if you rely on low-fat sauces and other toppings.

One of our favorite lunches is a fluffy baked potato served with nonfat or light sour cream, picante sauce and a little shredded reduced-fat Cheddar cheese.

Other appealing toppings include recipes from this book:

Light Cheese Sauce (with steamed vegetables, such as
  zucchini, carrots and cauliflower)
Chili con Carne
Curried Cauliflower and Carrots
Curry Sauce
Microwave Baked Beans
Nonfat Topping for Vegetables
Ratatouille
Shrimp in Curried Tomato Sauce
Turkey Sloppy Joes (filling)
Vegetarian Chili

spacing them at least one inch apart so the microwaves can circulate properly.

Microwave on high power—baking time will vary greatly depending on the number, weight and shape of the potatoes. Here are some rough guidelines: Two eight-ounce potatoes will require approximately 6 to 9 minutes; four will take 10 to 14 minutes. To encourage even baking, stop once during the process and roll each potato over and rotate a quarter turn. Do this even if you have a turntable.

To test for doneness, pierce each potato at the thickest part using a sharp, thin knife; the knife should slide through the flesh easily. Note that the potatoes may not all be done at the same time. Be aware also that they will continue to cook after you remove them from the microwave, so be careful not to overdo them.

If you like a crisp skin on your spuds, microwave them until just tender, then pop them into a conventional oven for a few minutes.

Rice or pasta. Neither of these foods cooks faster in a microwave than on the stove. But both reheat very nicely and can provide you with an instant low-fat pilaf or a bed for meat or vegetables. Place each rice or pasta serving on a microwave-safe dinner plate and cover with wax paper. Microwave on high until heated through, about 30 to 45 seconds for a three-quarter-cup serving. To do a larger batch, spread the rice or pasta in a shallow layer in a large microwave-safe dish or platter. Cover with wax paper and microwave on high until heated through. The exact time will depend on the amount of food being heated.

Risotto. As we said, microwaving rice is not a quick way to cook it. However, the microwave takes virtually all the work—and time-consuming, arm-tiring stirring—out of risotto. See our recipes for Easy Risotto and Seafood Risotto for details.

Sweet potatoes. Bake them using exactly the same method as for white potatoes. Since they bake a bit more rapidly, allow 4 to 8 minutes for two eight-ounce sweet potatoes. Four potatoes should take 8 to 12 minutes.

A READY REFERENCE

Consider this chapter the quick reference section of 100% *Pleasure. If you want low-fat tips on buying or preparing a particular kind of food, such as bread, dairy products or meat, or if you need strategies for keeping the fat in desserts or snacks to a minimum, check out these suggestions. This is a compilation of the things we learned during our years of low-fat cooking.*

Bread

From dark, flavorful European rye to buttery croissants, there are dozens of breads to choose from. The surprise is how much they vary in fat content. With croissants, "buttery" is the operative word. Each has about 17 grams of fat, compared with 1 gram or less in a whole French baguette. So read labels before you buy.

■ Many bakeries sell muffins along with their doughnuts and Danish pastries. Although muffins *can* be low in fat, most commercial ones are not. Check labels if they're available or inquire about the fat content before you buy.

■ For sandwiches, choose low-fat breads such as pita, French bread or a loaf specifically advertised as reduced in fat or calories. (Check the label to make sure the claims hold up.)

■ Try some of our quick and easy recipes for low-fat homemade breads and muffins. They all get less than 30 percent of their calories from fat—often far less.

Dairy Products

Not so long ago the only nonfat dairy products widely available were skim milk, nonfat dry milk and some brands of buttermilk. Now there's a low- or reduced-fat version of everything from sour cream to ricotta cheese. And all are a boon to low-fat cooking. If you haven't already sampled these products, give some of them a try. The ones you like best will be a matter of individual taste. Here's how to take full advantage of the low-fat products:

■ Use nonfat yogurt in place of regular yogurt.

■ Replace whole milk or two percent fat milk with skim or one percent fat milk.

■ Switch from full-fat cheeses to reduced-fat varieties. Note that feta cheese is lower in fat than most other hard cheeses.

■ Choose sharp Cheddar over the milder variety. It provides more taste per ounce. Of the full-fat cheeses, Parmesan, blue and Roquefort taste so robust that you need very little.

■ If nonfat cheeses are too bland for your taste, combine them with regular or reduced-fat cheese. This is often a good idea for dips and spreads.

■ For quick, low-fat pizza, use a store-bought crust and nonfat or low-fat pizza sauce. Top with nonfat or reduced-fat mozzarella. For extra flavor and texture, add chopped or sliced vegetables such as zucchini, mushrooms, onions and green peppers. Skip the pepperoni, ground beef or sausage, or at least go very light on them.

■ Make grilled cheese sandwiches in a nonstick skillet or a microwave (see page 59). Or use a toaster oven to melt shredded cheese sprinkled on bread slices or bagel halves.

■ Never use full-fat cream cheese as a spread for bread—it's just too high in fat. Light cream cheese has one-third less fat and tastes almost the same. For even less fat, try some of the nonfat cream cheese spreads. If you want, combine them with light cream cheese for added texture and flavor.

■ Replace all or part of the cream cheese in homemade spreads with nonfat ricotta or fat-free cream cheese.

■ For cooking, switch from stick to tub-style margarine. The latter has less hydrogenated fat.

■ As a spread for bread, try diet tub-style margarine. It's particularly good with some herbs stirred in.

Desserts and Baked Goods

One persistent bit of conventional wisdom is that you have to give up desserts to eat a low-fat diet. But that's not really true. All of the sweet treats and baked products in *100% Pleasure* are designed to fit into a diet that gets 30 percent or fewer calories from fat. Many, like our Apricot Bars and our Fresh Cherry Compote, are in the 5 to 15 percent range. A few others are higher but still have less fat than conventional versions of the same desserts. Tips:

■ Choose desserts that rely on fruits, spices or cocoa rather than butter, eggs, nuts or chocolate for their flavor.

■ Switch from regular ice cream to ice milk, light ice cream, low-fat frozen yogurt or low-fat yogurt pops. Read labels since the fat content of these products can vary considerably.

■ If plain fruit seems too plain, try dressed-up fruit desserts like baked apples, poached pears or berries with a creamy low-fat sauce, such as Vanilla Custard Pudding.

■ For pies, tarts and cobblers, a single crust obviously contributes less fat than a double one. In many cases, you can simply omit the top crust. If the top of the pie seems bare, use a streusel topping or add a few decorative pastry cut-outs or perhaps a very open lattice crust. Rolling the pastry dough *very* thin can likewise eliminate some excess fat.

Flavor Enhancers

Use commercial or homemade salsa, picante sauce, chutney or one of our low-fat sauces to spice up foods that would otherwise seem plain. Try combinations like picante sauce on vegetable quesadillas or chutney on vegetable curry. Or use flavorful chopped fresh herbs, such as fresh dill on salmon or chives and parsley on baked or boiled potatoes. Experiment with lemon juice, lime juice, hot sauce, vinegar, soy sauce, chicken broth, beef broth and wine.

Meat and Poultry

A whopping portion of the fat in the typical American diet comes from meat. But that doesn't mean you have to banish a favorite food from your table in order to eat healthfully. In fact, it's possible to consume a diet with as little as 20 to 25 percent calories from fat and still enjoy meat on a regular basis. All you have to do is buy low-fat cuts, control portion size and take our fat-trimming tips to heart.

Remember that most guidelines recommend a serving size of only three ounces. If you routinely cook a big roast and serve the whole thing on a platter, you'll be encouraging overconsumption. Instead, emphasize interesting dishes like stir-fries, skillet dinners, one-pot meals, stews and soups. The idea is to cut the meat into small serving pieces and combine it with lots of vegetables and grains or beans. If you like to serve larger pieces, cut them into very thin slices to make a modest amount of meat look generous. In addition:

■ Buy low-fat cuts such as round of beef, pork loin, turkey breast and chicken breasts.

■ Before cooking, trim all visible fat. This simple step can make a surprising difference. For example, three ounces of untrimmed beef chuck arm has 21.9 grams of fat. Trimmed, the same cut has 7.4 grams.

■ Pull off and discard poultry skin. If the skin is difficult to hold, grasp it with a paper towel. Also be sure to trim off the yellow bits of fat right under the skin. These two steps will remove about half the fat from a chicken breast.

■ When browning ground beef, always remove the excess fat by draining the meat on a plate lined with paper towels.

■ Give soups a rich, meaty flavor—without actually adding meat to them—by preparing the stock with beef, pork, lamb or veal bones. Since bones, especially marrow bones, contain considerable fat, be sure to skim the stock well before using it. The best way is to refrigerate it until the fat hardens and then lift it off. Alternatively, remove the fat by skimming it off with a large, shallow spoon or by pouring the stock into a spouted skimmer device.

■ Use any of these same methods when making gravy. In addition, make gravy with low-fat ingredients like defatted broth and low-fat milk or water.

■ Several times a week, replace the meat on your table with low-fat fish and seafood such as cod, flounder, grouper, haddock, hake, turbot, clams and shrimp.

Salads

You may think salads *must* be healthy since they're chock-full of crunchy fresh vegetables and leafy greens. But unless you go easy on the dressing or other add-ons, a salad can also be chock-full of fat. Made the traditional way, a salad dressing can blow your fat budget for the entire day. Toss on some nuts, seeds, bacon bits, fried croutons, olives and cheese cubes, and the fat count can go through the roof. Here are some ways to make sure salad *is* a healthy part of your diet:

■ Just a little dab of dressing will do ya! If you must have a traditional dressing, serve it on the side and use it sparingly.

■ When making dressings, use more lemon juice or vinegar and less oil than conventional recipes call for. For extra flavor, experiment with highly flavored oils such as walnut or extra-virgin olive oil. Try different types of vinegar, including raspberry, tarragon, balsamic and rice wine.

■ Try a selection of nonfat or reduced-fat salad dressings to find ones you like. Or make your own from low-fat buttermilk, nonfat ricotta cheese or tomato juice.

■ For rich flavor with a lot less fat, replace some of the oil in marinated salads with defatted chicken broth.

■ Cut back on the amount of mayonnaise used in such dishes as tuna salad. One tablespoon of mayonnaise (or at most two) is sufficient to dress a six-ounce can of water-packed tuna. Also, try reduced-fat or nonfat mayonnaise instead of regular. For a zippy flavor, mix mayonnaise with nonfat yogurt, nonfat sour cream or buttermilk.

■ Instead of making a traditional salad and feeling that you must have some dressing, opt for a plate of crunchy raw vegetables such as carrot and celery sticks, broccoli and cauliflower florets, sweet pepper rings and fresh mushrooms. Serve with a low-fat dip or enjoy them plain.

Snacks

Contrary to what Mom may have told you, there's nothing inherently wrong with eating between meals. In fact, for some of us, small, nutritious meals throughout the day make sense. Nevertheless, it's essential to be aware of what you're nibbling on. Grabbing a handful of the wrong cookies, crackers or chips can easily add a whopping 20 or even 30 grams of fat to your daily intake. So, when it comes to munching, read labels and make your selections carefully:

■ Stock up on low-fat snack foods such as plain or light popcorn, pretzels and rice cakes. You may also enjoy munching on plain low-fat cereal.

■ Investigate the expanded lines of low- and reduced-fat crackers, corn chips and cookies. At some markets, you'll even find nonfried substitutes for potato chips. Some of these products are just as tasty as much fattier versions.

■ Keep a supply of cut-up raw vegetables in the refrigerator so you can grab a handful when you're feeling hungry. For variety, steam them.

■ Keep fresh fruit such as apples, bananas, grapefruit, grapes, melons, oranges, pears, pineapple and strawberries on hand.

■ For a sweet treat without fat, try dried fruit such as apples, apricots, figs, pears, prunes or raisins.

■ If you enjoy an occasional piece of candy, select hard candy, which usually has no fat.

Vegetables, Fruits and Complex Carbohydrates

Fruits, vegetables, grains and pasta should be the backbone of a low-fat diet. But don't cancel out the benefits of these super foods by using a lot of extra fat in their preparation. Instead:

■ Rely on low-fat sautéing techniques that use nonstick cookware, a minimum amount of fat and some broth or other liquid to keep the food from sticking to the pan.

■ Avoid plain vegetables topped with butter or margarine. Instead, seek out low-fat vegetable side dishes that get great taste from herbs, spices and other flavorful ingredients.

■ Experiment with different types of grains such as barley, brown rice, couscous and bulgur. They're a nice change from white rice and pasta. And each has its own distinctive flavor.

■ For a filling meal, try a hearty baked potato and a low-fat topping, such as Ratatouille, Chili con Carne or Shrimp in Curried Tomato Sauce.

■ Work at least one carbohydrate—potatoes, pastas, grains and such—into every meal.

■ Enjoy low-fat vegetarian main dishes once or twice a week. However, don't make the mistake of assuming that all vegetarian dishes are automatically low in fat. Many are loaded with high-fat cheese, butter and nuts. And some feature textured vegetable protein (like fake bacon bits), which can be just as high in fat as meat.

Chapter 9

RECIPES FOR SUCCESS

We've become convinced that the only truly effective way to keep people eating low-fat food is to make it delicious. Recipes need to be more than just highly nutritious. They need to look good and taste good—they need to pass muster not only on paper but also on the plate and in the mouth!

So, during development, all the recipes in this book were both profession-ally analyzed to make sure they were low in fat and sampled and critiqued solely for their eye and taste appeal. Any that fell even a little short taste-wise were dropped—no matter how "good for you" they were.

Through long experience with low-fat cooking, we've learned that a mod-erate approach usually works best. Instead of squeezing every last molecule of fat from a recipe, we pare as much as possible without affecting good texture and taste. This is why we don't automatically use the lowest-fat product available in every recipe and don't completely eschew ingredients like oil, margarine and full-fat cheese.

Even so, the vast majority of our dishes *still derive* less than 30 percent of their calories from fat. Many contain far less than that—15 to 20 percent—which makes it quite easy to put together dozens of healthy meals and menus.

Here is some additional information about the recipes.

■ All recipes were tested at least three times (and some many more times) to ensure good results.

■ Procedures were streamlined wherever possible, and utensils were kept to the minimum needed to produce tempting dishes.

■ The emphasis is on readily available, fresh ingredients, but there is selected use of prepared items (such as canned tomatoes, frozen spinach and commercial salsas, picante sauces and such) for convenience, economy and shortened preparation time.

■ We aimed to appeal to normal American tastes, while at the same time emphasizing low-fat and other healthful ingredients and minimizing sugar and salt.

■ The recipes introduce a wide variety of fat-reducing techniques—such as browning meat under a broiler rather than in a pan with oil and using nonfat yogurt as a replacement for sour cream in some baked goods.

■ Where appropriate, recipes incorporate time-saving or fat-reducing microwave techniques. However, conventional ovens and burners are called for when they produce better taste or texture.

■ Many recipes incorporate suggestions for serving and garnishing. We also often give ideas for suitable accompaniments or provide background nutritional information to enhance the recipes' usefulness.

Nutritional Analyses

All recipes were analyzed by a registered dietitian using the latest professional nutritional analysis computer software. The analyses provide the number of calories, the grams of total fat, the percentage of calories from fat, the grams of saturated fat and the milligrams of cholesterol in one serving of the dish.

With regard to portion sizes, our goal has been to keep estimates realistic and in line with the quantities people really eat. Indeed, we've leaned in the direction of ample, even generous servings, not artificially small ones that would make the number of grams of fat and calories per serving seem low. The reason is that *appetites* aren't fooled by what's on paper—if portions are too small, people simply go back for seconds and thirds.

Keep in mind that each nutritional analysis is necessarily based on the specific ingredients and techniques detailed in a recipe. To ensure that your dish actually has the amount of fat and calories indicated, it's necessary to prepare the recipe as written. For example, if the ingredient list calls for extra-lean ground round of beef and you use regular ground beef, the fat and calories will be higher than the analysis states. Likewise, if the directions call for carefully skimming fat from a broth and you skip this step, your dish will contain more grams of fat and more calories than are shown.

Here are some other details of the nutritional analyses:

■ When a choice of ingredients is offered (for example, orange juice or Grand Marnier), the analysis is based on the first one.

■ If a quantity range is given (for example, ⅓–½ cup buttermilk), the analysis is based on the first number.

■ When an ingredient is listed as optional, it is not included in the recipe analysis.

Chapter 10

S U M P T U O U S
S O U P S

The pleasure of soup starts with a pot of flavorful ingredients simmering on the back of the stove and filling the kitchen with tempting aromas. Then comes the first satisfying mouthful—smooth and creamy or chunky and hearty.

It's no accident that we've started the recipe section with an inviting selection of soups. Some, like our Herbed Broccoli Bisque and our Manhattan-Style Clam Chowder, make a perfect first course or light luncheon fare. Others, like our White Bean and Pasta Soup and Hearty Split Pea, Bean and Barley Soup, are so robust that they can easily be the main event at supper. Accompany them with a salad and bread (perhaps our Buffins or Spicy Cornbread) to round out the meal.

Herbed Broccoli Bisque

Leeks contribute a subtle, pleasing flavor to this easy soup, which gets its creamy texture from pureed potatoes and broccoli. We prefer to use a blender, but you may puree the soup in a food processor. In that case, the texture of the soup will not be quite as smooth.

- 3 medium leeks
- 1 garlic clove, minced
- 2 teaspoons nondiet tub-style canola or corn-oil margarine or butter
- 3 cups defatted chicken broth, divided
- 4 cups small broccoli florets
- 1 pound boiling potatoes (about 4 medium), peeled and cut into ¾" cubes
- 1 teaspoon dried basil leaves
- 1 teaspoon dried thyme leaves
- ¼ teaspoon ground white pepper
- 1½ cups 2% fat milk
- 1 teaspoon lemon juice
- ½ teaspoon salt, or to taste
  Tiny blanched broccoli florets or fresh broccoli leaves (garnish)

Clean the leeks by trimming off the root ends and all but about 1" of the green tops; discard. Peel off and discard 1 or 2 layers of the tough outer leaves. Then, beginning at the green end, slice down about 1" into the leeks. Put the leeks in a colander. Wash them thoroughly under cool running water. Wash again to remove all traces of dirt. Set them aside until well drained. Cut into ½" pieces.

In a Dutch oven or other large heavy pot, combine the leeks, garlic, margarine or butter and 3 tablespoons of the broth. Cook over medium heat, stirring frequently, for 10 minutes, or until the leeks are tender but not browned. (Add a bit more broth if the liquid begins to evaporate.) Add the 4 cups broccoli, potatoes, basil, thyme, pepper and the remaining broth. Bring to a boil.

Cover, reduce the heat and simmer for 11 to 14 minutes, or until the potatoes and broccoli are tender. Remove from the heat and let cool slightly.

Working in batches, puree the mixture in a blender on low speed for 10 seconds. Raise the speed to high and process until completely smooth. Return the puree to the pot. Add the milk, lemon juice and salt. Mix well. Cook for an additional 4 to 5 minutes; do not boil.

Garnish individual servings with the blanched florets or leaves.

Makes 5 servings.

Per serving: 207 calories, 3.5 g. total fat (15% of calories), 1.2 g. saturated fat, 5 mg. cholesterol

Creamy Garden-Vegetable Soup

This mild, homey soup looks and tastes creamy, yet it contains no cream or even whole milk. The illusion of richness is created by pureeing some of the vegetables—most notably the corn—in a blender until smooth. The puree adds welcome body and flavor to the soup. If possible, use white corn in this recipe. Because its taste is very mellow and its color pale, it does a particularly good job of passing for cream.

1	large onion, chopped
1	large celery stalk, chopped
1/3	cup chopped sweet red peppers
1½	teaspoons nondiet tub-style canola or corn-oil margarine or butter
2½	cups defatted chicken broth
1	tablespoon all-purpose or unbleached white flour
1	large carrot, peeled and diced
2¼	cups diced boiling potatoes
½	cup shredded green cabbage or cauliflower florets
2	large bay leaves
1	teaspoon dried marjoram leaves
1	cup loose-pack frozen white corn kernels, divided
¼	cup chopped fresh chives or scallion tops
2	cups 2% fat milk
1/8	teaspoon ground white pepper
	Salt, to taste (optional)

In a Dutch oven or other large heavy pot, combine the onions, celery, red peppers and margarine or butter. Cook over medium-high heat, stirring frequently, for 3 to 4 minutes, or until the onions are limp. (If the mixture begins to dry out, add a little broth, as needed, to prevent sticking and burning.)

Stir in the flour. Cook, stirring, for 30 seconds longer. Gradually add the broth, stirring vigorously, until the mixture is well blended and smooth. Add the carrots, potatoes, cabbage or cauliflower, bay leaves and marjoram. Bring to a boil, stirring occasionally.

Cover, reduce the heat and simmer for 5 minutes. Stir in ½ cup of the corn. Continue to simmer, stirring occasionally, for 6 to 7 minutes longer, or until the vegetables are cooked through. Remove and discard the bay leaves.

Scoop out about 1 cup of the vegetables and 1/3 cup of the broth; transfer to a blender. Add the remaining ½ cup corn. Blend on low speed for 10 seconds. Raise the speed to medium and process until completely smooth. Pour the puree into the pan.

Stir in the chives or scallions. Simmer, stirring frequently, for 2 minutes. Stir in the milk, white pepper and salt (if using). Heat through but do not boil.

Makes 5 servings.

Per serving: 204 calories, 4 g. total fat (17% of calories), 1.6 g. saturated fat, 7 mg. cholesterol

Fiesta Corn Chowder

The combination of pureed corn and potatoes gives this Tex-Mex soup a remarkably creamy texture.

1	medium onion, chopped
1	garlic clove, minced
2	teaspoons olive oil
2½	cups defatted chicken broth, divided
3	cups peeled and cubed boiling potatoes
2	cups 1% fat milk
1	large bay leaf
½	teaspoon dried thyme leaves
¼	teaspoon dry mustard
¼	teaspoon ground white pepper
2	cups loose-pack frozen yellow corn kernels
4	ounces reduced-fat sharp Cheddar cheese, shredded (about 1 cup)
1	can (4 ounces) chopped mild green chili peppers
¼	teaspoon salt (optional)

In a Dutch oven or other large heavy pot, combine the onions, garlic, oil and 2 tablespoons of the broth. Cook on medium heat, stirring frequently, for 5 minutes, or until the onions are tender. Add the potatoes, milk, bay leaf, thyme, mustard, white pepper and the remaining broth. Bring to a boil.

Cover, reduce the heat and simmer, stirring occasionally, for 10 to 11 minutes, or until the potatoes are tender. Add the corn, bring the liquid to a simmer again and cook for 6 to 8 minutes, or until the corn is cooked through. Remove and discard the bay leaf. Using a ladle, transfer about half of the vegetables and liquid to a blender. Blend on medium speed until thoroughly pureed.

Add the puree to the pot. With the heat on medium-low, slowly add the cheese and stir until melted. Stir in the chili peppers and salt (if using). Heat, stirring, for about 1 minute; do not boil.

Makes 4 servings.

Per serving: 351 calories, 9.6 g. total fat (24% of calories), 1.4 g. saturated fat, 19 mg. cholesterol

White Bean and Pasta Soup

There's only a small amount of ham per serving in this Italian-style soup. But the meat makes an important contribution to the rich broth. Since the pasta absorbs liquid, you may need to add a bit of extra water when reheating.

1½	cups dry Great Northern beans, washed and sorted
1	large onion, chopped
2	garlic cloves, chopped
2	teaspoons olive oil
7	cups defatted chicken broth, divided
1	cup water
12	ounces fully cooked thick-cut boneless ham slices, trimmed of all visible fat and cut into small pieces
2	large carrots, peeled and sliced
2	large celery stalks, including leaves, sliced
2	large bay leaves
1½	teaspoons dried basil leaves
1½	teaspoons dried thyme leaves
¼	teaspoon ground black pepper
1	generous cup medium pasta, such as cut fusilli
1	can (16 ounces) tomatoes, with juice

Place the beans in a large heavy pot. Cover with 2" of water and bring to a boil over high heat. Reduce the heat and boil for 2 minutes. Remove the pot from the heat, cover and let stand for 1 hour. Drain the beans in a colander, discarding the soaking water.

In the same pot, combine the onions, garlic, oil and 3 tablespoons of the broth. Cook over medium heat, stirring frequently, for 5 to 6 minutes, or until the onions are soft. (Add a bit more broth if the liquid begins to evaporate.) Add the remaining broth and the water.

Add the ham, carrots, celery, bay leaves, basil, thyme, pepper and the beans. Bring the soup to a boil.

Cover, reduce the heat and simmer for 1¼ to 1½ hours, or until the beans are tender. Remove and discard the bay leaves. With a large shallow spoon, skim any fat from the top of the soup. Bring the soup to a full boil, stirring occasionally. Add the pasta. Reduce the heat and boil for 12 to 16 minutes, or until the pasta is tender.

Add the tomatoes (with juice); break up the tomatoes with a spoon. Cook, stirring occasionally, for an additional 2 to 3 minutes.

Makes 7 servings.

Per serving: 239 calories, 4.5 g. total fat (17% of calories), 1.4 g. saturated fat, 27 mg. cholesterol

H e a r t y   S p l i t   P e a ,   B e a n   a n d   B a r l e y   S o u p

This hearty soup is a great way to use a ham bone left over from a special occasion. You can also purchase ham bones at shops that specialize in sliced ham. If you substitute smoked pork hocks, the flavor will be less intense. This soup is wonderful when reheated. However, be sure to stir it carefully to prevent the split peas from sticking. If the soup thickens too much in the refrigerator, thin it with a little more water during reheating.

13	cups water
1	pound split peas, washed and sorted
1	meaty ham bone or 2 large pork hocks (about 2 pounds total)
1	cup dry navy beans, washed and sorted
¼	cup pearl barley
3	bay leaves
	About 5 beef bouillon cubes, divided
2	large onions, coarsely chopped
1	large carrot, peeled and thinly sliced
2	large celery stalks, including leaves, thinly sliced
2	garlic cloves, minced
1½	teaspoons dried thyme leaves
¼	teaspoon ground celery seeds
	Salt and ground black pepper, to taste

In a Dutch oven or other large heavy pot, combine the water, split peas, ham bone or pork hocks, beans and barley. Add the bay leaves, 3 bouillon cubes, onions, carrots, celery, garlic, thyme and celery seeds. Bring to a boil over high heat.

Cover, reduce the heat and simmer, stirring occasionally, for 2 to 2½ hours, or until the beans are tender. (As the mixture thickens, lower the heat even further and stir more frequently to prevent the split peas from sticking to the bottom of the pan.)

Taste the soup. If it is not robust enough, add 1 or 2 more bouillon cubes. Then add salt and pepper. Remove and discard the bay leaves.

Remove the ham bone or pork hocks. (If you used pork hocks, discard them. If you used a ham bone, reserve it and let cool slightly. Cut the meat into bite-size pieces and return them to the pan. Discard the bone.)

Skim any fat from the top of the soup with a large shallow spoon. Bring the soup to a boil again. Stir well before serving.

Makes 12 servings.

Per serving: 196 calories, 1.1 g. total fat (5% of calories), 0.2 g. saturated fat, 2 mg. cholesterol

Homemade Stock

You may store this stock in the refrigerator for three to four days. Freeze for longer storage.

To easily defat stock, refrigerate it until the fat solidifies. Then you can lift the fat off and discard it. If time is too short, very carefully skim the fat from the surface using a large shallow spoon.

Chicken Stock

You can use this lightly salted stock in any recipe calling for chicken stock or broth. If you are on a sodium-restricted diet, simply omit the salt from the recipe. The stock requires long, slow cooking but very little attention during that time.

1	broiler-fryer chicken (3½ pounds), quartered
2	large onions, quartered
2	large celery stalks, cut into 1" pieces
2	large carrots, peeled and cut into ½" pieces
1	medium turnip, very coarsely chopped
3	quarts water
⅔	cup chopped fresh parsley
1	large bay leaf
1	teaspoon coarsely crushed black peppercorns
½	teaspoon dried thyme leaves
¾	teaspoon salt, or to taste

In an 8-quart stock pot or other very large pot, combine the chicken, onions, celery, carrots, turnips and water. Bring to a boil over medium-high heat. Adjust the heat so the mixture simmers briskly, and simmer for 15 minutes. Skim off and discard any scum and fat using a large shallow spoon.

Add the parsley, bay leaf, peppercorns and thyme. Adjust the heat so the mixture simmers gently. Cook for 2½ to 3 hours.

Remove the pot from the heat. Stir in the salt. Strain the stock through a fine sieve. Discard the chicken and vegetables.

Measure the stock. If there's more than 8 cups of liquid, return it to the pot and boil until it reduces to about 8 cups. If there's less than 8 cups, add some water.

Makes 8 cups.

Per cup: 14 calories, <0.1 g. total fat (1% of calories), 0 g. saturated fat, 0 mg. cholesterol

Beef Stock

Beef stock makes an excellent base for many soups and stews. Browning the bones contributes significantly to the richness of the stock. Because beef bones exude a surprising amount of fat, it's essential to skim the fat off the stock.

3	pounds beef soup bones, preferably marrow bones, sawed into 2" pieces
3	pounds meaty beef plate ribs
4	large onions, chopped
2	large carrots, peeled and cut into chunks
2	large celery stalks, cut into 3" pieces
1	medium turnip, sliced
2	garlic cloves, chopped
3	large bay leaves
6–7	parsley sprigs
1	teaspoon dried thyme leaves
1	teaspoon salt, or to taste
¼	teaspoon ground black pepper
2	whole cloves
12½	cups water, divided

Preheat the broiler.

Rinse and drain the bones and ribs. Pat them dry with paper towels. Spread in a single layer in a very large roasting pan. Broil 5" from the heat for 7 to 8 minutes, or until nicely browned. Turn the pieces and broil for an additional 8 minutes.

Meanwhile, in an 8-quart stock pot or other very large pot, combine the onions, carrots, celery, turnips, garlic, bay leaves, parsley, thyme, salt, pepper, cloves and 11 cups of the water. Bring to a boil over high heat.

Add the bones. Discard the fat from the roasting pan. Put the remaining 1½ cups water in the pan. With a large spoon, scrape up any browned bits sticking to the bottom. Transfer the water and the brown bits to the pot. Cover, reduce the heat and simmer gently for 1 hour. Skim any scum from the surface using a large shallow spoon. Cover again and simmer for an additional 3 to 4 hours, checking occasionally to make sure the liquid is not boiling vigorously.

Remove the pot from the heat. Strain the stock through a fine sieve. Discard the bones and vegetables.

Makes 12 cups.

Per cup: 17 calories, 0.5 g. total fat (26% of calories), 0.3 g. saturated fat, 0 mg. cholesterol

Old-Fashioned Turkey-Vegetable Soup

This tempting soup is brimming with chunky vegetables and succulent turkey meat. It is also convenient and economical, since turkey wings are often available—usually at a very reasonable price. (Note that while turkey wings are not as lean as turkey breast meat, much of the excess fat is removed from this recipe by carefully skimming the top of the broth.) The soup is hearty enough to serve as a light supper. You may make it ahead and store it in the refrigerator for up to four days. When reheating it, stir frequently to prevent the vegetables from sticking to the pot. If the soup thickens during storage, thin it with a little water.

2½ pounds turkey wings
 3 cups defatted chicken broth
 3 cups water
 2 large onions, chopped
 3 celery stalks, chopped
 ½ cup chopped fresh parsley leaves
 3 cups thinly sliced carrots
 ½ teaspoon dried marjoram leaves
    Generous ¼ teaspoon dried thyme leaves
 ¼ teaspoon ground black pepper, or to taste
 1 can (14½ ounces) Italian (plum) tomatoes, with juice
 1 package (10 ounces) frozen succotash
 1 can (15 ounces) white beans, rinsed and drained
    Salt, to taste (optional)
 2 tablespoons finely chopped fresh parsley leaves (garnish)

In a Dutch oven or other large heavy pot, combine the wings, broth, water, onions, celery and ½ cup chopped parsley. Bring to a boil over high heat.

Cover, reduce the heat and simmer for 1¾ hours, or until the wings are almost tender. Remove them from the pot and set them aside until cool enough to handle.

Using a large shallow spoon, skim off all the fat from the soup surface. (Alternatively, refrigerate the mixture for at least 4 hours, until the fat solidifies on the surface. Then skim it off and discard. Reheat the soup thoroughly.)

Add the carrots, marjoram, thyme and pepper to the pot. Cover and continue simmering for 30 minutes.

Meanwhile, remove the turkey meat from the bones and cut it into bite-size pieces. Break up the tomatoes with a spoon, reserving the juice.

Add the turkey, tomatoes (with juice), succotash and beans to the pot. Simmer for 15 minutes, or until the vegetables are tender and the flavors are blended. Add the salt (if using). Serve garnished with finely chopped parsley.

Makes 8 servings.

Per serving: 289 calories, 7.1 g. total fat (22% of calories), 1.9 g. saturated fat, 68 mg. cholesterol

Creole Vegetable Soup

The combination of ingredients gives this easy vegetable soup quite a pleasing flavor. For a very quick and satisfying meal, just add a salad and bread.

1	large onion, chopped
1	celery stalk, sliced
1	garlic clove, minced
2	teaspoons olive oil
5¼	cups defatted chicken broth, divided
2	cans (16 ounces each) kidney beans, rinsed and drained
1	can (15 ounces) tomato sauce
1	large carrot, peeled and sliced
½	large green pepper, seeded and chopped
1¼	teaspoons dried thyme leaves
1	teaspoon dried marjoram leaves
⅛	teaspoon ground black pepper, or to taste
3	drops hot-pepper sauce (optional)
¼	cup uncooked long-grain white rice

In a Dutch oven or other large heavy pot, combine the onions, celery, garlic, oil and 3 tablespoons of the broth. Cook over medium heat, stirring occasionally, for 5 to 6 minutes, or until the onions are tender. (Add a bit more broth if the liquid begins to evaporate.)

Add the beans, tomato sauce, carrots, green peppers, thyme, marjoram, black pepper, hot-pepper sauce (if using) and the remaining broth. Stir to mix well. Bring to a boil.

Add the rice. Cover, reduce the heat and cook at a gentle boil for 25 minutes, or until the rice is tender and the soup has thickened slightly.

Makes 6 servings.

Per serving: 244 calories, 3.5 g. total fat (12% of calories), 0.5 g. saturated fat, 1 mg. cholesterol

Manhattan-Style Clam Chowder

Bacon is extraordinarily fatty, but much of the fat can be removed by handling bacon properly. We like to cook it in the microwave, then carefully blot it with paper towels before crumbling the strips. The greatly defatted meat lends a rich, smoky flavor to dishes, such as this full-bodied chowder. The chowder is hearty enough to serve for dinner, especially if accompanied with one of our yeast breads or a batch of our savory muffins.

2	bacon strips
1	large onion, finely chopped
2	large celery stalks, including leaves, diced
1	medium green pepper, seeded and diced
1	tablespoon nondiet tub-style canola or corn-oil margarine or butter
2	cans (10½ ounces each) minced clams, with juice
	About 1 cup bottled clam juice
3½	cups peeled and diced boiling potatoes
2	tablespoons finely chopped fresh parsley leaves
1	large bay leaf
	Generous ½ teaspoon dried thyme leaves
¼	teaspoon dried marjoram leaves
¼	teaspoon dry mustard
⅛	teaspoon ground black pepper
3	drops hot-pepper sauce (optional)
1	can (16 ounces) stewed tomatoes, with juice
½	cup tomato sauce

Lay the bacon strips side by side on a triple thickness of paper towels; cover with 3 more towels. Place the towels on a microwave-safe plate. Microwave on high power for 45 seconds. Rotate the plate a quarter turn; microwave for another 45 seconds. Check the bacon for doneness; if necessary, microwave for up to 1 minute longer. Transfer the bacon to clean paper towels and set aside.

In a Dutch oven or other large heavy pot, combine the onions, celery, green peppers and margarine or butter. Cook over medium heat, stirring frequently, for 5 minutes, or until the onions are tender.

Drain the liquid from the clams into a 4-cup glass measure. Add enough bottled clam juice to make 2¾ cups of liquid. Add the liquid to the pan, along with the potatoes. Bring to a boil. Cover, reduce the heat and simmer, stirring occasionally, for 10 minutes.

Crumble the bacon and add to the pan. Add the parsley, bay leaf, thyme, marjoram, mustard, black pepper and hot-pepper sauce (if using).

Chop any large pieces of stewed tomatoes. Stir the tomatoes (with juice) and the tomato sauce into the pan. Add the clams. Cover and simmer for 7 minutes longer, or until the potatoes are just tender and the flavors are well blended. Remove and discard the bay leaf.

Makes 6 servings.

Per serving: 281 calories, 5.2 g. total fat (17% of calories), 0.9 g. saturated fat, 68 mg. cholesterol

Indian-Style Lentil Soup

This tasty, filling soup is extra-low in fat because the onions and some of the other vegetables are cooked in the microwave instead of in oil or margarine on top of the stove. The red lentils called for are available at some grocery stores and most health food stores.

1	cup chopped onions
1	medium carrot, peeled and thinly sliced
1	large celery stalk, sliced
2	cups water, divided
6	cups defatted chicken broth
1½	cups dry red lentils, washed and sorted
2	teaspoons mild curry powder, or to taste
½	teaspoon ground cumin
¼	teaspoon salt (optional)
⅛	teaspoon ground black pepper
1	medium boiling or red-skinned potato, peeled and cubed
1½	cups small cauliflower florets

Combine the onions, carrots and celery in a 4-cup glass measure. Add 1 cup of the water. Cover with wax paper. Microwave on high power for 12 to 18 minutes, or until the onions have softened and about half the water has evaporated.

Meanwhile, in a Dutch oven or other large heavy pot, combine the broth, lentils, curry powder, cumin, salt (if using), pepper and the remaining 1 cup water. Bring to a boil over medium-high heat.

Cover, reduce the heat and simmer, stirring occasionally, for 20 minutes. Add the onion mixture. Stir in the potatoes and cauliflower. Bring to a boil again.

Reduce the heat and simmer, stirring occasionally, for an additional 15 to 18 minutes, or until the potatoes are tender.

Makes 6 servings.

Per serving: 139 calories, 1.6 g. total fat (10% of calories), 0.5 g. saturated fat, 1 mg. cholesterol

Bahamas-Style Fish Chowder

*This soup is zesty and colorful, not to mention very low in fat.
Served along with crusty bread, it makes a nice lunch or light one-
dish supper.*

1½	cups chopped onions
1	cup chopped celery
1	cup diced carrots
½	cup diced sweet red peppers
2½	teaspoons nondiet tub-style canola or corn-oil margarine or butter
2	cups bottled clam juice
2	cups diced thin-skinned boiling potatoes
2	large bay leaves
1	teaspoon Worcestershire sauce
1	teaspoon mild curry powder
¼	teaspoon dried thyme leaves
⅛	teaspoon ground black pepper, or to taste
1⅔	cups defatted chicken broth
¾	cup loose-pack frozen yellow corn kernels
3½	tablespoons ketchup
1	pound skinless, boneless cod, scrod, haddock or other mild white fish fillets, cut into 1" chunks
1	tablespoon chopped fresh parsley leaves (garnish)
	Corn cob slices (garnish)

In a Dutch oven or other large heavy pot, combine the onions,
celery, carrots, red peppers and margarine or butter. Cook over
medium-high heat, stirring frequently, for 5 to 7 minutes, or until
the vegetables are limp and beginning to brown. (Add a bit of clam
juice if needed to prevent the vegetables from burning.)

Stir in the clam juice, potatoes, bay leaves, Worcestershire sauce,
curry powder, thyme and black pepper. Adjust the heat so the mixture simmers gently; cook, stirring occasionally, for 15 minutes, or
until the carrots and potatoes are just barely tender when pierced
with a fork.

Add the broth, corn and ketchup; mix well. Stir in the fish. Cover
and simmer for 4 to 5 minutes, or until the corn is just tender and
the fish pieces flake when touched with a spoon. Remove and discard the bay leaves. Serve the chowder garnished with the parsley
and corn cob slices.

Makes 5 servings.

*Per serving: 269 calories, 3.5 g. total fat (12% of calories), 0.6 g. saturated fat,
36 mg. cholesterol*

Vegetable Minestrone

This quick and easy soup makes a warm, filling lunch or a light supper entrée. For a vegetarian version, substitute vegetable bouillon for the chicken broth. If cannellini beans are unavailable, use a 16-ounce can of kidney beans.

1   large onion, chopped
1   celery stalk, thinly sliced
1   garlic clove, minced
2   teaspoons olive oil
5   cups defatted chicken broth, divided
2   cups coarsely shredded cabbage
1   cup sliced zucchini and/or yellow squash
1   carrot, peeled and thinly sliced
1   bay leaf
1   teaspoon dried thyme leaves
1   teaspoon dried basil leaves
½   teaspoon dried oregano leaves
⅛   teaspoon ground black pepper
    Dash of ground celery seeds
1   can (19 ounces) cannellini beans, rinsed and drained
½   cup radiatore (pinwheel-shaped pasta) or other small pasta shapes
1   can (8 ounces) tomato sauce

In a Dutch oven or other large heavy pot, combine the onions, celery, garlic, oil and 3 tablespoons of the broth. Cook over medium heat, stirring frequently, for 5 to 6 minutes, or until the onions are soft. Add the cabbage, zucchini and/or squash, carrots, bay leaf, thyme, basil, oregano, pepper, celery seeds and the remaining broth. Bring to a boil.

Cover, reduce the heat and simmer for 15 minutes, or until the vegetables are almost tender. Add the beans and pasta. Simmer for 8 to 11 minutes, or until the pasta is tender. Remove and discard the bay leaf. Stir in the tomato sauce.

Makes 5 servings.

Per serving: 200 calories, 3 g. total fat (13% of calories), 0.6 g. saturated fat, 0 mg. cholesterol

Pumpkin-Carrot Soup

Give this recipe a try and you'll find that pumpkin is a rich-tasting soup base that goes well with the carrot and spices. What's more, both pumpkin and carrots are high in beta-carotene, a nutrient that helps prevent cancer. Be sure to use plain canned pumpkin and not pumpkin-pie filling, which has spices already added.

1	medium onion, finely chopped
1	celery stalk, finely chopped
2	teaspoons nondiet tub-style canola or corn-oil margarine or butter
2¼	cups defatted chicken broth, divided
⅔	cup solid-pack canned pumpkin
1	large carrot, peeled and grated or shredded
1	tablespoon mild honey, such as clover
⅛	teaspoon ground ginger
⅛	teaspoon ground cinnamon
⅛	teaspoon ground allspice
⅛	teaspoon ground black pepper
½	tablespoon cornstarch
1½	cups 1% fat milk
	Salt, to taste (optional)

In a large saucepan, combine the onions, celery, margarine or butter and 2 tablespoons of the broth. Cook over medium heat, stirring frequently, for 5 to 6 minutes, or until the onions are soft. Add the pumpkin, carrots, honey, ginger, cinnamon, allspice, pepper and the remaining broth. Stir until smooth. Bring to a boil.

Cover, reduce the heat and simmer for 15 minutes, or until the vegetables are tender. (The celery will be crisp-tender.)

Place the cornstarch in a 2-cup measure. Gradually stir in the milk to maintain a smooth consistency. Stir into the simmering soup. Turn up the heat and cook for 2 minutes, or until thickened. Add salt (if using).

Makes 4 servings.

Per serving: 128 calories, 3.1 g. total fat (22% of calories), 1 g. saturated fat, 3 mg. cholesterol

A P P E A L I N G A P P E T I Z E R S A N D S N A C K S

Quick trips to the refrigerator or pantry to see what's available for snacking have become a way of life for many people. Actually, there's nothing wrong with eating between meals—if you make the right selections. We've cut the fat but none of the pleasure from some of our favorite snacks, such as Tex-Mex Dip, White Pizza and our Fruit Spread for bagels, crackers or bread.

And we've included a nice selection of traditional appetizers like Cocktail Meatballs and Shrimp Rémoulade—only we've slimmed them down to meet today's emphasis on health. When looking for first courses and appetizers, remember that you can often serve smaller portions of full-size recipes. Two that work particularly well for us are our Marinated Vegetable Antipasto Salad and our Spicy Crab Cakes.

Cocktail Meatballs

Absolutely no one ever guesses that these delicious meatballs are low in fat. The secret is in using lean ground round along with some cooked beans, and then baking the meatballs rather than frying them. (Baking also cuts down on preparation time.) You may prepare the recipe with extra-lean ground beef, but the meatballs will have almost twice as much fat. You can make the meatballs ahead and refrigerate or freeze them. (If they're frozen, allow them to thaw in the refrigerator before reheating.) Provide toothpicks to serve the meatballs.

MEATBALLS

1	cup rinsed and drained canned kidney beans
½	cup quick-cooking rolled oats
3	large egg whites
1½	tablespoons mild chili powder
1¼	teaspoons Worcestershire sauce
½	teaspoon salt
1	large onion, chopped
1	pound lean ground round of beef

SAUCE

½	cup ketchup
½	cup tomato sauce
½	cup water
1½	tablespoons Worcestershire sauce
2	tablespoons packed light brown sugar
1	teaspoon mild chili powder
⅛	teaspoon ground black pepper

To prepare the meatballs: Preheat the oven to 375°. Generously coat a large jelly-roll pan with nonstick spray.

In a food processor, combine the beans, oats, egg whites, chili powder, Worcestershire sauce and salt. Process for 2 minutes, or until the mixture is pureed. Add the onions and process with on/off pulses until very finely chopped but not pureed.

Transfer to a large bowl. Add the beef and mix until thoroughly combined. Form the mixture into scant ¾-inch meatballs. Place, slightly separated, on the prepared pan.

Bake on the center oven rack for 20 to 25 minutes, or until nicely browned and cooked through.

Using a slotted spoon, transfer the meatballs to a tray lined with a double thickness of paper towels to blot away any remaining fat.

To prepare the sauce: In a Dutch oven or other large heavy pot, stir together the ketchup, tomato sauce, water, Worcestershire sauce, sugar, chili powder and pepper until evenly blended.

Bring the sauce to a simmer over medium heat. Simmer for 1 minute or until the sugar dissolves and the ingredients are well blended. Add the meatballs. Heat, gently stirring occasionally, for 5 to 10 minutes. Transfer to a large serving dish.

Makes 60 meatballs.

Per meatball: 25 calories, 0.6 g. total fat (20% of calories), 0.2 g. saturated fat, 5 mg. cholesterol

Cheese, Pimiento and Olive Spread

Traditional cheese, pimiento and olive spread was one of our all-time favorites. But we'd given it up until the advent of nonfat cream cheese. By combining this product with green olives and non-fat Cheddar, we have created a rich, creamy spread with real Cheddar and olive taste. We serve it as an appetizer with crackers or French bread. The spread will keep in the refrigerator for up to a week.

1   container (8 ounces) nonfat tub-style cream cheese
3   ounces nonfat Cheddar cheese, shredded (about ¾ cup)
3   ounces reduced-fat Cheddar cheese, shredded (about ¾ cup)
1   tablespoon sliced canned pimientos
1   teaspoon instant minced onion flakes
½   teaspoon Worcestershire sauce
¼   teaspoon dry mustard
8   medium pimiento-stuffed green olives
2   tablespoons chopped celery
    Chopped canned pimientos (optional)

In a food processor, combine the cheeses, sliced pimientos, onion flakes, Worcestershire sauce and mustard. Process until well combined.

Cut 2 or 3 slices from one of the olives and reserve them as a garnish. Chop the remaining olives. Stir the olives and celery into the spread.

Transfer to a crock. Garnish with the olive slices and chopped pimientos (if using). Cover and refrigerate several hours until the flavors are blended.

Makes 1½ cups; 36 servings (2 teaspoons each).

Per serving: 16 calories, 0.6 g. total fat (31% of calories), 0 g. saturated fat, 2 mg. cholesterol

Smoked Salmon Mousse

Prepared in a fish-shaped (or other decorative) mold and presented on a bed of sliced cucumbers, this makes a tempting, elegant party dish. Although smoked salmon is pricey, a little goes a long way in this recipe. Serve the mousse with low-fat crackers and small, thin slices of dark bread. Provide not only knives for spreading the mousse but also forks for spearing the cucumber slices.

2	tablespoons water
1½	teaspoons unflavored gelatin
2	containers (8 ounces each) nonfat tub-style cream cheese
4	ounces reduced-fat tub-style cream cheese
4	ounces smoked salmon, cut into 2" pieces
1	teaspoon tomato paste
1	teaspoon dried dillweed
¼	teaspoon dry mustard
3	tablespoons minced celery
5	teaspoons finely chopped fresh chives
2	medium cucumbers, peeled (garnish)
	Dill sprigs (garnish)

Place the water in a small microwave-safe cup or bowl; sprinkle with the gelatin. Let stand for 5 minutes, or until the gelatin softens. Microwave on high power for 20 seconds. Stir. Microwave for another 10 to 20 seconds, or until the mixture is hot and the gelatin has completely dissolved. Set aside.

In a food processor, combine all the cream cheese, salmon, tomato paste, dill and mustard. Process until smooth. Add the gelatin mixture through the feed tube and continue processing until evenly incorporated. Stir in the celery and chives.

Transfer the mixture to a 2- to 3-cup fish mold or other decorative mold. Refrigerate for at least 1½ hours, until set.

If desired, draw the tines of a fork down the length of each cucumber all the way around to produce decorative ridges. Cut the cucumbers into thin slices. Arrange the cucumber slices to form a bed on a serving platter.

Dip the mold almost to its rim in a pan of warm water for a few seconds. Loosen one side of the mousse with a table knife. Carefully unmold the mousse onto the cucumbers. Garnish with the dill.

Makes 1⅞ cups; 60 servings (1½ teaspoons each).

Per serving: 15 calories, 0.4 g. total fat (26% of calories), 0 g. saturated fat, 2 mg. cholesterol

Marinated Mussels

This appealing dish was inspired by one from a now-defunct restaurant in Seekonk, Massachusetts, called Café in the Barn. The mussels are equally appropriate as a first course or an appetizer.

2	pounds mussels in the shell
1/3	cup water
1/3	cup chopped sweet red peppers
2	tablespoons chopped scallions
1	large garlic clove, minced
2	teaspoons extra-virgin olive oil
3	tablespoons red wine vinegar
1/2	teaspoon dried basil leaves
1/4	teaspoon dried oregano leaves
1/4	teaspoon dried thyme leaves
	Pinch of ground black pepper
	Pinch of salt
	Curly endive leaves (garnish)

Rinse and drain the mussels. Wash them in several changes of water, scrubbing the shells with a vegetable brush. Trim off any dark, rootlike debris using kitchen shears or a sharp knife. Continue changing the water until it is clear and no sand remains. Then cover the mussels with cold water and let them soak for at least 2 to 3 hours to allow them to disgorge any more sand. Rinse again. (Alternatively, soak the mussels in cold water sprinkled with a handful of cornmeal for about 1 hour. Then rinse and drain well.)

Place the water in a 6-quart or larger pot. Insert a steamer basket or colander. Cover and bring to a boil over medium-high heat. Add the mussels; cover and steam for about 5 minutes, or until the shells open. Set aside until the mussels are cool enough to handle.

Remove the mussels from their shells, discarding any closed ones, and transfer them to a small deep bowl. Measure 2 tablespoons of cooking liquid from the pot and add it to the bowl.

In a 12" nonstick skillet, combine the red peppers, scallions, garlic and oil. Cook over medium-high heat, stirring, until tender, about 5 minutes. Transfer to a medium nonreactive bowl.

Add the vinegar, basil, oregano, thyme, black pepper and salt. Stir in the mussels and cooking liquid. Cover and refrigerate for at least 30 minutes and up to 24 hours. Allow to warm almost to room temperature before serving. Serve on a bed of endive.

Makes 6 servings.

Per serving: 70 calories, 2.8 g. total fat (36% of calories), 0.2 g. saturated fat, 32 mg. cholesterol

White Pizza

After enjoying white pizza as an appetizer in a trendy Boston restaurant, we immediately set out to make a low-fat version that would taste just as good. Our recipe relies on a trio of cheeses combined with chopped fresh vegetables for texture and flavor. The ricotta and mozzarella have virtually no fat. And the feta is low in fat, with six grams per ounce. Serve these mini pizzas piping hot as appetizers or as part of a brunch or light lunch. You can easily double the recipe. You may also prepare the ricotta-vegetable mixture several hours ahead and refrigerate it until needed.

3	English muffins, halved
⅓	cup nonfat ricotta cheese
⅓	cup thinly sliced scallion tops
⅓	cup finely chopped zucchini
¼	cup finely chopped sweet red peppers
½	teaspoon dried oregano leaves
¼	teaspoon dried basil leaves
¼	cup finely crumbled feta cheese
1	ounce nonfat or reduced-fat mozzarella cheese, shredded (about ¼ cup)
	Hot-pepper flakes (optional)

Preheat the broiler.

Arrange the English muffin halves, cut side up, on a baking sheet and set aside.

In a small bowl, mix the ricotta, scallions, zucchini, peppers, oregano and basil. Divide the mixture among the English muffins and spread it evenly. Sprinkle each muffin with 2 teaspoons of the feta, then with 2 teaspoons of the mozzarella.

Broil 2" from the heat for 2 minutes, or until the mozzarella has melted. Sprinkle with the pepper flakes (if using).

Makes 6 servings.

Per serving: 106 calories, 2.8 g. total fat (24% of calories), 1.4 g. saturated fat, 10 mg. cholesterol

Shrimp Rémoulade

Here's a recipe so rich, full-bodied and satisfying that it couldn't possibly be low in fat. But it is! Serve this spicy shrimp as an appetizer with fat-free crackers or melba toast. Or serve as a luncheon entrée, either on a bed of greens and vegetables or on rolls. A half-cup of the mixture has 108 calories and 2.4 grams of total fat.

⅔   cup ketchup
½   cup nonfat ricotta cheese
2   tablespoons reduced-fat mayonnaise
1¼   teaspoons prepared horseradish
½   teaspoon mild chili powder
12   ounces small cooked and peeled shrimp
1   celery stalk, finely chopped
2   tablespoons chopped fresh chives or scallion tops

In a food processor, combine the ketchup, ricotta, mayonnaise, horseradish and chili powder. Process, stopping and scraping down the sides of the container once or twice, until the mixture is well blended. Transfer to a medium serving bowl.

Stir in the shrimp, celery and chives or scallions. Cover and refrigerate for several hours, until the flavors are well blended.

Makes 2½ cups; 60 servings (2 teaspoons each).

Per serving: 9 calories, 0.2 g. total fat (18% of calories), 0 g. saturated fat, 9 mg. cholesterol

Chutney Dip

This dip tastes wonderful served with apple wedges or crackers. To keep apple wedges from discoloring on a party table, soak them for a few minutes in pineapple or orange juice. If all the ingredients are very fresh, this dip will keep in the refrigerator for four to five days. You may use any brand of prepared chutney; we prefer Cross and Blackwell's Major Grey.

¾   cup nonfat ricotta cheese
3   tablespoons reduced-fat tub-style cream cheese
¼   teaspoon curry powder
     Pinch of salt
4   tablespoons prepared chutney, divided

In a food processor, combine the ricotta and cream cheese. Process until smooth, stopping and scraping down the container if necessary. Transfer the mixture to a small serving bowl. Stir in the curry powder and salt.

Lightly stir in 3 tablespoons of the chutney, leaving swirls of chutney visible. Spread the remaining 1 tablespoon chutney on top and swirl it attractively with the tip of a spoon.

Makes 1⅛ cups; 27 servings (2 teaspoons each).

Per serving: 13 calories, 0.3 g. total fat (22% of calories), 0.2 g. saturated fat, 1 mg. cholesterol

Hot Artichoke Spread

After enjoying an artichoke-cheese spread at a local restaurant, we came up with this version, which is just as tasty but a lot lower in fat. We serve it with slices of crusty French or sourdough bread or with nonfat crackers. You may prepare the spread up to 24 hours ahead and refrigerate it until needed. Just keep in mind that chilled spread will take longer to heat than that at room temperature.

1	jar (14 ounces) water-packed artichoke heart quarters, well drained
¼	cup grated Parmesan cheese
2	tablespoons nonfat tub-style cream cheese
1	small garlic clove, minced
3	drops hot-pepper sauce

In a food processor, combine the artichokes, Parmesan, cream cheese, garlic and hot-pepper sauce. Process until almost completely smooth. Transfer to a small glass or ceramic microwave-safe bowl or crock.

Cover with wax paper and microwave on high power, occasionally giving the bowl a quarter turn and stirring the mixture, for 1½ to 4 minutes, or until heated through.

Makes 1⅓ cups; 32 servings (2 teaspoons each).

Per serving: 11 calories, 0.3 g. total fat (22% of calories), 0.2 g. saturated fat, 1 mg. cholesterol

Tex-Mex Dip

This spicy, colorful, layered dip is always a big hit at parties, and nobody realizes we've removed almost all the fat. We like to serve it in a glass dish so that the layers show. For dipping, we provide fat-free corn chips or toasted pita triangles. The dip will keep for three to four days in the refrigerator.

1	can (16 ounces) kidney beans, rinsed and drained
1	teaspoon mild chili powder
1	cup mild or medium-hot picante sauce, divided
¾	cup nonfat sour cream
2	ounces nonfat Cheddar cheese, shredded (about ½ cup)
2	ounces reduced-fat sharp Cheddar cheese, shredded (about ½ cup)
1	medium tomato, chopped

In a food processor, combine the beans and chili powder. Process until the beans are partially pureed. Stir in ¼ cup of the picante sauce. Transfer the mixture to a round 8" glass dish or shallow casserole. Spread it evenly with the back of a spoon.

Spread the sour cream over the beans in an even layer. Spread the remaining picante sauce evenly over the sour cream. Sprinkle evenly with the cheeses. Top with the tomatoes.

Cover and refrigerate for at least 2 hours and up to 24 hours before serving.

Makes 1⅔ cups; 40 servings (2 teaspoons each).

Per serving: 23 calories, 0.4 g. total fat (16% of calories), 0 g. saturated fat, 1 mg. cholesterol

Blue Cheese Spread

Here's a recipe that takes advantage of the distinctive flavor of blue cheese—combining a little with reduced-fat Cheddar and nonfat ricotta for a very rich-tasting spread. Serve it with crackers, melba toast or flatbreads. If all the ingredients are very fresh, this dip will keep in the refrigerator for four to five days.

1	ounce reduced-fat Cheddar cheese, shredded (about ¼ cup)
	Generous 1 tablespoon crumbled blue cheese
1	cup nonfat ricotta cheese
1	medium celery stalk, finely chopped
2	teaspoons instant minced onion flakes
½	teaspoon prepared horseradish
3	drops hot-pepper sauce
	Pinch of garlic powder
	Pinch of salt

In a 1-cup glass measure, combine the Cheddar and blue cheese. Cover with wax paper and microwave on high power for 25 to 40 seconds, or until the cheeses are melted. Transfer to a food processor bowl.

Add the ricotta and process until smooth, stopping several times to scrape down the sides of the container. Transfer the mixture to a medium bowl.

Stir in the celery, onion flakes, horseradish, hot-pepper sauce, garlic powder and salt. Mix well. Cover and chill for several hours before serving.

Makes 1 cup; 48 servings (1 teaspoon each).

Per serving: 7 calories, 0.3 g. total fat (37% of calories), 0.1 g. saturated fat, 1 mg. cholesterol

Fruit Spread

This spread can be served with vegetables, crackers or melba toast. Or use it to stuff celery sticks or Belgian endive leaves. The nonfat cream cheese provides a rich texture, and the dried fruit gives the spread crunch and a slightly nutty taste. We like to use Del Monte mixed fruit, but you may use a combination of dried apricots, apples and prunes. We serve the spread at parties and also keep it in the refrigerator to use with bagels or toast. If made with very fresh cream cheese, the dip can be kept up to five days in the refrigerator.

1	container (8 ounces) nonfat tub-style cream cheese
½	cup well-drained juice-packed crushed pineapple
1	teaspoon mild honey, such as clover (optional)
½	cup chopped mixed dried fruit, divided

In a medium bowl, combine the cream cheese, pineapple and honey (if using). Stir until well combined. Add all but 1 tablespoon of the fruit and mix well. Transfer to a small serving bowl. Refrigerate for at least 2 hours to allow the flavors to blend and the dried fruit to soften slightly. Sprinkle with the reserved fruit.

Makes 1¾ cups; 42 servings (2 teaspoons each).

Per serving: 10 calories, <0.1 g. total fat (1% of calories), 0 g. saturated fat, <1 mg. cholesterol

Mulled Cider

When friends and family gather at our houses on chilly fall and winter days, we love to greet them with steaming apple cider. We leave a pot of this sweet, spicy drink warming on the stove so they can help themselves whenever they like. We're often asked for our recipe. And people are usually surprised at how simple it is. Fresh-pressed unpasteurized cider works best. But, since the flavor can vary, you may want to zip it up with orange juice or ginger ale.

1	gallon apple cider
2	short (2") cinnamon sticks
15	whole cloves
10	whole allspice berries (optional)
3½	cups orange juice or ginger ale (optional)

In a large heavy pot, combine the cider, cinnamon, cloves and allspice (if using). Taste the mixture. If the cider lacks flavor, add the orange juice or ginger ale.

Warm over medium heat for about 45 minutes. *Do not boil.* With a slotted spoon, remove the cloves and allspice. Serve hot in mugs.

Makes 16 servings (8 ounces each).

Per serving: 94 calories, 0 g. total fat (0% of calories), 0 g. saturated fat, 0 mg. cholesterol

Curried Vegetable Spread

This spicy appetizer is reminiscent of an East Indian dal—a cooked lentil dish. Red lentils are much milder in flavor and more pleasing in color than the regular green or brown types, and they cook much faster. Red lentils are available at health food stores and some grocery stores. Serve the spread on pita bread or fat-free crackers. The spread will keep in the refrigerator for four to five days.

- ¾   cup dry red lentils, washed and sorted
- 1   medium onion, chopped
- 1   celery stalk, diced
- 1   small carrot, peeled and grated or shredded
- 1   garlic clove, minced
- 2   tablespoons reduced-fat mayonnaise
- ½   teaspoon mild curry powder
- ¼   teaspoon ground cumin
- ¼   teaspoon ground ginger
- ¼   teaspoon salt, or to taste
- ⅛   teaspoon ground turmeric
-     Pinch of ground cinnamon
- 1   teaspoon fine nonfat cracker crumbs

In a medium saucepan, combine the lentils, onions, celery, carrots and garlic. Cover with 3" of water. Bring to a boil over medium-high heat. To keep the lentils from foaming up and boiling over, reduce the heat and simmer for 18 to 25 minutes, or until the lentils are tender.

Pour the lentils into a fine sieve and let drain completely. Do not shake the strainer, as the lentils may start to come through.

While the lentils are draining, combine the mayonnaise, curry powder, cumin, ginger, salt, turmeric and cinnamon in a medium bowl. Add the lentils and cracker crumbs. Mix well.

Refrigerate for at least 1 hour and up to 24 hours before serving.

Makes 2 cups; 48 servings (2 teaspoons each).

Per serving: 10 calories, 0.1 g. total fat (13% of calories), 0 g. saturated fat, 0 mg. cholesterol

Chapter 12

SENSATIONAL SALADS

This is a large chapter because we had so many different kinds of wonderful salads we wanted to include: hearty main-dish and filling side-dish salads featuring meat, seafood, pasta, potatoes and beans; light, crunchy-crisp slaws and raw vegetable medleys; zesty cooked marinated vegetable combinations and both sweet and savory molded salads and simple fruit mixtures.

Low-fat and reduced-fat salads such as the ones in this book are an excellent way to add appealing color, texture and variety to lunch and dinner menus. Many can be made ahead—and even improve upon storage—so they also make convenient additions to meals. Moreover, since most contain vegetables or fruits, and many include rice, pasta or other grains, they are high on the list of foods we can enjoy often without guilt.

Ginger-Sesame Chicken and Pasta Salad

Because this oriental-style pasta salad is colorful, tempting and can be prepared well ahead, it is great for a buffet supper or luncheon. You may omit the chicken for a vegetarian dish.

3	tablespoons sesame seeds
1	large boneless, skinless chicken breast half, cut into 1½" × ⅛" strips
1	cup scallion shreds (2" × ¼")
1	cup sweet red pepper strips (2" × ⅛")
⅔	cup shredded carrots
2	teaspoons peanut oil
1⅔	cups very coarsely shredded celery cabbage
1	cup Chinese pea pods, trimmed and halved lengthwise
1	can (14 ounces) baby corn ears, well drained
1	can (8 ounces) sliced water chestnuts, well drained
5	tablespoons reduced-sodium soy sauce
2	tablespoons rice wine vinegar or 1½ tablespoons white vinegar
1	tablespoon peeled and minced ginger root
2½	teaspoons packed light brown sugar
2	teaspoons oriental sesame oil
¼	teaspoon mild chili powder
3	drops hot-pepper oil, or to taste (optional)
4	cups cooked vermicelli or other thin spaghetti, cut into 2½" lengths

Place the sesame seeds in a 12" nonstick skillet. Place over medium-high heat and stir frequently for 2 to 3 minutes, or until the seeds are fragrant and lightly browned. Remove the skillet from the heat. Transfer the seeds to a small bowl. Set aside.

Return the skillet to the heat and add the chicken, scallions, peppers, carrots and peanut oil. Cook for 3 minutes, or until the scallions are limp. Stir in the cabbage and pea pods; cook for 1 minute longer.

Remove the skillet from the heat. Stir in the corn, water chestnuts, soy sauce, vinegar, ginger, sugar, sesame oil, chili powder and hot-pepper oil (if using). Transfer to a large nonreactive bowl.

Add the vermicelli or spaghetti and 1½ tablespoons of the sesame seeds. Toss until well combined. Cover and refrigerate for at least 1 hour and up to 24 hours, stirring once or twice during this time.

Place the salad in a serving bowl. Just before serving, sprinkle with the remaining 1½ tablespoons sesame seeds.

Makes 8 servings.

Per serving: 247 calories, 5.4 g. total fat (19% of calories), 0.8 g. saturated fat, 9 mg. cholesterol

Potato Salad

This is a traditional potato salad prepared with a mayonnaise dressing. However, we've removed a lot of the usual fat by using a combination of reduced-fat mayonnaise and nonfat ricotta cheese and whirring them in a blender or food processor until completely smooth.

DRESSING

½	cup reduced-fat mayonnaise
⅓	cup nonfat ricotta cheese
3½	tablespoons dill pickle juice
1	teaspoon Worcestershire sauce
1	teaspoon Dijon mustard
1	teaspoon granulated sugar
¼	teaspoon dried thyme leaves
¼	teaspoon ground white pepper
¼	teaspoon mustard seeds (optional)
¼	teaspoon dried dillweed
⅛	teaspoon celery salt

SALAD

5⅓	cups chunked cooked boiling or red-skinned potatoes
1½	cups chopped celery
⅔	cup chopped dill pickles
2	tablespoons chopped fresh chives or scallions, including tops

To prepare the dressing: In a food processor or blender, combine the mayonnaise, ricotta, pickle juice, Worcestershire sauce, mustard, sugar, thyme, pepper, mustard seeds (if using), dill and celery salt. Process until completely smooth, stopping and scraping down the sides of the container as needed.

To prepare the salad: In a large bowl, combine the potatoes, celery, pickles and chives or scallions. Add the dressing and toss until the potatoes are evenly coated. Cover and refrigerate for at least 45 minutes and up to 24 hours to allow the flavors to blend.

Makes 6 servings.

Per serving: 147 calories, 1.5 g. total fat (9% of calories), 0.6 g. saturated fat, 10 mg. cholesterol

Marinated Potato Salad

A small amount of chicken broth added to the oil-based dressing helps keep this zesty potato salad surprisingly low in fat. Potatoes that are cooked until just a little bit crisp work best in this salad, since they hold together when stirred into the dressing and also do not absorb as much liquid (and fat) as very tender potatoes.

5	medium red-skinned potatoes, cut into ¼" slices
2	tablespoons canola oil
2	tablespoons defatted chicken broth
2	teaspoons balsamic vinegar
1	large celery stalk, thinly sliced
¼	cup finely chopped fresh parsley leaves
2	tablespoons chopped red onions
¾	teaspoon dried marjoram leaves
¾	teaspoon dried thyme leaves
½	teaspoon Dijon mustard
½	teaspoon lemon juice
¼	teaspoon salt, or to taste
	Pinch of ground white pepper

Place the potatoes in a medium saucepan. Add enough cold water to cover them. Cover and bring to a boil over medium-high heat. Reduce the heat and simmer for 9 to 13 minutes, or until the potatoes are tender but not soft when pierced with a fork.

Transfer the potatoes to a colander. Cool slightly under cold running water and drain well.

In a large bowl or serving dish, mix the oil, broth and vinegar. Add the celery, parsley, onions, marjoram, thyme, mustard, lemon juice, salt and pepper. Stir to mix well.

Add the potatoes. Stir carefully with a large spoon to coat them with the dressing mixture. Be careful not to break up the potatoes. Cover and refrigerate for several hours; stir occasionally to allow the flavors to blend.

Makes 5 servings.

Per serving: 137 calories, 2 g. total fat (13% of calories), 0.1 g. saturated fat, 0 mg. cholesterol

Microwave option: Combine the potatoes and 2 to 3 tablespoons of water in a microwave-safe 2-quart casserole. Microwave on high power for a total of 8 to 12 minutes, or until the potatoes are tender but not soft when pierced with a fork; during that time stop twice to stir the potatoes and give the casserole a quarter turn. Transfer the potatoes to a colander and continue with the recipe.

Marinated Vegetable Antipasto Salad

This tangy, colorful vegetable salad can play a delicious supporting role in a summer meal. It can also star as an appetizer course. In that case, serve it with forks and small plates or drain off the dressing and let guests spear the vegetables with toothpicks. If you serve the salad as an appetizer, cut the vegetables into larger pieces (make the red peppers 1" squares and the zucchini ½" thick rounds).

DRESSING

⅓   cup defatted chicken broth
¼   cup chopped fresh parsley leaves
2   tablespoons olive oil, preferably extra-virgin
2   tablespoons thinly sliced scallion tops
2   teaspoons lemon juice
1   teaspoon apple cider vinegar
1   teaspoon dried thyme leaves
1   teaspoon dried basil leaves
3   drops hot-pepper sauce

SALAD

½   large cauliflower head, cut into small florets
1   cup water
2   jars (14 ounces each) water-packed artichoke heart quarters, well drained
1   large celery stalk, sliced
1   large carrot, peeled and sliced
1   large sweet red pepper, seeded and diced
1   medium zucchini, cubed

To prepare the dressing: In a large, nonreactive bowl, combine the broth, parsley, oil, scallions, lemon juice, vinegar, thyme, basil and hot-pepper sauce. Stir to mix well. Set aside.

To prepare the salad: In a medium saucepan, combine the cauliflower and water. Cover, bring to a boil over high heat, then reduce the heat to medium. Cook for 2 to 3 minutes, until the cauliflower is just crisp-tender. Transfer to a colander and cool under cold running water. Drain well.

Add the cauliflower, artichokes, celery, carrots, peppers and zucchini to the bowl with the dressing. Stir to coat the vegetables. Marinate at room temperature for 10 to 15 minutes, stirring occasionally, or cover and refrigerate for at least 3 hours.

Makes 6 servings.

Per serving: 93 calories, 4.9 g. total fat (43% of calories), 0.7 g. saturated fat, 0 mg. cholesterol

Marinated White Bean Salad

Colorful and tasty, this hearty salad is perfect for alfresco summer dining.

1½	cups dry Great Northern or navy beans, washed and sorted
8	cups water
⅓	cup defatted chicken broth
¼	cup ketchup
2	tablespoons olive or canola oil
1	teaspoon lemon juice
1	teaspoon dried thyme leaves
1	teaspoon dried basil leaves
½	teaspoon salt, or to taste
⅛	teaspoon ground black pepper
3	drops hot-pepper sauce (optional)
¾	cup chopped sweet red peppers
¾	cup diced zucchini
¾	cup diced yellow squash
¼	cup thinly sliced scallion tops
¼	cup chopped fresh parsley leaves
1	large celery stalk, thinly sliced

Place the beans in a Dutch oven or other large heavy pot. Cover with 2" of water and bring to a boil over high heat. Reduce the heat and boil for 2 minutes. Remove the pot from the heat, cover and let stand for 1 hour. Drain the beans in a colander, discarding the soaking water.

Return the beans to the pot in which they were soaked. Cover with 8 cups water. Cover and bring to a boil over high heat. Reduce the heat and simmer for 1¼ to 1½ hours, or until the beans are tender. Transfer to a colander. Cool slightly under cold running water. Drain well.

In a large bowl, combine the broth, ketchup, oil, lemon juice, thyme, basil, salt, black pepper and hot-pepper sauce (if using). Stir to mix well.

Add the red peppers, zucchini, squash, scallions, parsley and celery. Stir to mix well. Add the beans and gently stir to coat with the dressing. Cover and refrigerate for 2 to 3 hours or overnight. Stir before serving.

Makes 7 servings.

Per serving: 213 calories, 4.7 g. total fat (19% of calories), 0.4 g. saturated fat, 0 mg. cholesterol

Confetti Rice Salad

The dressing ingredients for this salad may seem a bit unusual, but they blend to make a very tangy, tasty combination.

1	cup uncooked long-grain white rice
3	cups coarsely chopped broccoli florets and tender stem pieces
1	tablespoon olive oil
2	tablespoons apple cider vinegar
1	tablespoon defatted chicken broth
¼	teaspoon salt, or to taste
⅛	teaspoon ground white pepper
½	cup buttermilk
3	tablespoons reduced-fat mayonnaise
2	tablespoons instant nonfat dry milk
1	tablespoon Dijon mustard
½	teaspoon granulated sugar
1	cup cubed zucchini
1	celery stalk, thinly sliced
¼	cup finely chopped red onions
½	sweet yellow or red pepper, seeded and chopped

Cook the rice according to the package directions. Set aside.

Place the broccoli in a medium saucepan. Add 1" of water. Cover and bring to a boil over high heat. Reduce the heat and cook for 1 to 2 minutes. Transfer to a colander and rinse under cold running water to set the color. Drain well and set aside.

In a large nonreactive bowl, combine the oil, vinegar, broth, salt and white pepper. Stir in the rice and broccoli; mix well. Let marinate at room temperature for 30 minutes.

In a small deep bowl, mix together the buttermilk, mayonnaise, dry milk, mustard and sugar. Blend well, using a wire whisk. Stir the dressing into the rice mixture. Add the zucchini, celery, onions and yellow or red peppers. Stir to mix well. Cover and refrigerate for at least 2 hours and up to 24 hours before serving.

Makes 7 servings.

Per serving: 159 calories, 3.7 g. total fat (21% of calories), 0.6 g. saturated fat, 2 mg. cholesterol

Roasted Sweet Pepper and Eggplant Salad

This salad goes well with many poultry and seafood dishes. It tastes best if made ahead so the flavors can blend.

VEGETABLES

2 large sweet red peppers, halved lengthwise and seeded
2 large green peppers, halved lengthwise and seeded
1 large (1 pound) eggplant, peeled and cut lengthwise into 1" thick slices
1 teaspoon extra-virgin olive oil
1 small garlic clove, crushed

DRESSING

2 tablespoons lemon juice
2 tablespoons chopped fresh chives or scallions, including tops
2 teaspoons extra-virgin olive oil
1 teaspoon dried marjoram leaves
¼ teaspoon salt, or to taste
⅛ teaspoon ground black pepper, or to taste
3 tablespoons finely chopped fresh cilantro or parsley leaves

To prepare the vegetables: Preheat the broiler.

Lay the red and green pepper halves in a single layer on a small foil-lined baking sheet. Lay the eggplant slices in a single layer on a separate foil-lined sheet. Stir together the oil and garlic. Brush the eggplant with the oil; discard the garlic.

Set the sheets 6" below the broiler element. Broil the eggplant for 4½ to 5½ minutes, or until browned and barely tender when pierced with a fork. Set aside until cool enough to handle. Cut into ½" × 1" pieces. Place in a glass bowl or other nonreactive serving bowl.

Broil the peppers for a total of 13 to 15 minutes, turning them with tongs every 3 to 4 minutes to ensure even cooking. The skins should be blistered and charred, the flesh just tender when pierced with a fork. Transfer to a large heatproof bowl and cover tightly with foil. Let stand until cool enough to handle. Peel off and discard the loosened skins. Cut the peppers into ¼" × 1½" pieces. Add to the bowl with the eggplant.

To prepare the dressing: In a small bowl, stir together the lemon juice, chives or scallions, oil, marjoram, salt and pepper. Pour over the vegetables. Gently stir until well blended. Cover and refrigerate for at least 3 hours (preferably 24 hours). Allow the salad to warm up just slightly before serving. Sprinkle with the cilantro or parsley.

Makes 5 servings.

Per serving: 61 calories, 3 g. total fat (40% of calories), 0.4 g. saturated fat, 0 mg. cholesterol

Cucumber Salad

This old-fashioned cucumber salad is not only fat free but also perfect to serve with dinner or to take on a picnic on a hot summer day. We like to use dill, as called for in the recipe. But you can omit it or replace it with oregano or basil if you prefer. The salad will keep for two to three days refrigerated.

¼   cup water
3   tablespoons apple cider vinegar
1½ tablespoons granulated sugar
1   teaspoon chopped fresh dill leaves or ½ teaspoon dried dillweed (optional)
2   medium cucumbers, peeled and sliced paper thin
¼   cup grated or shredded carrots
¼   cup thinly sliced scallion tops

In a shallow nonreactive dish or bowl, combine the water, vinegar, sugar and dill (if using). Stir to mix well. Add the cucumbers, carrots and scallions. Stir to coat with the dressing. Cover and refrigerate for at least 1 hour before serving.

Makes 6 servings.

Per serving: 27 calories, 0.1 g. total fat (4% of calories), 0 g. saturated fat, 0 mg. cholesterol

Asparagus Salad

Here's an example of how a very little bit of a high-fat ingredient can go a long way. Because the Parmesan is added as a garnish, you need only a sprinkling to set off these fresh asparagus spears.

¼   cup finely chopped fresh parsley leaves
¼   cup coarsely chopped green or sweet red peppers
3   tablespoons canola oil
3   tablespoons defatted chicken broth
2   tablespoons lemon juice
¼   teaspoon celery salt
¼   teaspoon dry mustard
⅛   teaspoon ground black pepper
2   pounds fresh untrimmed asparagus spears
    Red or Boston lettuce leaves
2   teaspoons grated Parmesan cheese (optional)

In a small bowl, combine the parsley, green or red peppers, oil, broth, lemon juice, celery salt, mustard and black pepper. Stir to mix well. Set aside for at least 20 minutes to blend the flavors.

Wash the asparagus well. Gently break off and discard the tough white part at the bottom of each spear. Lay the spears in a large skillet and cover them with water. Cover the skillet and bring the water to a boil over high heat. Reduce the heat and gently simmer for 4 to 8 minutes, or until the spears are crisp-tender; do not overcook.

Transfer the asparagus to a colander and cool slightly under cold running water. Drain.

Arrange the lettuce and asparagus on a serving platter. Drizzle with the dressing. Garnish with the Parmesan (if using), sprinkling it evenly over the spears. Cover and refrigerate for at least 30 minutes before serving.

Makes 6 servings.

Per serving: 61 calories, 3.2 g. total fat (41% of calories), 0.4 g. saturated fat, 0 mg. cholesterol

Marinated Tomatoes with Oregano

This is a fine way to take advantage of an abundance of succulent, sun-ripened tomatoes. Since the dish is prepared ahead, it makes an easy, wonderfully savory addition to a summer luncheon or buffet supper. Tomatoes peel easily if dipped in boiling water for a few seconds.

- 3 tablespoons red wine vinegar
- 1 tablespoon chopped fresh chives or scallions, including tops
- 2½ teaspoons extra-virgin olive oil
- ¾ teaspoon dried oregano leaves
- ¾ teaspoon granulated sugar
- ¼ teaspoon celery salt, or to taste
- ¼ teaspoon ground black pepper, or to taste
- 6 large sun-ripened red or yellow tomatoes, peeled and cored

In a 1-cup glass measure, stir together the vinegar, chives or scallions, oil, oregano, sugar, celery salt and pepper until well blended.

Slice the tomatoes ¼" thick, or cut into wedges. Arrange a layer of tomatoes in a nonreactive serving plate or bowl. Drizzle with some of the dressing. Add another layer of tomatoes and more dressing. Repeat until all the tomatoes and dressing have been used. Cover and refrigerate for at least 1 hour and up to 8 hours before serving.

Makes 6 servings.

Per serving: 44 calories, 2.3 g. total fat (41% of calories), 0.3 g. saturated fat, 0 mg. cholesterol

Pasta-Turkey Salad with Tarragon

Tarragon adds an unusual, elegant and very appealing touch to this main-dish salad. The salad can be prepared with leftover roast turkey breast or with breast meat poached in a little water or chicken broth. Although turkey meat is leaner than chicken, you could substitute chicken breast meat if that's what's on hand. Notice that this recipe calls for cooking the pasta in a mixture of water and chicken broth. This adds rich, satisfying flavor without any extra fat.

DRESSING

½	cup reduced-fat mayonnaise
2½	tablespoons tarragon vinegar or white wine vinegar
½	cup defatted chicken broth
2	tablespoons chopped fresh chives or 1 tablespoon dried chives
1½	teaspoons dried tarragon leaves
¼	teaspoon ground white pepper
⅛	teaspoon salt (optional)

SALAD

4½	cups water
3	cups defatted chicken broth
2½	cups pasta ruffles or pasta twists
2½	cups diced cooked turkey breast
1	cup coarsely diced yellow squash
1	cup chopped celery
3	tablespoons finely chopped fresh chives or scallions, including tops
3	tablespoons coarsely diced sweet red peppers
	Tomato wedges (garnish)

To prepare the dressing: In a small deep bowl, whisk together the mayonnaise, vinegar, broth, chives, tarragon, pepper and salt (if using) until well blended.

To prepare the salad: In a large pot, bring the water and broth to a rolling boil. Add the pasta and bring back to a boil. Cook for 7 to 9 minutes, or until the pasta is cooked through but still slightly firm. Transfer to a colander and rinse under cold running water. Let stand until thoroughly drained and cooled.

Meanwhile, in a large bowl, stir together the turkey, squash, celery, chives or scallions and peppers. Stir in the dressing until evenly incorporated. Add the pasta and stir until well blended. Cover and refrigerate until thoroughly cooled, at least 1 hour and up to 24 hours. Just before serving, garnish with the tomatoes.

Makes 6 servings.

Per serving: 232 calories, 8.7 g. total fat (33% of calories), 0.8 g. saturated fat, 64 mg. cholesterol

Carrot and Sweet Pepper Salad with Garbanzo Beans

Colorful and zesty, this makes a nice addition to a warm-weather buffet or picnic. Serve the salad chilled or at room temperature.

SALAD

- 1 pound carrots, peeled and thinly sliced
- 1 small sweet red pepper, seeded and cut into 1" chunks
- 1 small green pepper, seeded and cut into 1" chunks
- 1 can (7¾ ounces) garbanzo beans, rinsed and drained

DRESSING

- ⅓ cup apple cider vinegar
- ¼ cup tomato sauce
- ¼ cup tomato paste
- 2½ tablespoons mild honey, such as clover
- 2 tablespoons olive oil, preferably extra-virgin
- 3 tablespoons chopped fresh chives or scallions, including tops
- 1 teaspoon Worcestershire sauce
- ¾ teaspoon Dijon mustard
- ¼ teaspoon celery seeds
- ⅛ teaspoon ground allspice
- ⅛ teaspoon ground black pepper, or to taste
- ⅛ teaspoon salt (optional)

To prepare the salad: Place the carrots in a medium saucepan; just barely cover with water. Cover the pan and bring to a boil over high heat. Reduce the heat and simmer for 3 to 5 minutes, or until the carrots are almost cooked through but still firm. Transfer to a colander. Cool under cold running water. Drain well.

Place the carrots in a large nonreactive serving bowl. Add the peppers and beans.

To prepare the dressing: In a small bowl, stir together the vinegar, tomato sauce, tomato paste, honey, oil, chives or scallions, Worcestershire sauce, mustard, celery seeds, allspice, pepper and salt (if using). Pour over the salad and stir to mix well. Cover and refrigerate for at least 1 hour and up to 24 hours before serving.

Makes 5 servings.

Per serving: 183 calories, 6.6 g. total fat (30% of calories), 0.5 g. saturated fat, 0 mg. cholesterol

Fruit Salad

This recipe is particularly convenient because it can be made ahead and the fruit will still retain its appealing color and texture. Be sure to use sweet orange marmalade, made from navel oranges rather than bitter Seville oranges.

3	tablespoons sweet orange marmalade
2	teaspoons Grand Marnier or orange juice
⅛	teaspoon peeled and finely minced ginger root
3	cups mixed melon balls or cubes
1½	cups fresh pineapple chunks
1	cup seedless green or red grapes
2	ripe kiwifruits, peeled and sliced
1	cup orange segments, seeded and membrane removed

In a small deep bowl, combine the marmalade, Grand Marnier or orange juice and ginger. Whisk or beat with a fork until well blended and syrupy. Set aside.

In a medium serving bowl, mix the melon, pineapple, grapes, kiwi and oranges. Gently stir in the syrup. Refrigerate for at least 30 minutes and up to 8 hours.

Makes 6 servings.

Per serving: 115 calories, 0.6 g. total fat (4% of calories), 0 g. saturated fat, 0 mg. cholesterol

Sesame Green Bean Salad

Soy sauce, oriental sesame oil and ginger give this bean salad a pleasing oriental flavor.

DRESSING

¼	cup reduced-sodium soy sauce
2	tablespoons oriental sesame oil
2	tablespoons defatted chicken broth
2	teaspoons sesame seeds
¾	teaspoon ground ginger
3	drops hot-pepper sauce

SALAD

2	packages (16 ounces each) whole frozen green beans
1	can (8 ounces) sliced water chestnuts, well drained and cut into thin strips
½	large sweet red pepper, seeded and julienned
¼	cup thinly sliced scallions

To prepare the dressing: In a medium bowl, combine the soy sauce, oil, broth, sesame seeds, ginger and hot-pepper sauce. Stir to mix well. Set aside.

To prepare the salad: Cook the beans according to the package directions. Place them in a colander and cool slightly under cold running water. Drain well.

Add the water chestnuts, peppers and scallions to the bowl with the dressing. Add the beans and stir to coat with the dressing. Cover and refrigerate for 6 to 8 hours before serving.

Makes 5 servings.

Per serving: 168 calories, 2.3 g. total fat (12% of calories), 0.4 g. saturated fat, 0 mg. cholesterol

Salsa Salad

Here's a simple, easy accompaniment to our Chili con Carne, Vegetarian Chili or Beans and Rice con Queso. Use medium or mild salsa for the dressing, depending on your preference. The recipe calls for blanching the broccoli, but this step can be omitted.

SALAD

- 2 cups small broccoli florets
- 1½ cups diced zucchini
- 1½ cups shredded iceberg lettuce
- 1 sweet yellow pepper, seeded and diced
- ½ cup sliced scallion tops

DRESSING

- ½ cup commercial salsa
- 1 tablespoon olive oil
- 1 tablespoon mild honey, such as clover

To prepare the salad: Place the broccoli in a medium saucepan. Add 1" of water. Cover and bring to a boil over high heat. Reduce the heat and cook for 1 to 2 minutes. Transfer to a colander and rinse under cold running water to set the color. Drain well. Place in a medium bowl.

Add the zucchini, lettuce, peppers and scallions. Toss to mix well.

To prepare the dressing: In a small bowl, combine the salsa, oil and honey. Mix well. Pour over the salad and toss well. Cover and refrigerate for 1 to 2 hours until the flavors are well blended.

Makes 5 servings.

Per serving: 68 calories, 3.5 g. total fat (40% of calories), 0.4 g. saturated fat, 0 mg. cholesterol

Curried Chicken Salad

Chicken salad is usually quite high in fat. But we've used a pleasing combination of flavorful ingredients to reduce both the fat and the calories—and come up with a distinctive, chunky salad that we serve as a luncheon entrée or as part of a summer buffet.

DRESSING

¼   cup reduced-fat mayonnaise
3   tablespoons plain nonfat yogurt
3   tablespoons nonfat ricotta cheese
1   tablespoon mild honey, such as clover
1¼   teaspoons mild curry powder, or to taste
      Salt and ground white pepper, to taste

SALAD

1   pound boneless, skinless chicken breast halves
1   can (20 ounces) juice-packed pineapple chunks, well drained
1   can (8 ounces) water chestnuts, well drained
1   medium red apple, cored and cubed
1   celery stalk, thinly sliced
⅓   cup sliced scallion tops
      Iceberg or other lettuce leaves

To prepare the dressing: In a food processor, combine the mayonnaise, yogurt, ricotta, honey, curry powder and salt and pepper. Process until smooth, stopping and scraping down the sides of the container, if necessary. Transfer the mixture to a large bowl. Set aside.

To prepare the salad: Cut each breast half into 2 or 3 large pieces; place in a 12" skillet. Cover with 1" of water and bring to a boil. Cover the pan, reduce the heat and simmer for 10 to 13 minutes, or until the chicken is cooked through. Transfer to a colander and cool under cold running water. Dry with paper towels and cut into bite-size pieces. Add to the bowl with the dressing.

Pat the pineapple chunks dry with paper towels. Add to the bowl. Add the water chestnuts, apples, celery and scallions. Toss to coat well.

Cover and refrigerate for several hours, stirring occasionally. Serve on a bed of lettuce.

Makes 6 servings.

Per serving: 236 calories, 4.7 g. total fat (18% of calories), 0.6 g. saturated fat, 35 mg. cholesterol

Molded Tomato-Shrimp Salad

Shrimp, crisp vegetables and herbs star in this tangy molded gelatin salad, which can be made up to 36 hours before serving.

1½	cups beef bouillon or defatted beef broth
2	envelopes unflavored gelatin
1	can (8 ounces) tomato sauce
1½	tablespoons lemon juice
2	teaspoons Worcestershire sauce
½	teaspoon prepared horseradish
¼	teaspoon mild chili powder
¼	teaspoon dried thyme leaves
	Pinch of ground white pepper
1	cup peeled, seeded and chopped cucumbers
1	medium tomato or 2 Italian (plum) tomatoes, seeded and chopped
1	cup small cooked and peeled shrimp
½	cup chopped scallions
	Endive or lettuce leaves (garnish)

Coat a 4-cup mold with nonstick spray and set aside.

Place the bouillon or broth in a small saucepan. Sprinkle with the gelatin. Let stand for one minute. Cook over medium heat, stirring, for 2 to 3 minutes, or just until the gelatin is dissolved. Remove the pan from the heat.

Stir in the tomato sauce, lemon juice, Worcestershire sauce, horseradish, chili powder, thyme and pepper.

Pour the mixture into the prepared mold. Refrigerate until thickened but not set, about 1 hour. (You can hurry this process by placing the mold in the freezer. Stir frequently so that the mixture at the sides of the mold does not freeze.)

Stir in the cucumbers, tomatoes, shrimp and scallions until evenly incorporated. Cover and refrigerate until set, about 2 hours.

To unmold the salad, dip the mold in warm water nearly up to the rim for 30 seconds. Loosen the edges with a knife and unmold onto a serving platter. Garnish with endive or lettuce.

Makes 5 servings.

Per serving: 54 calories, 0.4 g. total fat (7% of calories), 0.1 g. saturated fat, 35 mg. cholesterol

Salmon and Pasta Salad

The chicken broth in the dressing of this filling salad substitutes for some of the fat that would normally be used. For a quick and easy variation, add a jar of well-drained water-packed artichoke hearts.

DRESSING

½   cup thinly sliced scallions
½   cup chopped fresh parsley leaves
¼   cup defatted chicken broth
3   tablespoons olive oil
2   teaspoons lemon juice
1½   teaspoons dried thyme leaves
1½   teaspoons dried basil leaves
¼   teaspoon salt
⅛   teaspoon ground white pepper
3   drops hot-pepper sauce

SALAD

2   cups cut fusilli or other medium pasta shapes
1   can (16 ounces) red salmon
2   cups cauliflower florets
1   cup cubed tomatoes
1   cup diced zucchini
2   tablespoons chopped fresh parsley leaves (garnish)
1   tablespoon sliced scallion tops (garnish)

To prepare the dressing: In a large serving bowl, mix the scallions, parsley, broth, oil, lemon juice, thyme, basil, salt, pepper and hot-pepper sauce. Set aside.

To prepare the salad: Cook the pasta according to the package directions. Transfer to a colander and cool under cold running water. Drain well. Set aside.

Remove and discard any skin, bones and dark meat from the salmon. Break the remaining meat into bite-size chunks. Add to the bowl with the dressing.

If desired, blanch the cauliflower: Place it in 1" of water in a medium saucepan. Cover and bring to a boil over high heat. Reduce the heat and cook for 2 to 3 minutes. Transfer to a colander; rinse under cold running water. Drain well. Add to the salmon.

Stir in the pasta, tomatoes and zucchini. Cover and refrigerate for several hours before serving. Garnish with the parsley and scallions.

Makes 6 servings.

Per serving: 275 calories, 10.4 g. total fat (34% of calories), 1.8 g. saturated fat, 26 mg. cholesterol

Herbed Broccoli Bisque (page 73)

Indian-Style Lentil Soup (page 83)

Bahamas-Style Fish Chowder (page 84)

Vegetable Minestrone (page 85)

Chutney Dip (page 93)

Fruit Spread (page 96)

Smoked Salmon Mousse (page 90)

Marinated Vegetable Antipasto Salad (page 102)

Marinated Tomatoes with Oregano (page 107)

Asparagus Salad (page 106)

Marinated White Bean Salad (page 103)

Taco Salad (page 132)

Sesame Green Bean Salad (page 110)

Fruit Salad (page 110)

Microwaved Vegetables and Cheese (page 150)

Pan-Grilled Peppers and Onions (page 153)

Molded Fresh Cranberry-Orange Salad

Zesty and colorful, this easy make-ahead salad is a nice addition to a holiday dinner or buffet, especially one featuring poultry. The salad is virtually fat free, so it's a particularly good choice with a rich, heavy meal. Note that the recipe calls for a relatively large quantity of gelatin. This is needed to compensate for the high acidity of the cranberries and cranberry juice.

¼ cup cold tap water
1 envelope + 1¾ teaspoons unflavored gelatin
1 cup granulated sugar
1½ teaspoons grated orange zest
¼ teaspoon peeled and finely minced ginger root (optional)
3 cups fresh or thawed frozen cranberries, divided
1 cup cranberry juice cocktail
1 cup orange segments, seeded and membrane removed
1 cup chopped celery
½ cup peeled, cored and chopped apples

Place the water in a small bowl and sprinkle the gelatin over it. Let stand for 5 minutes, until the gelatin softens.

Combine the sugar, orange zest and ginger (if using) in a food processor bowl. Process for about 1 minute or until the ginger and orange zest are very fine. Add 1½ cups of the cranberries and process with on/off pulses just until the berries are chopped. Transfer to a large saucepan.

Place the remaining 1½ cups cranberries in the food processor; chop using on/off pulses. Transfer to the saucepan.

Stir in the cranberry juice. Bring the mixture just to a boil. Lower the heat and gently simmer for 3 minutes. Stir in the gelatin mixture and continue stirring until the gelatin dissolves. Set aside until cooled.

Place the oranges in the food processor; coarsely chop with on/off pulses and add to the cranberries. Add the celery and apples and mix well.

Spoon into a 6-cup (or slightly larger) ring mold or other decorative mold. Refrigerate; stir several times during the first hour to ensure the fruit is evenly distributed. Refrigerate for at least 2 more hours and up to 48 hours.

Makes 8 servings.

Per serving: 157 calories, 0.2 g. total fat (1% of calories), 0 g. saturated fat, 0 mg. cholesterol

Taco Salad

We've removed a considerable amount of fat but none of the zippy taste from this popular Tex-Mex salad. Made the old way, a serving of taco salad has around 37 grams of fat. Ours has only 6.5! The recipe calls for nonfat Cheddar. Although this product is bland when used alone, it works very well in concert with the many flavorful ingredients in the dish. You'll find the salad is hearty enough to serve as a summer entrée.

8	ounces ground round of beef
1	large onion, chopped
1	garlic clove, minced
1	can (16 ounces) kidney beans, rinsed and drained
1½	teaspoons mild chili powder, or to taste
⅛	teaspoon salt (optional)
⅛	teaspoon ground black pepper
6	cups shredded iceberg lettuce
1	medium cucumber, peeled and cubed
2	medium tomatoes, cubed, divided
4	ounces nonfat Cheddar cheese, shredded (about 1 cup), divided
1	cup mild or medium commercial salsa or picante sauce
1½	cups crumbled nonfat tortilla chips or taco shells

In a large saucepan, combine the beef, onions and garlic. Cook over medium heat, stirring frequently and breaking up the meat with a spoon, until browned. Transfer the mixture to a plate lined with paper towels. When the fat has been absorbed by the paper towels, return the mixture to the pan.

Stir in the beans, chili powder, salt (if using) and pepper. Remove the pan from the heat and set aside.

In a large bowl, combine the lettuce, cucumbers, three-quarters of the tomatoes and ¾ cup of the cheese. Toss to mix. Add the salsa or picante sauce. Toss to coat.

To serve, divide the lettuce mixture among individual serving plates. Mound equal portions of the meat mixture in the center. Sprinkle the chips in a circle around the meat mixture. Sprinkle with the remaining tomatoes and cheese.

Makes 6 servings.

Per serving: 218 calories, 6.5 g. total fat (27% of calories), 2 g. saturated fat, 22 mg. cholesterol

Savory Cabbage Slaw

This zesty slaw is loaded with some of the most healthful vegetables, notably cabbage, carrots and sweet peppers. And it contains far less fat than slaws made with mayonnaise. Since it is also easy and can be prepared ahead, it makes a good addition to a buffet or informal company meal. This recipe can be doubled if you like. The mustard seeds make the slaw slightly peppery. For a less zippy version, simply omit them. This dish keeps well in the refrigerator for up to a week.

⅓	cup apple cider vinegar
2	tablespoons chopped fresh chives or 1 tablespoon dried chives
1	tablespoon granulated sugar
1½	teaspoons canola or safflower oil
½	teaspoon Dijon mustard
¼	teaspoon mustard seeds (optional)
¼	teaspoon celery seeds
¼	teaspoon celery salt
¼	teaspoon ground black pepper
5	cups lightly packed shredded green cabbage
2	medium carrots, peeled and shredded
¼	cup finely chopped sweet red peppers
¼	cup finely chopped celery

In a large nonreactive bowl, combine the vinegar, chives, sugar, oil, mustard, mustard seeds (if using), celery seeds, celery salt and black pepper until well blended. Stir in the cabbage, carrots, red peppers and celery. Mix well. Cover and refrigerate for at least 15 minutes (preferably 1 hour). Toss briefly before serving.

Makes 6 servings.

Per serving: 48 calories, 1.4 g. total fat (22% of calories), 0.2 g. saturated fat, 0 mg. cholesterol

Piquant Rice and Bean Salad

Rice and two kinds of beans combine with crunchy bits of vegetables in this colorful make-ahead salad.

⅓	cup + 2 tablespoons apple cider vinegar
⅓	cup chopped fresh chives or scallions, including tops
3½	tablespoons olive oil, preferably extra-virgin
2	tablespoons granulated sugar
½	teaspoon ground allspice
¼	teaspoon dried thyme leaves
¼	teaspoon celery salt
¼	teaspoon ground black pepper, or to taste
4	cups cooked long-grain white or brown rice
1	can (16 ounces) kidney beans, rinsed and drained
1	can (16 ounces) black beans, rinsed and drained
¾	cup chopped sweet red peppers
¾	cup chopped green peppers
⅔	cup finely chopped celery
2	tablespoons finely chopped fresh parsley
	Thinly sliced sweet red pepper rings, halved (garnish)

In a large nonreactive bowl, stir together the vinegar, chives or scallions, oil, sugar, allspice, thyme, celery salt and black pepper until well blended.

Add the rice, kidney beans, black beans, red peppers, green peppers, celery and parsley. Toss until well mixed.

Cover and refrigerate for at least 1 hour and up to 24 hours before serving. Garnish with the pepper rings.

Makes 8 servings.

Per serving: 302 calories, 6.7 g. total fat (19% of calories), 0.9 g. saturated fat, 0 mg. cholesterol

Bulgur-Parsley Salad

Bulgur, partially ground and cooked grains of wheat, is a staple in many Middle Eastern cuisines. It has a slightly chewy texture and a mild, nutty taste. We love it in this satisfying salad.

- 1 **cup uncooked bulgur**
- 1¼ **cups water**
- 1 **cup lightly packed chopped fresh parsley leaves**
- ⅔ **cup rinsed and drained canned garbanzo beans**
- ⅔ **cup diced tomatoes**
- 3 **tablespoons chopped fresh chives or 1 tablespoon dried chives**
- 3 **tablespoons lemon juice**
- 1½ **tablespoons olive oil, preferably extra-virgin**
- ¼ **teaspoon salt**
- ¼ **teaspoon ground black pepper**
  Cucumber slices or lettuce leaves (garnish)

In a medium saucepan, combine the bulgur and water. Bring to a simmer over medium-high heat. Simmer for 3 to 4 minutes, or until the bulgur is just barely tender. Stir, remove from the heat and set aside for 15 minutes, or until cooled to room temperature.

Stir in the parsley, beans, tomatoes and chives until evenly incorporated.

In a small bowl or cup, stir together the lemon juice, oil, salt and pepper. Toss with the bulgur mixture until well combined. Garnish with the cucumbers or lettuce.

Makes 5 servings.

Per serving: 177 calories, 5.2 g. total fat (25% of calories), 0.7 g. saturated fat, 0 mg. cholesterol

Chapter 13

SAVORY
AND SWEET
SAUCES
AND GRAVIES

Salad dressings, sauces and gravies are often the finishing touches that make the difference between an ordinary meal and a memorable one. Think of a tangy chutney with a curry dish. Or the perfect dressing on fresh greens. Or a rich-tasting cheese sauce that complements steamed vegetables.

Traditionally, these extra touches add a lot of excess fat to the dinner or dessert plate. But they won't if they're made the 100% Pleasure way. Try our Tomato-Pear Chutney, Russian Dressing or Light Cheese Sauce. And while you're at it, top burritos with our Fresh Chunky Green Salsa or add flavor to your next cookout with No-Fat Ginger-Soy Marinade. You'll find the recipes in this chapter won't bust your fat budget—but they'll add considerable pizzazz to your meals.

Tomato-Pear Chutney

Chutney can lend zip and flavor to dishes without contributing any fat. This easy version is especially appealing, providing color and texture as well as the characteristic sweet-and-sour accent. We like to serve it with such dishes as Shrimp in Curried Tomato Sauce, Tandoori Spice Turkey Cutlets and Curried Chicken Salad. Be sure to use slightly underripe pears; they hold their shape and add a pleasant chunkiness. Store the chutney, covered and refrigerated, for up to two months.

- 1 cup apple cider vinegar
- 1 cup granulated sugar
- 1 large onion, finely chopped
- 1 tablespoon peeled and finely chopped fresh ginger root
- 1½ teaspoons mustard seeds
- 3 medium slightly underripe Bartlett pears
- 2 medium fully ripe tomatoes, peeled and cut into 1¼" chunks

In a medium nonreactive saucepan, stir together the vinegar, sugar, onions, ginger and mustard seeds until the sugar dissolves. Bring to a boil over high heat. Adjust the heat so the mixture boils gently and cook for 15 minutes to reduce the mixture slightly. Remove the pan from the heat.

Peel and core the pears. Cut them into 1" chunks. Immediately stir them into the vinegar mixture to prevent discoloring.

Return the saucepan to the heat. Bring the mixture to a simmer over medium-high heat. Add the tomatoes. Reduce the heat and simmer, stirring occasionally, for 50 minutes longer, or until the pears have cooked down and are softened but still retain some shape. (The chutney will be just slightly fluid but will thicken when chilled.) Let cool briefly.

Pour into glass storage jars. Cover and refrigerate for at least 3 hours, or until thoroughly chilled and slightly thickened, before serving.

Makes 4 cups; 32 servings (2 tablespoons each).

Per serving: 35 calories, 0.1 g. total fat (2% of calories), 0 g. saturated fat, 0 mg. cholesterol

Nonfat Topping for Vegetables

This virtually fat-free topping has a lot more character than plain nonfat sour cream. It tastes wonderful on baked potatoes and on cooked broccoli. And it can be the centerpiece of an appetizer platter of lightly steamed vegetables. If the yogurt and ricotta are very fresh, the topping will keep in the refrigerator for three to four days.

¾   cup plain nonfat yogurt
½   cup nonfat ricotta cheese
2   teaspoons chopped fresh chives or 1 teaspoon dried chives
    Generous ½ teaspoon dried dillweed
¼   teaspoon granulated sugar
¼   teaspoon celery salt
⅛   teaspoon salt, or to taste
    Pinch of ground white pepper

In a food processor, combine the yogurt and ricotta. Process until smooth, stopping and scraping down the sides of the container, if necessary. Transfer the mixture to a small bowl.

Add the chives, dill, sugar, celery salt, salt and pepper. Stir to mix well. Refrigerate for at least ½ hour before serving.

Makes 1¼ cups; 20 servings (1 tablespoon each).

Per serving: 9 calories, 0.1 g. total fat (7% of calories), 0 g. saturated fat, 0 mg. cholesterol

Leek-and-Carrot Sauce

Gourmet cooking doesn't have to mean using lots of high-fat ingredients and sauces, as this tasty garnish proves. Essentially a savory mix of finely diced and braised vegetables, it is the perfect way to enhance fish, chicken or even meat without adding a lot of fat. A local French restaurant first introduced us to this sauce, using it as a base for fresh salmon. While our version is leaner than the original, it retains the subtle flavor. To serve, spoon the leeks and carrots onto individual serving plates to form an attractive and savory bed for your entrée.

2   very large leeks
1   large carrot, peeled and grated or shredded
1   small garlic clove, minced
1   tablespoon nondiet tub-style canola or corn-oil margarine or butter
1   cup defatted chicken broth, divided
    Generous pinch of ground white pepper

Trim off the root end of the leeks and all but about ½" of the green tops; discard. Peel off and discard 1 or 2 layers of the tough outer leaves. Beginning at the green end, slice down about 1" into the leeks. Put the leeks in a colander. Wash them thoroughly under cool running water, separating the layers to remove any grit trapped between them. Wash again to remove all traces of grit. Then set them aside until well drained.

Cut the leeks into thin slices and place them in a medium saucepan. Add the carrots, garlic, margarine or butter and 3 tablespoons of the broth. Cook over medium heat, stirring frequently, for 8 to 10 minutes, or until the leeks are very tender. Add the remaining broth and the pepper. Bring to a boil.

Cover, reduce the heat and simmer for 10 minutes. Uncover and cook for 10 to 12 minutes, or until the vegetables are very tender and most of the liquid has evaporated.

Makes 4 servings.

Per serving: 81 calories, 3.5 g. total fat (36% of calories), 0 g. saturated fat, 0 mg. cholesterol

Light Cheese Sauce

If you like to splurge occasionally and dress up vegetables with cheese sauce, here's a recipe with significantly less fat than a traditional sauce (which can have ten grams of fat per serving). We use sharp Cheddar because a small amount contributes a lot of flavor.

1½	tablespoons all-purpose or unbleached white flour
	Generous ½ teaspoon dry mustard
¼	teaspoon ground white pepper
½	teaspoon salt, or to taste
2	cups 1% fat milk
8	ounces reduced-fat sharp Cheddar cheese, shredded (about 2 cups)

In a small saucepan, stir together the flour, mustard, pepper and salt. Slowly add the milk, stirring with a wire whisk to keep the mixture from lumping. Whisk until the flour is completely incorporated.

Cook over medium heat, whisking constantly, for 3 to 4 minutes, or until thickened. Gradually add the cheese, continuing to whisk until it is completely melted.

Makes 2 cups; 8 servings (½ cup each).

Per serving: 114 calories, 5.6 g. total fat (44% of calories), 0.4 g. saturated fat, 16 mg. cholesterol

No-Fat Ginger-Soy Marinade

A marinade is one of the best ways to bring out flavor and add moistness to meats without relying on fat. Unlike many marinades, this one is fat free. It is also more versatile than most recipes, complementing chicken, turkey, beef, pork and fish. After marinating the cuts or pieces, you can grill, bake, broil or, in the case of fish, even steam them.

- ⅓ cup dry or medium-dry white wine
- ¼ cup reduced-sodium soy sauce
- 1 tablespoon mild honey, such as clover
- 1 tablespoon peeled and finely chopped ginger root
- 1 tablespoon chopped scallions
- 1 small garlic clove, minced (optional)
- 2 teaspoons Worcestershire sauce
- ⅛ teaspoon ground black pepper
- 2 drops hot-pepper sauce (optional)

In a small deep bowl, stir together the wine, soy sauce and honey until the honey is smoothly incorporated. Add the ginger, scallions, garlic (if using), Worcestershire sauce, pepper and hot-pepper sauce (if using). Use the marinade immediately or transfer it to a glass jar and refrigerate it for up to a week.

Makes about ¾ cup; enough to prepare 1½–1¾ pounds meat, poultry or fish.

Per ¾ cup: 166 calories, 0 g. total fat (0% of calories), 0 g. saturated fat, 0 mg. cholesterol

Note: To use the marinade, pour half of it into a flat glass baking dish large enough to hold the meat, poultry or fish in a single layer. Add the pieces and pour the remaining marinade over the top. Cover and refrigerate for at least 2 hours, turning occasionally. Marinate meat and poultry for at least 8 hours and up to 24 hours. Marinate fish for 2 to 8 hours. Drain off the marinade and reserve it for basting. Cook the marinated pieces as desired, basting them several times during the cooking period. Discard any marinade not used for basting.

Nearly Fat-Free Chicken or Turkey Gravy

Most people assume that because old-fashioned homemade gravy is usually fatty, it just naturally has to be that way. Happily, we've discovered that this isn't the case at all. By altering the classic preparation steps a bit, we've created a very savory, rich-tasting gravy containing practically no fat. What's more, our easy fat-busting method yields lump-free gravy every single time.

	Pan juices and drippings from a roasted 6–7½ pound chicken or 6–7 pound turkey breast
	About 1½ cups defatted chicken broth, divided
1	teaspoon cornstarch
½	teaspoon reduced-sodium soy sauce
	Pinch of ground black pepper, or to taste
	Pinch of marjoram leaves (optional)
¼	cup all-purpose or unbleached white flour

Pour the juices and drippings from the roasting pan into a 2-cup glass measure. Add ½ cup of the broth to the roasting pan and scrape the pan surface with a wooden spoon to loosen browned bits and thickened juices. Pour the mixture into the measuring cup.

Chill in the refrigerator or freezer until the fat solidifies on the surface. Skim it off and discard it. (If time is short, transfer the mixture to a gravy skimmer. Let stand until the juices and fat separate, then carefully pour the juices into the measuring cup.)

Add enough additional broth to the cup to measure 1¾ cups. Pour into a blender or food processor. Add the cornstarch, soy sauce, pepper and marjoram (if using). Let stand.

Place the flour in a 4-quart saucepan or pot. Working over medium heat, use a long-handled wooden spoon to stir the flour constantly for 3 to 4 minutes, or until it turns light brown but does not burn. Immediately remove from the heat.

Add the flour to the blender or food processor. Process the mixture until very smooth.

Wipe out the saucepan used to brown the flour. Pour in the blended mixture. Stirring constantly, bring the mixture to a simmer. Continue to stir and simmer for 1½ to 2 minutes longer, or until the gravy thickens. If necessary, thin it with a little broth or water.

Makes 5 servings.

Per serving: 33 calories, 0.3 g. total fat (10% of calories), 0.1 g. saturated fat, 0 mg. cholesterol

Variation: To make beef gravy, use the pan juices and drippings from a beef roast and use defatted beef broth.

Fresh Chunky Green Salsa

Tomatillos are small, firm, green Mexican vegetables related to tomatoes. They taste a bit like very green tomatoes, having a similar appealing acidity and bite. They combine well with cilantro to make an easy, crunchy-crisp salsa. This colorful relish is good sprinkled over many Mexican dishes, including our Taco Casserole. Tomatillos are usually sold with their thin, papery husks intact. Simply peel these off before using the vegetables. Don't store the salsa too long or the tomatillos will lose their appealing crispness.

1¼   cups coarsely chopped tomatillos
½   cup loosely packed chopped fresh cilantro leaves
2   tablespoons chopped fresh chives or scallions, including tops
1½   tablespoons white wine vinegar or apple cider vinegar
¼   teaspoon dried basil leaves
¼   teaspoon salt
2   slivers jalapeño peppers, minced (optional); wear plastic gloves when handling

In a nonreactive bowl, stir together the tomatillos, cilantro, chives or scallions, vinegar, basil and salt. Add the peppers (if using).
Chill for at least 15 minutes and up to 8 hours.

Makes about 1⅛ cups; 6 servings (3 tablespoons each).

Per serving: 8 calories, 0.1 g. total fat (12% of calories), 0 g. saturated fat, 0 mg. cholesterol

Honey-Mustard Dressing

This creamy dressing tastes good on fruit or vegetable salads. For a quick variation, stir in ½ teaspoon poppy seeds just before serving. It will keep in the refrigerator for three to four days.

½   cup plain nonfat yogurt
¼   cup reduced-fat mayonnaise
¼   cup nonfat ricotta cheese
1½   tablespoons mild honey, such as clover
1   teaspoon Dijon mustard

In a food processor, combine the yogurt, mayonnaise, ricotta, honey and mustard. Process until smooth. Transfer to a small bowl or jar and refrigerate for 1 to 2 hours before serving.

Makes 1 cup; 16 servings (1 tablespoon each).

Per serving: 23 calories, 1 g. total fat (42% of calories), 0 g. saturated fat, 1 mg. cholesterol

Russian Dressing

Rich and tangy, this creamy dressing is surprisingly low-fat. It will keep for up to four days refrigerated, if you use very fresh ricotta.

¾	cup ketchup
½	cup nonfat ricotta cheese
1	tablespoon reduced-fat mayonnaise
2	teaspoons sweet pickle relish

In a food processor, combine the ketchup, ricotta and mayonnaise. Process, stopping and scraping down the sides of the container once or twice, until the mixture is well blended. Stir in the relish. Transfer to a small bowl, cover and refrigerate for at least ½ hour and up to 24 hours before using.

Makes 1 cup; 16 servings (1 tablespoon each).

Per serving: 17 calories, 0.3 g. total fat (16% of calories), 0 g. saturated fat, 1 mg. cholesterol

Spicy Herbed Mustard Sauce

This zippy sauce goes well with most winter vegetables—cabbage, rutabagas, turnips, parsnips, carrots and onions are particularly good. Or, use it to dress up grilled or broiled chicken. It will keep in the refrigerator for up to two days. Stir well and reheat before using.

1	tablespoon cornstarch
1	tablespoon packed light brown sugar
1	cup defatted chicken broth
¼	cup nonfat sour cream
2	tablespoons Dijon mustard
1¼	teaspoons dried tarragon leaves

In a small saucepan, stir together the cornstarch and sugar until blended. Stir in the broth until the mixture is smooth. Cook over medium-high heat, stirring constantly, for 2 minutes, or until the mixture turns clear. Remove from the heat.

In a small deep bowl, whisk together the sour cream, mustard and tarragon. Whisk into the cornstarch mixture until blended. Return to the heat and heat until piping hot but not boiling. Serve immediately.

Makes 1¼ cups; 8 servings (2½ tablespoons each).

Per serving: 25 calories, 0.3 g. total fat (11% of calories), 0 g. saturated fat, 0 mg. cholesterol

Curry Sauce

This aromatic, slightly spicy sauce is good served with cooked broccoli, onions, cauliflower and/or carrots. It also makes an easy low-fat topping for baked potatoes. You can make it ahead and store it in the refrigerator for three to four days; reheat before using.

½	cup chopped onions
¼	cup peeled and chopped apples
2	teaspoons nondiet tub-style canola or corn-oil margarine or butter
2½	tablespoons all-purpose or unbleached white flour
1	cup defatted chicken broth
¼	cup tomato sauce
¼	cup instant nonfat dry milk
1½	teaspoons curry powder
½	teaspoon ground coriander

In a medium saucepan, combine the onions, apples and margarine or butter. Cook over medium heat, stirring frequently, for 4 minutes, or until the onions are limp. Stir in the flour until incorporated; the mixture will not be completely smooth. Cook, stirring, for 30 seconds.

Gradually stir in the broth and tomato sauce until well incorporated. Bring to a boil and cook, stirring, for 2 minutes.

Transfer the mixture to a food processor or blender. Add the dry milk, curry powder and coriander. Process for 1 minute, or until completely smooth.

Makes 1½ cups; 6 servings (¼ cup each).

Per serving: 45 calories, 1 g. total fat (30% of calories), 0.1 g. saturated fat, 0 mg. cholesterol

Creamy Vanilla Sauce for Fruit

To come up with a smooth, creamy dessert sauce without using heavy cream, we took advantage of nonfat cream cheese and yogurt. The sauce seems decadent even though it's lean. It's appealing spooned over any mixed fruit salad or over bowls of individual fruit, such as strawberries, raspberries or peaches. For best results, use marmalade made from sweet oranges, such as navel oranges.

3	tablespoons plain nonfat yogurt
2½	tablespoons mild honey, such as clover
2	tablespoons sweet orange marmalade
1¼	teaspoons vanilla extract
1	container (8 ounces) nonfat tub-style cream cheese

In a blender or food processor, combine the yogurt, honey, marmalade and vanilla. Process until completely smooth. With the motor running, add spoonfuls of the cream cheese. Process until smooth, stopping and scraping down the sides of the container several times. Cover and chill for at least 1 hour and up to 3 days. Stir before using.

Makes 1¼ cups; 10 servings (2 tablespoons each).

Per serving: 51 calories, 0 g. total fat (0% of calories), 0 g. saturated fat, 4 mg. cholesterol

Fresh Ginger-Peach Sauce

Tart and tangy, this easy microwave peach sauce is a nice accompaniment to our Creamy Cheesecake in place of its usual Raspberry Glaze. It's also good as a pancake sauce. Or, use it to dress up raspberry or strawberry ice milk or frozen yogurt. The sauce will keep for about five days in the refrigerator. If you prefer a less spicy sauce, omit the ginger.

4	cups sliced peaches
½	cup granulated sugar
2	teaspoons peeled and minced ginger root
2	teaspoons lemon juice
	Pinch of ground cinnamon

Combine the peaches, sugar, ginger, lemon juice and cinnamon in a 4-cup glass measure. Stir carefully so you don't break up the peach slices.

Cover with wax paper. Microwave on high power for 5 to 8 minutes, or until the mixture is bubbly and the peaches are cooked; halfway through the cooking time, give the container a quarter turn and stir the peaches.

Cool slightly. Transfer about half of the mixture to a food processor and puree it. Stir the puree back into the container. Refrigerate for 4 to 5 hours to allow the flavors to blend.

Makes 2½ cups; 20 servings (2 tablespoons each).

Per serving: 33 calories, <0.1 g. total fat (1% of calories), 0 g. saturated fat, 0 mg. cholesterol

V I B R A N T
V E G E T A B L E
A N D   F R U I T
S I D E   D I S H E S

One of the secrets to creating tempting vegetable and fruit side dishes is simply to view them as vital elements, and not afterthoughts, of meals. Both of us cook for vegetarian family members occasionally, and this has encouraged us to give these recipes more attention. After all, some of those at the table are eating only the vegetable and fruit dishes, and we don't want them to be shortchanged.

Interestingly, we've found that meat eaters appreciate appealing side dishes as much as the vegetarians do. Fresh vegetables and fruits that are carefully prepared and seasoned to preserve their succulence and varied textures and flavors (not to mention their vitamins and minerals) are greeted as enthusiastically as the rest of the menu. Sometimes these foods add such interest to a meal that they actually outshine everything else.

Pepper-Corn Pudding Baked in Sweet Pepper Shells

This recipe features corn pudding enlivened with green chili peppers and spices and baked in sweet red pepper halves. (Substitute green or yellow peppers if red are unavailable.) Serve as a festive side dish or plan on two halves per person for a light vegetarian main dish.

4	large sweet red peppers, halved lengthwise and seeded
⅔	cup finely chopped onions
⅓	cup chopped sweet red peppers
2½	teaspoons nondiet tub-style canola or corn-oil margarine or butter
2	cups loose-pack frozen yellow corn kernels, thawed and well drained
½	cup liquid egg substitute
¼	cup whole milk
3	tablespoons yellow cornmeal
½	teaspoon Worcestershire sauce
½	teaspoon dry mustard
¼	teaspoon mild chili powder
½	teaspoon salt (optional)
¼	teaspoon ground black pepper
2	drops hot-pepper sauce (optional)
3	tablespoons canned chopped mild green chili peppers, well drained
2	ounces reduced-fat sharp Cheddar cheese, shredded (about ½ cup)
¼	teaspoon paprika (optional)

Preheat the oven to 350°.

Arrange the pepper halves, cut side up, in a glass baking dish in which they will fit snugly.

In a 12" nonstick skillet, combine the onions, chopped red peppers and margarine or butter. Cook over medium heat, stirring frequently, for 5 minutes, or until the onions are tender.

In a blender, combine the corn, egg substitute, milk, cornmeal, Worcestershire sauce, mustard, chili powder, salt (if using), black pepper and hot-pepper sauce (if using). Blend for 1 minute or until fairly smooth.

Stir (do not blend) the cooked vegetables, chili peppers and cheese into the blended mixture until evenly distributed. Pour the mixture into the pepper halves, dividing it equally among them. Sprinkle with the paprika (if using).

Bake for 25 to 35 minutes, or until the filling is set when the peppers are jiggled. Let stand for 5 minutes before serving.

Makes 8 servings.

Per serving: 109 calories, 3.4 g. total fat (26% of calories), 1.2 g. saturated fat, 6 mg. cholesterol

Microwave Cabbage, Tomato and Potato Bake

Though not often served together, cabbage, tomatoes and potatoes make a very tasty—not to mention healthful—combination. Since the casserole cooks in the microwave, it's ready in about 15 minutes. You can even prepare it ahead and reheat just before serving.

⅔   cup finely chopped onions
2   teaspoons nondiet tub-style canola or corn-oil margarine or butter
3   medium all-purpose potatoes, peeled and cut into ⅛" slices
½   cup whole milk, divided
½   teaspoon dried marjoram leaves
½   teaspoon salt, or to taste
⅛   teaspoon ground black pepper, or to taste
8   ounces green cabbage (half a small head), cut into ¼" slices
2   tablespoons chopped fresh parsley leaves, divided
1   large tomato, peeled and cut into ¼" slices

In a 10" pie plate, combine the onions and margarine or butter. Loosely cover with wax paper and microwave on high power for 1½ to 2 minutes, or until the onions are limp and tender.

Lay the potato slices, slightly overlapping, in the plate. Pour ¼ cup of the milk over them. Cover again with wax paper and microwave on high power for 5 minutes.

Stir the marjoram, salt and pepper into the remaining ¼ cup milk until well blended and the salt dissolves. Rearrange the potato slices so the center slices are at the outer edge. Lay the cabbage slices over the potatoes in a ring around the perimeter of the plate; leave the center of the casserole open.

Pour 2 tablespoons of the milk mixture over the cabbage. Sprinkle with 1 tablespoon of the parsley. Cover the plate with wax paper. Microwave on high power for 6 minutes; halfway through the cooking time, give the plate a quarter turn.

Arrange the tomato slices in a ring over the cabbage, still leaving the center open. Pour the remaining 2 tablespoons milk mixture over the casserole. Sprinkle with the remaining 1 tablespoon parsley.

Cover the plate again with wax paper and microwave on high for 3 to 5 minutes, or until the cabbage and potatoes are just tender when pierced with a fork. Let stand for 5 minutes before serving.

Makes 5 servings.

Per serving: 123 calories, 2.6 g. total fat (18% of calories), 0.8 g. saturated fat, 3 mg. cholesterol

Baked Stuffed Zucchini

*This is a festive, substantial and very tasty side dish or light vege-
tarian entrée. Although it takes a bit of time to prepare the stuffing
and fill the zucchini, this can be done well ahead. Then, at dinner-
time, simply slip the zucchini into the oven and bake them.*

3	medium (6½" long) zucchini, halved lengthwise
3	teaspoons olive oil, preferably extra-virgin, divided
1	small onion, chopped
½	cup chopped mushrooms
¼	cup chopped sweet red peppers
1	large garlic clove, minced
½	cup cooked long-grain white rice
¼	cup tomato sauce
1¼	teaspoons mild chili powder
1	teaspoon paprika
½	teaspoon dried marjoram leaves
½	teaspoon salt
¼	teaspoon dried thyme leaves
⅛	teaspoon ground black pepper
	Pinch of ground red pepper (optional)

Preheat the oven to 375°.

Using a teaspoon, form "boats" with the zucchini halves by scoop-
ing out the pulp and leaving a shell about ⅛" thick. Chop the pulp
and set it aside. Using 1 teaspoon of the oil, brush the insides of the
boats.

In a 12" nonstick skillet over medium heat, warm the remaining 2
teaspoons oil until hot but not smoking. Add the onions, mushrooms, chopped red peppers, garlic and reserved zucchini pulp.
Cook, stirring frequently, for 5 minutes, or until the vegetables are
soft. Add the rice, tomato sauce, chili powder, paprika, marjoram,
salt, thyme, black pepper and ground red pepper (if using). Mix
well.

Arrange the zucchini shells in a flat baking dish just large enough
to hold them in a single layer. Mound the vegetable mixture in the
shells, dividing it equally among them. Cover tightly with foil.

Bake for 40 minutes. Uncover and bake for 10 to 15 minutes
longer, or until the shells are tender when pierced at the thickest
part with a fork.

Makes 6 servings.

*Per serving: 72 calories, 2.5 g. total fat (30% of calories), 0.3 g. saturated fat,
0 mg. cholesterol*

Microwaved Vegetables and Cheese

Oh so quick and easy, this vegetable-cheese combination makes a wonderful side dish or even a light luncheon main dish. You may either peel the potatoes or leave the skins on before slicing them.

- 2   cups thinly sliced boiling or red-skinned potatoes
- 1   small onion, finely chopped
- 1   sweet red or yellow pepper, seeded and diced
- 2   cups small broccoli florets
- 2   cups thinly sliced zucchini or yellow squash
- 3   ounces reduced-fat sharp Cheddar cheese, shredded (about ¾ cup)
- ¼   teaspoon salt (optional)

In a 2½-quart microwave-safe casserole, combine the potatoes and onions. Cover with a lid and microwave on high power for 5 to 8 minutes; halfway through the cooking time, stir the vegetables and give the casserole a quarter turn.

Add the peppers, broccoli and zucchini or squash. Cover and microwave on high power for 5 or 7 minutes, until the vegetables are tender; halfway through the cooking time, stir the vegetables and give the casserole a quarter turn.

Add the cheese and salt (if using). Stir until the cheese melts.

Makes 5 servings.

Per serving: 124 calories, 3.3 g. total fat (23% of calories), 0 g. saturated fat, 8 mg. cholesterol

Sweet Potato Casserole

Some people think of sweet potatoes only as a holiday side dish. But we like to serve them on a regular basis because they are not only delicious but also an excellent source of beta-carotene and fiber. Since sweets cook particularly well in the microwave, this casserole is both quick and easy. For a change of pace, try substituting maple syrup for the honey.

- 3   large sweet potatoes
- ⅔   cup orange juice
- ½   cup coarsely chopped or diced dried apricots
- ⅓   cup dark or golden raisins
- 2   tablespoons mild honey, such as clover
- 2   tablespoons diet tub-style canola or corn-oil margarine or butter
- ½   teaspoon ground ginger

Pierce the sweet potatoes several times with a knife or fork. Place on a plate and arrange like the spokes of a wheel. Microwave on high power for 10 to 14 minutes, or until tender when tested with a knife; halfway through the cooking time, give the plate a quarter turn. Cool slightly.

Halve the sweet potatoes and scoop out the flesh; discard the skin. Place the flesh in a 2-quart microwave-safe casserole and mash with a fork to break up any large lumps. Stir in the orange juice and mix well. Add the apricots, raisins, honey, margarine or butter and ginger. Stir to mix well.

Spread the mixture evenly in the casserole. Cover with a lid or wax paper and microwave on high power for 6 to 7 minutes, or until heated through; halfway through the cooking time, give the casserole a quarter turn.

Makes 5 servings.

Per serving: 265 calories, 1.6 g. total fat (5% of calories), 0.3 g. saturated fat, 0 mg. cholesterol

Broccoli and Sweet Red Pepper Stir-Fry

Sesame oil and reduced-sodium soy sauce flavor this simple and colorful stir-fry—which we like to serve as an accompaniment to Quick-Baked Seasoned Fish and Pork Loin, Carribean-Style.

1	small garlic clove, minced
1	teaspoon oriental sesame oil
1½	tablespoons reduced-sodium soy sauce, divided
4	cups small broccoli florets and tender stem pieces
1	medium sweet red pepper, seeded and cut into thin strips
½	teaspoon sesame seeds

In a 12" nonstick skillet, stir together the garlic, oil and 1 table-spoon of the soy sauce. Add the broccoli and stir to coat it with the oil. Cook over medium heat, stirring frequently, for 5 minutes. Add the peppers, sesame seeds and the remaining ½ tablespoon soy sauce. Cook, stirring, for 3 to 4 minutes, or until the broccoli is crisp-tender and the pepper is still very crisp.

Makes 4 servings.

Per serving: 64 calories, 1.9 g. total fat (20% of calories), 0.3 g. saturated fat, 0 mg. cholesterol

Dilly Carrots

This is a quick, nearly fat-free way to dress up carrots. Try to use fresh dill; it has a livelier, more distinct flavor than dried dill.

1	cup defatted chicken broth
2	tablespoons chopped fresh dill or 1 teaspoon dried dillweed
2	teaspoons mild honey, such as clover
2½	cups finely sliced carrots

In a 12" nonstick skillet, stir together the broth, dill and honey. Bring to a boil over medium-high heat. Boil for 1 minute. Add the carrots.

Adjust the heat so the carrots simmer. Cook, stirring occasionally, for 5 to 8 minutes, or until the carrots are cooked through but are still slightly firm. (If the liquid evaporates from the pan before the carrots are done, add a little water and continue cooking.)

Makes 4 servings.

Per serving: 50 calories, 0.5 g. total fat (8% of calories), 0.1 g. saturated fat, 0 mg. cholesterol

Curried Cauliflower and Carrots

Quick and easy, this spicy side dish goes well with broiled chicken breasts and white rice.

1	medium onion, chopped
1	garlic clove, minced
2	teaspoons nondiet tub-style canola or corn-oil margarine or butter
½	cup defatted chicken broth, divided
1½	teaspoons mild curry powder
	Scant ½ teaspoon ground ginger
½	teaspoon granulated sugar
	Pinch of ground cinnamon
¼	cup orange juice
½	cup 1% fat milk, divided
4	cups small cauliflower florets and stem pieces
1	large carrot, peeled and very thinly sliced
⅛	teaspoon salt (optional)
1	tablespoon cornstarch
	Chives (garnish)

In a large saucepan, combine the onions, garlic, margarine or butter and 2 tablespoons of the broth. Cook over medium heat, stirring frequently, for 5 to 6 minutes, or until the onions are tender.

Add the curry powder, ginger, sugar and cinnamon. Cook, stirring, for 1 minute longer. Add the orange juice, ¼ cup of the milk and the remaining broth. Stir to mix well. Stir in the cauliflower and carrots. Add the salt (if using).

Bring to a boil. Cover, reduce the heat and simmer, stirring occasionally, for 6 to 8 minutes, or until the cauliflower and carrots are tender.

In a small cup, stir together the cornstarch and the remaining ¼ cup milk. Stir into the cauliflower mixture. Bring to a boil over medium heat, then lower the heat and simmer for an additional 2 minutes, or until the sauce thickens. Garnish with chives.

Makes 5 servings.

Per serving: 74 calories, 2 g. total fat (24% of calories), 0.4 g. saturated fat, 1 mg. cholesterol

Pan-Grilled Peppers and Onions

Try this colorful, robust vegetable combo with just about any well-seasoned poultry, meat, shrimp or fish entrée. It's one of our favorites. You may cook the vegetables ahead and reheat them later, if desired.

3	medium onions, quartered
2	medium green peppers, seeded and cut into ¼" × 1¼" strips
1	medium sweet red pepper, seeded and cut into ¼" × 1¼" strips
1	large garlic clove, minced
1	teaspoon nondiet tub-style canola or corn-oil margarine or butter
1	teaspoon olive oil, preferably extra-virgin
¼	cup diced tomatoes
¼	teaspoon salt, or to taste
⅛	teaspoon ground black pepper, or to taste
½	teaspoon lemon juice

In a 12" nonstick skillet, combine the onions, green peppers, red peppers, garlic, margarine or butter and oil. Cook over medium heat, stirring frequently, for 9 to 10 minutes, or until the vegetables are nicely browned.

Stir in the tomatoes. Cook for 2 minutes longer. Stir in the salt, black pepper and lemon juice.

Makes 6 servings.

Per serving: 54 calories, 1.6 g. total fat (25% of calories), 0.2 g. saturated fat, 0 mg. cholesterol

Chinese Pea Pods with Sesame Seeds

This goes well not only with Asian-style menus but also with simple American dishes like roast chicken or pork. To preserve the appealing crispness of the pea pods, be careful not to overcook them. The sesame seeds add a pleasant crunch.

1½	teaspoons sesame seeds
1	scallion, finely chopped
1	teaspoon oriental sesame oil
4	cups trimmed Chinese pea pods
2½	teaspoons reduced-sodium soy sauce

In a 12" nonstick skillet over medium-high heat, toast the sesame seeds, stirring constantly, for 2 to 3 minutes, or until fragrant and lightly browned. Transfer to a small bowl and set aside.

In the same skillet, combine the scallions and oil. Cook, stirring, for 30 seconds. Add the pea pods and soy sauce. Cook, stirring, for 1 to 2 minutes longer, or until the peas are heated through. Stir in the sesame seeds.

Makes 5 servings.

Per serving: 64 calories, 1.6 g. total fat (21% of calories), 0.2 g. saturated fat, 0 mg. cholesterol

Easy Eggplant-Vegetable Skillet

Eggplant is often difficult to incorporate into low-fat casseroles and stir-fry dishes because it sticks and burns unless cooked with a large quantity of oil. This problem can easily be avoided, however, by partially cooking the eggplant in a microwave before adding it to the rest of the ingredients. This rich-tasting side dish goes well with chicken, beef or pork entrées, especially robust, well-seasoned ones. You may make this dish ahead and rewarm it over medium heat.

4¼	cups peeled and coarsely cubed eggplant
1½	tablespoons water, divided
1⅔	cups coarsely sliced mushrooms
½	cup diced sweet red or green peppers
2	tablespoons sliced scallions
1½	teaspoons olive oil, preferably extra-virgin
1	tablespoon reduced-sodium soy sauce
¾	teaspoon mild chili powder
	Ground black pepper, to taste

Place the eggplant in a colander; rinse with cold water and drain well. Spread evenly on a large microwave-safe plate. Sprinkle with 1 tablespoon of the water. Cover the plate with wax paper. Microwave on high for 3½ to 5 minutes, or until the pieces give slightly when tested with a fork but are not quite tender. Transfer to the colander and let drain.

Meanwhile, in a 12" nonstick skillet, combine the mushrooms, diced peppers, scallions and oil. Cook over medium-high heat, stirring frequently, for about 5 minutes, or until the mushrooms and onions brown and most of the juices evaporate from the pan. Add the eggplant.

In a cup, combine the soy sauce, chili powder and the remaining ½ tablespoon water. Add to the pan, tossing to coat the vegetables. Lower the heat and gently simmer for 2 to 3 minutes, or until most of the liquid evaporates and the eggplant is tender. Add the black pepper.

Makes 5 servings.

Per serving: 43 calories, 1.6 g. total fat (31% of calories), 0.2 g. saturated fat, 0 mg. cholesterol

Pan-Grilled Summer Squash

The process of searing the squash in a hot skillet and cooking away excess moisture helps bring out its delicate flavor. Since we use both yellow squash and zucchini, the dish is quite colorful.

1½   teaspoons olive oil, preferably extra-virgin
2   medium (6½" long) yellow squash, cut into thick diagonal slices
2   medium (6½" long) zucchini, cut into thick diagonal slices
1   tablespoon chopped onions
1   large garlic clove, minced
¼   teaspoon salt, or to taste
    Pinch of ground black pepper, or to taste

In a 12" nonstick skillet over medium-high heat, warm the oil until hot but not smoking. Add the squash, zucchini, onions and garlic. Cook, stirring frequently, for 6 to 8 minutes, or until the slices are nicely browned. Stir in the salt and pepper.

Makes 5 servings.

Per serving: 57 calories, 1.9 g. total fat (26% of calories), 0.3 g. saturated fat, 0 mg. cholesterol

Ratatouille

Classic ratatouille is a robust Mediterranean stew of summer vegetables. We've adapted the dish, reducing the amount of oil, replacing the traditional eggplant with yellow squash and modifying the seasonings to come up with a savory topping for baked potatoes (or pasta). Serve as a hearty side dish or a light entrée. For a vegetarian dish, substitute vegetable bouillon or water for the chicken broth.

1	medium onion, cut lengthwise into thin strips
1	large sweet red or green pepper, seeded and cut into ¼" × 2" strips
2	large garlic cloves, halved
2	teaspoons olive oil, preferably extra-virgin
5½	cups julienned mixed zucchini and yellow squash
½	cup chopped fresh parsley leaves, divided
1	can (14½ ounces) Italian (plum) tomatoes, with juice
1	can (6 ounces) tomato paste
¾	cup defatted chicken broth
1	teaspoon mild honey, such as clover
1½	teaspoons mild chili powder
½	teaspoon paprika
½	teaspoon dried marjoram leaves
¼	teaspoon ground black pepper, or to taste
¼	teaspoon salt (optional)
5	large warm baked potatoes, halved lengthwise

In a 12" nonstick skillet, combine the onions, red or green peppers, garlic and oil. Cook over medium heat, stirring frequently, for 5 minutes, or until the onions are limp and beginning to brown. Discard the garlic.

Add the zucchini and squash and ¼ cup of the parsley. Cook, stirring frequently, for 5 minutes longer. Add the tomatoes (with juice). Break up the tomatoes with a spoon.

In a small bowl, stir together the tomato paste, broth, honey, chili powder, paprika, marjoram and black pepper until well blended. Stir the mixture into the skillet.

Adjust the heat so the mixture simmers gently. Cook, stirring occasionally, for 15 to 20 minutes, or until the vegetables are tender and the liquid has cooked down slightly. Stir in the salt (if using) and the remaining ¼ cup parsley.

Fluff the potato flesh with a fork, then spoon on the ratatouille.

Makes 5 servings.

Per serving: 245 calories, 2.9 g. total fat (10% of calories), 0.5 g. saturated fat, 0 mg. cholesterol

Stir-Fried Vegetable Medley

Touches of mustard and sherry combine with the more typical oriental stir-fry ingredients to yield this zesty vegetable combo. Although this may seem like a large quantity of vegetables, they cook down considerably.

SAUCE

- 2 teaspoons cornstarch
- 1 teaspoon packed light or dark brown sugar
- 2½ tablespoons reduced-sodium soy sauce
- 1 tablespoon orange juice
- 2 teaspoons peeled and finely minced ginger root
- 1½ teaspoons prepared mustard
- 1½ teaspoons dry sherry
- ¼ cup water

VEGETABLES

- 1½ teaspoons peanut oil
- ½ cup cut (½" pieces) scallions
- 1 large garlic clove, minced
- 1¼ cups small cauliflower florets
- 1¼ cups small broccoli florets
- 3 tablespoons water
- 3 cups very coarsely sliced celery cabbage
- 1 can (8 ounces) sliced water chestnuts, well drained

To prepare the sauce: In a small bowl, stir together the cornstarch and sugar until blended. Stir in the soy sauce until smoothly incorporated. Whisk in the orange juice, ginger, mustard and sherry until smoothly incorporated. Stir in the water and set aside.

To prepare the vegetables: In a 12" nonstick skillet, combine the oil, scallions and garlic. Cook over medium-high heat, stirring, for 1 minute. Add the cauliflower, broccoli and water. Cook, stirring, for 3 minutes longer, or until the scallions are limp. Add the cabbage and cook, stirring, for 2 minutes.

Stir in the water chestnuts and the reserved sauce. Cook for 2 minutes, or until the sauce is thickened and clear.

Makes 5 servings.

Per serving: 153 calories, 2.1 g. total fat (12% of calories), 0.3 g. saturated fat, 0 mg. cholesterol

Roasted Winter Vegetables

Roasted vegetables are so easy, tasty and healthful that we serve them often. (They also smell wonderfully aromatic as they roast.) We prefer to use extra-virgin olive oil in this recipe because we think it brings out the taste of the vegetables. However, a very mild olive, canola or safflower oil may be substituted. Note that we have carefully specified what sizes the cut-up vegetables should be. This is so they will all be done at the same time. If you don't have small onions, use three large ones and quarter them.

1	large rutabaga, peeled and cut into ¾" chunks
⅓	cup defatted chicken broth
3	medium carrots, cut into ¾" lengths
12	small (1½" diameter) white onions, peeled and halved
3	large all-purpose potatoes, cut into 1¼" chunks
1½	tablespoons olive oil, preferably extra-virgin
¼	teaspoon dried thyme leaves
⅛	teaspoon ground black pepper
	Generous ¼ teaspoon salt

Preheat the oven to 375°.

Combine the rutabagas and broth in a large roasting pan or jelly-roll pan. Place on the center oven rack and roast, stirring occasionally, for 20 minutes.

In a large bowl, stir together the carrots, onions, potatoes, oil, thyme and pepper until well combined. Add the rutabagas and any remaining broth. Transfer the vegetables to the pan previously used for the rutabagas. Spread the vegetables out evenly.

Roast, stirring occasionally, for 40 to 50 minutes, or until the carrots and rutabagas are just tender when pierced with a fork. Sprinkle with the salt and mix well.

Makes 5 servings.

Per serving: 201 calories, 4.6 g. total fat (20% of calories), 0.7 g. saturated fat, 0 mg. cholesterol

Escalloped Cranberries, Apples and Pears

Using the microwave to cook the fruit really reduces the preparation time of this zesty, not-too-sweet casserole. Serve this as a brunch, luncheon or dinner side dish. It also makes a healthful dessert.

TOPPING

¼	cup all-purpose or unbleached white flour
¼	cup packed light or dark brown sugar
1	tablespoon nondiet tub-style canola or corn-oil margarine or butter
¼	teaspoon ground cinnamon
4	teaspoons light corn syrup
⅔	cup dry bread crumbs

FRUIT

¼	cup packed light or dark brown sugar
½	teaspoon ground cinnamon
1	tablespoon apple cider, unsweetened apple juice or cranberry juice cocktail
3	medium Bosc or Bartlett pears, peeled, cored and sliced
3	medium Winesap or Granny Smith apples, peeled, cored and sliced
1¼	cups fresh or thawed frozen cranberries

To prepare the topping: Combine the flour, sugar, margarine or butter and cinnamon in a food processor. Process with on/off pulses until the margarine or butter is evenly cut into the dry ingredients and no bits of it remain visible.

Add the corn syrup and process with on/off pulses just until evenly incorporated. Add the bread crumbs and process with on/off pulses just until incorporated; do not overmix. Set aside.

To prepare the fruit: Preheat the oven to 425°.

In a 10" pie plate, combine the sugar, cinnamon and cider or juice. Stir until well mixed. Stir in the pears and apples. Cover loosely with wax paper and microwave on high power for 3 minutes; halfway through the cooking time, stop and stir the fruit.

Stir in the cranberries. Cover again with wax paper. Microwave for 4 to 5 minutes, or until the fruit slices are almost tender and the cranberries are beginning to pop; halfway through the cooking period, stop and stir the fruit.

Stir well. Sprinkle with the crumb topping. Bake in the preheated oven for 10 to 13 minutes, or until the top is browned and the fruit is bubbly.

Makes 6 servings.

Per serving: 255 calories, 3.1 g. total fat (10% of calories), 0.5 g. saturated fat, 0 mg. cholesterol

Sautéed Apples

Although we call these sautéed apples, they're cooked in apple cider with just a smidgen of margarine or butter. As the cider evaporates, the slices become glazed and take on a golden-brown color. For best results, use Golden Delicious apples. This is a great side dish for breakfast, brunch or supper. It's even good as a light dessert. For a more decadent dessert, spoon the apples over small scoops of vanilla ice milk, light ice cream or frozen yogurt.

1	cup apple cider
2	tablespoons packed light or dark brown sugar
¼	teaspoon ground cinnamon
1	teaspoon nondiet tub-style canola or corn-oil margarine or butter
6	large Golden Delicious apples, peeled, cored and cut into eighths

In a measuring cup, mix the cider, sugar and cinnamon until the sugar dissolves.

In a 12" nonstick skillet over medium-high heat, melt the margarine or butter. Add the apples and stir to coat them with the margarine or butter. Add ⅓ cup of the cider mixture. Raise the heat to high. Cook the apples, stirring frequently, until almost all the liquid has evaporated; if the apples begin to burn, lower the heat slightly.

Add ⅓ cup of the remaining cider mixture. Cook, stirring, until the liquid has almost completely evaporated. Test the apples for doneness by piercing the center of several slices with the tines of a fork; they should give slightly but not be soft.

If the slices are almost tender, cook, stirring, just until all the juice has evaporated from the pan. If the slices are still firm, add the remaining ⅓ cup cider mixture and continue cooking until all the liquid evaporates and the slices are glazed. Serve immediately.

Makes 5 servings.

Per serving: 143 calories, 1.3 g. total fat (8% of calories), 0.2 g. saturated fat, 0 mg. cholesterol

Chapter 15

GLORIOUS GRAINS, LEGUMES, PASTA AND POTATOES

The beauty of grains, legumes, pasta and potatoes is that they fill you up without filling you out. Not only that, but these foods are the very ones that form the base of the new Food Guide Pyramid that is revolutionizing how Americans eat for good health. (See page 27 for more on the Food Guide Pyramid.)

Since the pyramid recommends 6 to 11 servings of these types of foods every day, you'll be particularly interested in the recipes in this chapter. Some are deliciously slimmed-down versions of old favorites like stuffed potatoes and barbecued beans. Others, like Garbanzos in Herbed Tomato Sauce, Easy Risotto and Corn and Rice Skillet with Cilantro, may be just the thing to give a new and delightful twist to your menus.

Caribbean Rice Skillet with Black Beans

This side dish is a lively, fragrant blend of flavors and textures. Since it uses cooked rice and canned black beans, you can put it together quickly. You can also make it ahead and reheat it. For variety, serve this as a super low fat meatless main dish.

1	cup chopped onions
1	cup chopped sweet red peppers
½	cup chopped celery, including leaves
1	large garlic clove, minced
1	tablespoon olive oil, preferably extra-virgin
1⅓	cups defatted chicken broth
1	cup chopped canned tomatoes, with juice
1½	teaspoons lemon juice
¾	teaspoon mild curry powder
½	teaspoon mild chili powder
½	teaspoon dried thyme leaves
½	teaspoon dried oregano leaves
½	teaspoon ground allspice
¼	teaspoon ground black pepper
¼	teaspoon salt, or to taste (optional)
	Pinch of ground red pepper (optional)
1	large bay leaf
1	can (16 ounces) black beans, rinsed and drained
4	cups cooked long-grain white rice
¼	cup chopped scallions, including tops
¼	cup chopped fresh cilantro leaves

In a 12" nonstick skillet, combine the onions, chopped red peppers, celery, garlic and oil. Cook over medium heat, stirring frequently, for 5 minutes, or until the onions are tender.

Stir in the broth, tomatoes (with juice), lemon juice, curry powder, chili powder, thyme, oregano, allspice, black pepper, salt (if using), ground red pepper (if using) and bay leaf. Bring to a simmer and cook for 5 minutes.

Stir in the beans, rice and scallions. Lower the heat so the mixture just barely simmers. Cover and cook, stirring once or twice, for 10 minutes longer, or until the liquid has been absorbed and the rice and beans are heated through. Remove and discard the bay leaf. Sprinkle with the cilantro.

Makes 6 servings.

Per serving: 310 calories, 3.4 g. total fat (10% of calories), 0.6 g. saturated fat, 0 mg. cholesterol

Sweet Potato Casserole (page 150)

Curried Cauliflower and Carrots (page 152)

Roasted Winter Vegetables (page 158)

Broccoli and Sweet Red Pepper Stir-Fry (page 151)

Noodle Pudding (page 190)

Stuffed Potatoes (page 187)

Easy Risotto (page 179)

Barbecued Beans (page 184)

Corn and Rice Skillet with Cilantro (page 181)

Pasta with Vegetables and Cheese (page 196)

Spanish-Style Scrambled Eggs (page 201)

Vegetarian Chili (page 192); Spicy Cornbread (page 309)

Stuffed Pita Pockets (page 200)

Red Snapper and Shrimp Étouffée (page 208)

Tuna Steaks with Mango-Pepper Salsa (page 212)

178   Grilled Fresh Salmon with Dill (page 209); Pan-Grilled Summer Squash (page 155)

Easy Risotto

Preparing risotto, a popular Italian rice dish, usually involves a lot of stirring and careful watching to avoid sticking. But this easy microwave version takes all the fuss out of the dish. You simply add the broth all at once and let the mixture cook until the rice is tender. The key to risotto's distinctive, creamy texture is the kind of rice used. Arborio rice is very absorbent and starchy, which accounts for its creamy, almost pudding-like consistency. Look for it in gourmet shops, some supermarkets, Italian markets and mail-order catalogs. A somewhat similar short-grained rice, called granza or paella rice, makes an acceptable substitute. Risotto is a mild yet savory accompaniment for all sorts of main dishes.

⅔	cup finely chopped onions
2	teaspoons olive oil, preferably extra-virgin
1¼	cups uncooked Arborio rice
3	cups defatted chicken broth, at room temperature
⅓	cup hot water
¼	cup finely chopped fresh parsley leaves
1	tablespoon finely chopped fresh chives or scallions, including tops
2	tablespoons grated Parmesan cheese
⅛	teaspoon ground black pepper

In a 1½-quart round microwave-safe casserole, stir together the onions and oil. Microwave on high power for 1½ to 2 minutes, or until the onions are cooked through and limp. Stir in the rice. Microwave on high power for 1½ minutes longer.

Stir in the broth and water. Loosely cover with wax paper and microwave on high power for 10 minutes. Stir the mixture well and give the casserole a quarter turn.

Microwave, uncovered, for 8 to 10 minutes longer, or until the rice is almost tender and most of the liquid has been absorbed; the mixture should still be slightly moist and soupy. Stir in the parsley, chives or scallions, Parmesan and pepper.

Cover the casserole lightly with wax paper and let stand for 5 minutes.

Makes 5 servings.

Per serving: 225 calories, 3.1 g. total fat (12% of calories), 0 g. saturated fat, 2 mg. cholesterol

Garbanzos in Herbed Tomato Sauce

Tomatoes and herbs are a perfect complement to the mild flavor of garbanzo beans. For a meatless meal, serve this dish with a salad and rice.

- 1 medium onion, chopped
- 1 garlic clove, minced
- 2 teaspoons olive oil
- 2 cans (15 ounces each) garbanzo beans, rinsed and drained
- 1 can (15 ounces) tomato sauce
- 1 large bay leaf
- 1¼ teaspoons dried thyme leaves
- ½ teaspoon dried marjoram leaves
  Salt and ground black pepper, to taste
- ½ teaspoon granulated sugar (optional)

In a medium saucepan, combine the onions, garlic and oil. Cook over medium heat for 5 to 6 minutes, or until the onions are tender. Add the beans, tomato sauce, bay leaf, thyme, marjoram and salt and pepper.

Taste the sauce. If it seems too acid, add the sugar. Bring to a boil. Cover, reduce the heat and simmer, stirring occasionally, for 15 to 20 minutes, or until the flavors are well blended. Remove and discard the bay leaf.

Makes 5 servings.

Per serving: 206 calories, 4.9 g. total fat (20% of calories), 0.7 g. saturated fat, 0 mg. cholesterol

Rice and Vegetable Pilaf

This colorful side dish is a nice change from ordinary white rice.

- 1 small onion, grated or shredded
- 1 small garlic clove, minced
- 1 teaspoon olive oil
- 4 cups defatted chicken broth, divided
- 2 cups uncooked long-grain white rice
- 1 medium carrot, peeled and grated or shredded
- 1 cup grated or shredded zucchini
- ¼ cup finely chopped fresh parsley leaves
- 1 large bay leaf
- 1 teaspoon dried thyme leaves
- 1 teaspoon dried basil leaves
  Ground black pepper, to taste

In a large saucepan, combine the onions, garlic, oil and 2 table-spoons of the broth. Cook over medium heat, stirring frequently, for 3 to 4 minutes, or until the onions are tender.

Add the remaining broth, rice, carrots, zucchini, parsley, bay leaf, thyme, basil and pepper. Stir to mix well. Bring to a boil over high heat. Cover, reduce the heat and cook, stirring occasionally, for 20 minutes, or until the rice is tender and all of the liquid has been absorbed. Remove and discard the bay leaf. Stir before serving.

Makes 7 servings.

Per serving: 233 calories, 1.9 g. total fat (7% of calories), 0.4 g. saturated fat, 0 mg. cholesterol

Corn and Rice Skillet with Cilantro

We like to keep cooked rice and frozen corn on hand so we can easily put together this zesty, hearty side dish. It has a Tex-Mex flavor that goes well with roasted or grilled poultry, beef, pork or fish.

¾	cup chopped scallions
½	cup lightly packed chopped fresh parsley leaves
1	large garlic clove, minced
½	tablespoon olive oil, preferably extra-virgin
1½	cups loose-pack frozen yellow corn kernels
2½	cups cooked long-grain white or brown rice
½	cup lightly packed chopped fresh cilantro leaves
1	can (8 ounces) tomato sauce
1	teaspoon mild chili powder
¼	teaspoon dried thyme leaves
⅛	teaspoon ground black pepper
¼	teaspoon salt (optional)

In a 12" nonstick skillet, combine the scallions, parsley, garlic and oil. Cook over medium heat, stirring frequently, for 5 minutes, or until the scallions are tender. Stir in the corn and cook, stirring, for 4 minutes, or until the corn is heated through.

Stir in the rice, cilantro, tomato sauce, chili powder, thyme, pepper and salt (if using). Bring to a simmer and cook for 5 minutes.

Makes 5 servings.

Per serving: 207 calories, 1.9 g. total fat (8% of calories), 0.3 g. saturated fat, 0 mg. cholesterol

Microwave Baked Beans

There's no need to spend hours in the kitchen to make delicious baked beans. Because these beans are cooked in the microwave, they're ready in a jiffy. We used canned vegetarian beans—which have virtually no fat. Look for them on the grocery shelf right next to the pork and beans. Incidentally, you can turn this casserole into a hearty main dish by adding two ounces of Canadian bacon, cut into thin strips, along with the seasonings. Canadian bacon is lean, so you'll add only four grams of fat to the whole recipe.

1	medium onion, finely chopped
3	cans (16 ounces each) vegetarian beans, with sauce
⅓	cup ketchup
2	tablespoons light molasses
2	tablespoons packed light brown sugar
1	tablespoon apple cider vinegar
½	teaspoon dry mustard
¼	teaspoon dried thyme leaves
¼	teaspoon ground ginger
⅛	teaspoon ground cloves

Place the onions in a 2½-quart microwave-safe casserole. Cover with a lid and microwave on high power for 4 to 6 minutes, or until the onions are softened; halfway through the cooking period, give the casserole a quarter turn.

Add the beans (with sauce), ketchup, molasses, sugar, vinegar, mustard, thyme, ginger and cloves. Stir to mix well. Cover and microwave on high power for 10 to 15 minutes, or until bubbly; halfway through the cooking period, give the casserole a quarter turn.

Makes 5 servings.

Per serving: 320 calories, 1.3 g. total fat (3% of calories), 0.3 g. saturated fat, 0 mg. cholesterol

Herbed Lentils and Rice with Tomatoes

This wonderfully savory side dish goes well with poultry dishes, such as Turkey Scaloppine with Lemon and Parsley.

¾	cup chopped celery, including leaves
1½	cups chopped onions
1	garlic clove, minced
1	tablespoon olive oil, preferably extra-virgin
2½	cups defatted chicken broth
⅓	cup dry brown lentils, washed and sorted
2	teaspoons dried basil leaves
½	teaspoon dried thyme leaves
½	teaspoon dried oregano leaves
¼	teaspoon ground black pepper
	Pinch of ground red pepper, or to taste
1	large bay leaf
¾	cup uncooked long-grain white rice
1	cup peeled and chopped tomatoes
¼	cup chopped scallions

In a Dutch oven or other large heavy pot, combine the celery, onions, garlic and oil. Cook over medium heat, stirring frequently, for 5 minutes, or until the onions are tender.

Add the broth, lentils, basil, thyme, oregano, black pepper, red pepper and bay leaf. Bring to a simmer. Cover and adjust the heat so the mixture simmers gently.

Cook for 15 minutes. Remove and discard the bay leaf. Add the rice. Cover and just barely simmer, stirring once or twice, for 20 to 25 minutes longer, or until the rice is just tender.

Stir in the tomatoes and scallions. Simmer for 5 minutes longer.

Makes 6 servings.

Per serving: 169 calories, 3.2 g. total fat (17% of calories), 0.5 g. saturated fat, 0 mg. cholesterol

Barbecued Beans

Tangy, flavorful and very low in fat, these beans go wonderfully well with Barbecued Chicken and Spicy Cornbread. You could also make them the centerpiece of a vegetarian meal.

1	cup dry Great Northern beans, washed and sorted
1	cup dry black-eyed peas, washed and sorted
1	medium onion, chopped
1	garlic clove, minced
3	quarts water
1	can (15 ounces) tomato sauce
1	cup ketchup
1	tablespoon light brown sugar
1	teaspoon dried thyme leaves
1	teaspoon mild chili powder
½	teaspoon prepared mustard
⅛	teaspoon ground cinnamon
	Pinch of ground cloves
3	drops hot-pepper sauce (optional)
	Salt and ground black pepper, to taste

Place the beans and peas in a Dutch oven or other large heavy pot. Cover with 2" of water and bring to a boil over high heat. Reduce the heat and boil for 2 minutes. Remove the pot from the heat, cover and let stand for 1 hour. Drain in a colander; discard the soaking water.

Return the beans and peas to the pot. Add the onions, garlic and 3 quarts water. Bring to a boil over high heat. Reduce the heat and simmer for 1¼ to 1½ hours, or until tender. Drain well in a colander.

Transfer back to the pot. Add the tomato sauce, ketchup, sugar, thyme, chili powder, mustard, cinnamon, cloves, hot-pepper sauce (if using) and salt and pepper. Gently stir to mix well.

Simmer for 20 to 25 minutes, stirring frequently, until the flavors are well blended.

Makes 6 servings.

Per serving: 197 calories, 0.8 g. total fat (4% of calories), 0.1 g. saturated fat, 0 mg. cholesterol

Bean and Pasta Skillet

Canadian bacon, beans and pasta blend felicitously in this rich and hearty skillet dinner.

   3   ounces Canadian bacon, trimmed of all visible fat and cut into thin strips
   1   medium onion, chopped
   1   large celery stalk, thinly sliced
   1   garlic clove, minced
   2   teaspoons olive oil, preferably extra-virgin
   1   can (16 ounces) stewed tomatoes
   1   teaspoon dried thyme leaves
   1   teaspoon dried basil leaves
   1   bay leaf
   ⅛   teaspoon ground black pepper
   1   can (19 ounces) white cannellini beans, rinsed and drained
   1½ cups cut fusilli or similar pasta shapes
   1   teaspoon cornstarch
   2   tablespoons cold water
   4   parsley sprigs (garnish)

In a 12" nonstick skillet, combine the bacon, onions, celery, garlic and oil. Cook over medium heat, stirring frequently, for 8 minutes, or until the onions are soft.

Add the tomatoes, thyme, basil, bay leaf and pepper. Stir to mix well. Stir in the beans. Bring to a boil. Reduce the heat and simmer for 15 to 20 minutes.

While the beans are simmering, cook the pasta according to the package directions. Drain and set aside.

In a cup, stir together the cornstarch and water. Bring the bean mixture to a boil. Add the cornstarch mixture and cook until the liquid thickens. Reduce the heat. Remove and discard the bay leaf.

Add the pasta and cook for an additional 2 to 3 minutes. Serve garnished with the parsley.

Makes 4 servings.

Per serving: 241 calories, 5.3 g. total fat (20% of calories), 1.1 g. saturated fat, 26 mg. cholesterol

Potato Slices

These tasty potato slices are very easy to make, and they're a great substitute for fried potatoes—with virtually no fat. Best piping hot, they can be served as a side dish, snack or part of a hearty break-fast. Try to cut the slices evenly for uniform browning. If you'd like slices that are more like potato chips, cut them thinner. However, you should keep a close watch on thin slices as they burn easily. For variety, replace the plain salt with seasoned salt, butter-flavored salt or herb seasoning. Or sprinkle on a little finely shredded Cheddar just before the last minute of broiling.

12 ounces potatoes, peeled or unpeeled and cut into ⅛" slices
 2 tablespoons water
    Salt, to taste

Spread the potatoes in 3 or 4 layers in an 8" or 9" pie plate. Add the water. Cover with wax paper. Microwave on high power for 3 to 5 minutes, or until partially cooked; halfway through the cooking time, give the dish a quarter turn.

Preheat the broiler. Coat a large baking sheet with nonstick spray; set aside.

Drain the potatoes in a colander, being careful not to break the slices. Turn them out onto the baking sheet and spread them in a single layer in the center of the sheet.

Broil 5" from the heat for 6 to 8 minutes, or until the slices have begun to bubble and are partially brown; halfway during the cooking period, give the sheet a half turn.

Turn over the slices with a spatula, transferring the browner slices from the center to the edges of the sheet. Broil for an additional 4 to 6 minutes, or until the slices are partially browned; halfway during the cooking period, give the sheet a half turn. (Remove thin slices if they become too crisp.)

Transfer the slices to a serving platter and sprinkle with the salt.

Makes 3 servings.

Per serving: 96 calories, 0.1 g. total fat (1% of calories), 0 g. saturated fat, 0 mg. cholesterol

Stuffed Potatoes

Although wonderfully satisfying and rich-tasting, these stuffed potatoes have very little fat. That's because we used only a small amount of regular cheese and combined it with other low-fat dairy products. You could bake the potatoes in the microwave, but the skins will have a firmer texture if you use a conventional oven.

4	large baking potatoes
1	ounce Cheddar cheese, shredded (about ¼ cup)
2¾	ounces nonfat Cheddar cheese, shredded (about ⅔ cup)
½	cup nonfat ricotta cheese
¾	cup plain nonfat yogurt
	About ⅓ cup 1% fat milk
2	teaspoons instant minced onion flakes, or to taste
	Salt and ground white pepper, to taste (optional)
2	tablespoons shredded Cheddar or nonfat Cheddar cheese (garnish)
	Paprika or chives (optional)

Wash and scrub the potatoes well; dry them with paper towels. Pierce the skins with a fork. Bake at 400° for 1 hour, or until the potatoes are tender when pricked with a long-tined fork. Using a pot holder or several layers of paper towels to hold the hot potatoes, cut each in half with a sharp knife.

Scoop out most of the flesh with a spoon, being careful not to tear the skins. Transfer the flesh to a large bowl. Place the skins on a baking sheet and set aside.

Break up the potato flesh with a potato masher or pastry cutter. Add the Cheddar cheeses (except 2 tablespoons for garnish) and mash well. When the cheese has melted, add the ricotta, yogurt, milk, onion flakes and salt and pepper (if using). Mix well. (If the mixture seems too stiff, add more milk.)

Evenly divide the potato mixture among the potato skins. Garnish with the 2 tablespoons Cheddar and paprika or chives (if using).

Broil about 5" from the heat until the potato mixture begins to brown and the topping cheese has melted slightly.

Makes 8 servings.

Per serving: 143 calories, 3.5 g. total fat (22% of calories), 2.1 g. saturated fat, 13 mg. cholesterol

Potato and Parmesan Casserole

Like other cheeses, Parmesan is relatively high in fat. Fortunately, it has a strong flavor, so a modest amount goes a long way. This casserole has only one-third cup, yet the flavor is surprisingly rich. To speed up the cooking time, you may partially cook the potatoes in the microwave before completing the process in the oven.

6	cups thinly sliced unpeeled red potatoes
1	small onion, chopped
1	small garlic clove, minced
2	cups 1% fat milk
1	tablespoon cornstarch
⅛	teaspoon ground white pepper
⅛	teaspoon salt (optional)
	Generous ⅓ cup grated Parmesan cheese

Coat a 2-quart casserole with nonstick spray. Add the potatoes, onions and garlic; mix well. Set aside.

In a medium saucepan, whisk together the milk, cornstarch, pepper and salt (if using). Bring to a simmer over medium heat, stirring frequently. Reduce the heat to medium-low and cook for 1 minute, or until the sauce has thickened.

Reduce the heat to low and gradually whisk in the Parmesan, stirring vigorously to break up any lumps. Cook for 1 minute. Pour the sauce over the potato mixture and stir well.

Cover and bake at 350° for 1¼ hours, or until the potatoes are tender. (For a crusty top, remove the cover during the last 20 minutes of baking.)

Remove from the oven and allow to stand for 5 minutes before serving.

Makes 7 servings.

Per serving: 163 calories, 2.6 g. total fat (15% of calories), 1.6 g. saturated fat, 8 mg. cholesterol

Microwave option: Combine the potatoes, onions and garlic in an ovenproof, microwave-safe 2-quart casserole. Microwave on high for 6 to 10 minutes, or until the potatoes are partially cooked; halfway through the cooking time, give the dish a quarter turn and stir the potatoes. Transfer to a colander to drain. Wipe out the casserole and coat it with nonstick spray. Return the potato mixture to the dish. Prepare the sauce as directed above. Bake, reducing the time to 25 to 35 minutes.

Potatoes and Spinach, Indian-Style

We've modified this classic Indian combination so that it is very low in fat. Serve it as a hearty side dish or an unusual light main course.

1	large onion, coarsely chopped
1	large garlic clove, minced
2	teaspoons canola oil
	About 1⅔ cups defatted chicken broth, divided
2	teaspoons finely chopped fresh mint leaves or 1 teaspoon dried mint leaves
1	teaspoon mild curry powder
1	teaspoon ground cumin
½	teaspoon ground ginger
3	drops hot-pepper sauce (optional)
4	cups peeled and diced potatoes
1	box (10 ounces) frozen chopped spinach, thawed and well drained
	Salt (optional)

In a 12" heavy nonstick skillet, combine the onions, garlic, oil and 3 tablespoons of the broth. Cook over medium heat, stirring frequently, for 5 to 6 minutes, or until the onions are tender. (If the liquid evaporates, add more broth.)

Stir in the mint, curry powder, cumin, ginger, hot-pepper sauce (if using) and the remaining broth. Cover, reduce the heat and simmer gently for 4 or 5 minutes, or until the flavors are well blended.

Add the potatoes and stir to coat them with the liquid. Raise the heat and bring the mixture to a boil. Lower the heat, cover the pan and simmer for 10 minutes, or until the potatoes are almost tender. (Stir occasionally during this time and check the liquid. If the mixture seems too dry, add a bit more broth.)

Stir in the spinach, distributing it evenly in the pan. Simmer, stirring occasionally, for an additional 3 to 4 minutes, or until the spinach is just heated through. Add more broth if the mixture seems dry. Stir in the salt (if using).

Makes 4 servings.

Per serving: 189 calories, 3.2 g. total fat (14% of calories), 0.5 g. saturated fat, 0 mg. cholesterol

Noodle Pudding

We've taken almost all of the fat but none of the flavor from this traditional Jewish side dish. It is an excellent source of calcium since it's made with dairy products. When buying the egg noodles, look for a brand that is low in fat and cholesterol. This recipe yields quite a few servings, which makes it perfect for a holiday gathering. The leftovers are also good cold or reheated.

4	cups uncooked medium no-yolk egg noodles
3	ounces reduced-fat tub-style cream cheese, at room temperature
⅓	cup + 3 tablespoons granulated sugar, divided
1	cup nonfat ricotta cheese
1	cup liquid egg substitute
¾	cup plain nonfat yogurt
1	teaspoon vanilla extract
¼	teaspoon salt
½	cup well-drained crushed pineapple
⅓	cup chopped dried apricots, currants or dark raisins
¼	teaspoon ground cinnamon

Preheat the oven to 375°. Coat a shallow 2-quart baking dish with nonstick cooking spray. Set aside.

Cook the noodles according to the package directions. Drain well and set aside.

While the noodles are cooking, in a large bowl, combine the cream cheese and ⅓ cup of the sugar. Using an electric mixer, beat on medium speed until well combined and smooth. Add the ricotta, egg substitute, yogurt, vanilla and salt. Beat on low speed until partially combined. Increase the speed to medium and beat until smooth.

Stir in the pineapple and apricots, currants or raisins. Fold in the noodles.

Transfer to the prepared dish and spread evenly, using the back of a large spoon.

In a cup, mix the cinnamon and the remaining 3 tablespoons sugar. Sprinkle evenly over the noodle mixture.

Bake for 30 to 35 minutes, until the mixture is just set and a toothpick inserted in the center comes out clean. Do not overbake.

Makes 15 servings.

Per serving: 118 calories, 2 g. total fat (14% of calories), 1 g. saturated fat, 6 mg. cholesterol

Chapter 16

VEGETARIAN DELIGHTS

Several years ago when one of our children announced that she had become a vegetarian, we decided that we'd better learn more about meatless cookery. While we're not vegetarians ourselves, we do appreciate the pleasure of many meat-free main dishes. In fact, we're likely to serve vegetarian meals at least once a week, using the recipes in this chapter or a combination of the bean, legume, pasta, potato and vegetable dishes from elsewhere in the book.

While we designed the recipes in this chapter to be lean as well as tasty, don't assume that all vegetarian fare is low in fat. In fact, it can be quite high if it's based on cheese, nuts and butter. So keep this in mind when adding other recipes to your repertory. Look for dishes that emphasize grains, pasta and potatoes—the very foods that should form the foundation of a healthy diet.

Vegetarian Chili

Ground vegetables and lentils add texture and richness to this hearty south-of-the-border main dish. And they help keep it extremely low in fat. If desired, replace the broccoli with celery.

1	can (16 ounces) tomatoes, with juice
2	large carrots, peeled and cut into 1" pieces
1	large broccoli stem, peeled and cut into 1" pieces
1	medium onion, chopped
1	garlic clove, minced
2	teaspoons olive oil
3	cans (16 ounces each) kidney beans, rinsed and drained
1	can (15 ounces) tomato sauce
1¼	cups water
¼	cup dry green lentils, washed and sorted
1	tablespoon chili powder, or to taste
1	teaspoon ground cumin
1	teaspoon granulated sugar (optional)
	Salt and ground black pepper, to taste (optional)
1½	cups uncooked long-grain brown or white rice

In a food processor, combine the tomatoes (with juice), carrots and broccoli. Process until the vegetables are finely chopped. Set aside.

In a Dutch oven or other large heavy pot, combine the onions, garlic and oil. Cook over medium heat, stirring frequently, for 5 to 6 minutes, or until the onions are tender.

Stir in the tomato mixture, beans, tomato sauce, water, lentils, chili powder and cumin. Taste the mixture; if the tomatoes seem acid, add the sugar. Add the salt and pepper (if using).

Bring to a boil. Cover, reduce the heat and simmer, stirring occasionally, for 1 hour, or until the lentils are very tender. (Stir more frequently as the mixture thickens.)

While the chili is simmering, prepare the rice according to the package directions. (If using brown rice, start it cooking as soon as the chili begins to simmer. If using white rice, start it cooking about 25 minutes before the chili will be ready.)

Stir the chili and serve over the rice.

Makes 6 servings.

Per serving: 430 calories, 3 g. total fat (6% of calories), 0.3 g. saturated fat, 0 mg. cholesterol

Beans and Rice con Queso

We love this hearty casserole. It tastes best made with freshly cooked dry black beans, but you may substitute a 16-ounce can of beans to simplify the recipe. Incidentally, we have found considerable variation in the amount of time needed to cook black beans—sometimes they take only an hour; other times they may need to cook for up to two hours.

¾ cup dry black beans, washed and sorted
8 cups water, divided
1 cup uncooked long-grain white rice
1 medium onion, chopped
1 garlic clove, minced
1 teaspoon chili powder
¼ teaspoon dry mustard
½ teaspoon salt, or to taste
⅛ teaspoon ground black pepper, or to taste
1 cup 1% fat cottage cheese
1 can (4 ounces) chopped mild green chili peppers, well drained
5 ounces reduced-fat sharp Cheddar cheese, shredded (about 1¼ cups)

Place the beans in a Dutch oven or other large heavy pot. Cover with 2" of water and bring to a boil over high heat. Reduce the heat and boil for 2 minutes. Remove the pot from the heat, cover and let stand for 1 hour. Drain the beans in a colander, discarding the soaking water.

Return the beans to the pot. Add 6 cups of the water. Bring to a boil over high heat. Reduce the heat and simmer for 1 to 2 hours, or until the beans are tender. Drain well in a colander.

While the beans are simmering, in a large saucepan, combine the rice, onions, garlic, chili powder, mustard, salt, black pepper and the remaining 2 cups water. Stir to mix well. Cover and bring to a boil. Reduce the heat and simmer for 20 minutes, or until the water has been absorbed and the rice is just tender.

Preheat the oven to 350°.

In a 2½-quart casserole, mix the rice, cottage cheese and chili peppers. Stir in the cheese. Gently stir in the beans and mix well.

Cover with a lid and bake for 25 to 30 minutes, or until heated through.

Makes 6 servings.

Per serving: 307 calories, 5.1 g. total fat (15% of calories), 0.4 g. saturated fat, 13 mg. cholesterol

Taco Casserole

Hearty and satisfying, this vegetarian Tex-Mex casserole brings together the appealing flavors and textures of tacos but is much easier to prepare. Since the filling is made from beans and rice rather than meat, it is also less fatty than traditional taco filling. By the way, nobody that we serve this dish to ever seems to notice that it is meatless.

1	package (4½ ounces) tostada shells, broken into bite-size pieces, divided
2	medium onions, finely chopped
2½	cups chopped mushrooms
1	small celery stalk, including leaves, finely chopped
1	garlic clove, minced
1	tablespoon canola or safflower oil
3	cups cooked long-grain brown or white rice
1	can (16 ounces) kidney beans, rinsed and drained
½	cup tomato sauce
1½	tablespoons mild chili powder
1	can (4 ounces) chopped mild green chili peppers, well drained
½	teaspoon dried oregano leaves
½	teaspoon salt (optional)
4	ounces reduced-fat sharp Cheddar cheese, coarsely shredded (about 1 cup)
3	medium tomatoes, coarsely diced
2	cups coarsely shredded iceberg lettuce
¼	cup chopped scallions (optional)
2	tablespoons chopped fresh cilantro leaves (optional)
	Fresh Chunky Green Salsa, page 142 (optional)
	Picante sauce (optional)

Preheat the oven to 350°. Lightly coat an 11" × 7" baking dish with nonstick spray. Spread a scant two-thirds of the broken shells in the dish.

In a 12" nonstick skillet, combine the onions, mushrooms, celery, garlic and oil. Cook over medium heat, stirring frequently, for 15 minutes, or until the vegetables are tender and most of the liquid has evaporated from the mushrooms.

In a food processor, combine the rice, beans, tomato sauce and chili powder. Process for 2 minutes, or until the mixture is pureed. Stir into the skillet.

Add the peppers, oregano and salt (if using). Mix well. Spread over the shells in the baking dish. Sprinkle with the remaining shells, then the cheese. Loosely cover with foil.

Bake for 15 to 20 minutes, or until heated through. Remove the foil and sprinkle with the tomatoes, lettuce, scallions (if using) and cilantro (if using). If desired, serve with the salsa and picante sauce.

Makes 6 servings.

Per serving: 376 calories, 11.3 g. total fat (26% of calories), 0.4 g. saturated fat, 9 mg. cholesterol

Bean Burritos

Amazingly low in fat, these tasty burritos are perfect for a light meal or snack. And the microwave makes warming them a snap. If you have leftover bean mixture, store it in the refrigerator for up to three days.

- 1 can (16 ounces) kidney beans, rinsed and drained
- 1 teaspoon chili powder
- 1⅓ cups mild or medium picante sauce, divided
- 4 large (8") flour tortillas
- 2 ounces nonfat Cheddar or mozzarella cheese, shredded (about ½ cup)
- 2 ounces reduced-fat sharp Cheddar cheese, shredded (about ½ cup)
- ⅓ cup nonfat sour cream (garnish)
  Mild or medium picante sauce (garnish)

In a food processor, combine the beans and chili powder. Process with on/off pulses until the beans are partially pureed. Stir in ⅓ cup of the picante sauce.

One at a time, lay the tortillas flat. Spoon a quarter of the bean mixture in a line down the center of each. Evenly divide the remaining 1 cup picante sauce among the tortillas, spreading it over the beans. Sprinkle with the cheeses.

Fold the tortillas into thirds, overlapping the edges and completely covering the bean mixture. Press lightly to flatten so the tortillas retain their shape.

Place 2 of the burritos side by side on a microwave-safe plate or small platter. Top with the remaining 2 burritos. Loosely cover with wax paper.

Microwave on high power for 2½ to 4 minutes; halfway through the cooking time, give the plate a quarter turn. Serve garnished with the sour cream and additional picante sauce.

Makes 4 servings.

Per serving: 295 calories, 6.1 g. total fat (18% of calories), 1 g. saturated fat, 9 mg. cholesterol

Pasta with Vegetables and Cheese

This quick and healthy version of macaroni and cheese has become a family favorite. Cooking the vegetables with the pasta helps keep preparation simple. Traditional macaroni and cheese has about 21 grams of fat per serving and 388 calories. Ours has considerably less. For variety, you may use other medium-size pasta shapes.

PASTA AND VEGETABLES

2	cups medium elbow macaroni
1	medium onion, chopped
1	garlic clove, chopped
2	medium carrots, peeled and thinly sliced
2½	cups small broccoli or cauliflower florets
2	cups cubed zucchini

SAUCE

1	tablespoon all-purpose or unbleached white flour
½	teaspoon dry mustard
¼	teaspoon ground white pepper
½	teaspoon salt (optional)
1½	cups 1% fat milk
6	ounces reduced-fat sharp Cheddar cheese, shredded (about 1½ cups)
¼	cup nonfat ricotta cheese

To prepare the pasta and vegetables: In a large pot of boiling water, cook the macaroni, onions and garlic for 3 minutes. Add the carrots, broccoli or cauliflower and zucchini. Cook for an additional 5 to 7 minutes, or until the macaroni is just tender.

Drain well in a colander, then return to the pot. Set aside.

To prepare the sauce: While the pasta is cooking, in a small saucepan, stir together the flour, mustard, pepper and salt (if using). Slowly whisk in the milk until the flour is completely incorporated.

Place over medium heat and cook, whisking, for 3 to 4 minutes, or until thickened. Gradually add the shredded cheese. Continue to whisk until it is completely melted. Add the ricotta and stir until incorporated.

Add the cheese sauce to the macaroni mixture. Stir well to incorporate. Place over low heat and warm, stirring frequently, for about 5 minutes.

Makes 6 servings.

Per serving: 280 calories, 6.6 g. total fat (21% of calories), 0.5 g. saturated fat, 17 mg. cholesterol

Vegetarian Spaghetti and Sauce

This hearty, satisfying pasta dish is a great way to increase vegetable consumption—and you won't miss the meat at all.

1	large onion, chopped
2	large garlic cloves, minced
1	tablespoon water
2	teaspoons olive oil
3	cans (15 ounces each) tomato sauce
2	cups small cauliflower or broccoli florets
½	large green pepper, seeded and chopped
2	cups diced zucchini
1	large celery stalk, finely chopped
1	teaspoon dried thyme leaves
1	teaspoon dried basil leaves
½	teaspoon dried oregano leaves
2	large bay leaves
¼	teaspoon ground black pepper
	Salt, to taste (optional)
2½	teaspoons sugar (optional)
1	box (16 ounces) thin spaghetti
4	tablespoons grated Parmesan cheese

In a Dutch oven or other large heavy pot, combine the onions, garlic, water and oil. Cook over medium heat, stirring frequently, for 5 to 6 minutes, or until the onions are soft.

Add the tomato sauce, cauliflower or broccoli, green peppers, zucchini, celery, thyme, basil, oregano, bay leaves, black pepper and salt (if using). Taste the sauce; if the tomatoes seem acid, add the sugar.

Bring to a boil. Cover, reduce the heat and simmer, stirring occasionally, for 40 to 45 minutes, or until the vegetables are tender and the flavors are blended. Remove and discard the bay leaves.

While the vegetables are cooking, cook the spaghetti according to the package directions. Drain and divide among dinner plates. Top with the sauce and sprinkle with the Parmesan.

Makes 6 servings.

Per serving: 420 calories, 4.5 g. total fat (9% of calories), 1.1 g. saturated fat, 2 mg. cholesterol

Creamy Broccoli and Cheese with Baked Potatoes

This is a nice lunch or supper entrée. Surprisingly, the topping actually contains potatoes, which help lend body and rich taste. For convenience, you may prepare the topping ahead and refrigerate it for up to three days. Reheat it just before serving.

2	medium broccoli heads
1	cup chopped scallions, including tops
1	tablespoon nondiet tub-style canola or corn-oil margarine or butter
3½	tablespoons all-purpose or unbleached white flour
2⅓	cups defatted chicken broth
	About ⅔ cup 2% fat milk
1⅓	cups peeled and coarsely chopped boiling potatoes
⅓	cup finely chopped fresh chives or 2½ tablespoons dried chives
1	tablespoon dried basil leaves
	Generous ⅛ teaspoon ground black pepper
6	very large hot baked potatoes
3	ounces reduced-fat sharp Cheddar cheese, grated or finely shredded (about ¾ cup)

Cut the florets from the broccoli heads and chop enough to yield 2½ cups of ¼" floret tips. Set aside. Coarsely chop enough of the remaining florets and tender peeled stem pieces from the broccoli to yield 2 cups and set aside.

In a large saucepan, combine the scallions and margarine or butter. Cook over medium heat, stirring frequently, for 4 minutes, or until the scallions are limp. Stir in the flour until well incorporated. Cook, stirring, for 30 seconds; the mixture will not be completely smooth.

Gradually stir in the broth, then the milk until well incorporated. Add the 2 cups chopped broccoli, chopped potatoes, chives, basil and pepper.

Bring the mixture to a boil over medium-high heat. Reduce the heat and simmer, stirring occasionally, for 12 to 14 minutes, or until the potatoes are tender.

Working in batches, process the mixture in a blender until completely smooth. Return the mixture to the saucepan. (If the mixture is too thick, thin it with a little more milk.) Add the 2½ cups broccoli florets. Bring to a simmer. Cook, stirring frequently, for 3 to 5 minutes longer, or until the florets are cooked through but still slightly crisp.

Cut the baked potatoes lengthwise to expose the flesh; fluff it up with a fork. Place in a microwave-safe or ovenproof serving dish.

Spoon the sauce over the potatoes, dividing it equally among them. Sprinkle with the cheese.

Heat the potatoes in the microwave or a conventional oven at 350° just until the cheese melts.

Makes 6 servings.

Per serving: 443 calories, 4.5 g. total fat (9% of calories), 1.3 g. saturated fat, 2 mg. cholesterol

Baked Ziti Casserole with Spinach and Cheese

This is reminiscent of vegetarian lasagna but is easier to put together. If using a commercial spaghetti sauce in this recipe, be sure to choose a reduced-fat or fat-free brand.

- 1 box (10 ounces) frozen leaf spinach, thawed
- 1 container (16 ounces) nonfat ricotta cheese
- 1 container (16 ounces) part-skim ricotta cheese
- ½ cup grated Parmesan cheese
- 2½ teaspoons dried basil leaves
- ¼ teaspoon salt
- ⅛ teaspoon ground black pepper
- 8 ounces ziti, cooked and drained
  About 3½ cups reduced-fat meatless spaghetti sauce
- 8 ounces part-skim mozzarella cheese, shredded (about 2 cups)

Preheat the oven to 350°. Lightly coat a 3-quart glass casserole with nonstick spray. Set aside.

Place the spinach in a colander. Press down with a spoon to extract as much moisture as possible. Transfer to a cutting board and chop finely, discarding any coarse stems.

In a large bowl, stir together the spinach, all the ricotta, Parmesan, basil, salt and pepper until well blended.

Spread half of the ziti in the prepared casserole. Top with half of the spinach mixture, half of the sauce and half of the mozzarella.

Repeat the layering process to use all the ingredients.

Bake for 40 to 45 minutes, or until the casserole is baked through and bubbly.

Makes 9 servings.

Per serving: 281 calories, 9.3 g. total fat (30% of calories), 3.9 g. saturated fat, 51 mg. cholesterol

Stuffed Pita Pockets

Bring the flavor of the Middle East to your table with these stuffed pitas. They make a nice change from ordinary sandwiches. The combination of spices and ingredients may seem a bit unusual, but it yields very pleasing results.

1	medium onion, chopped
1	large celery stalk, thinly sliced
1	garlic clove, minced
½	tablespoon olive oil
¾	cup uncooked bulgur
1	can (16 ounces) tomatoes, with juice
1	can (15 ounces) garbanzo beans, rinsed and drained
¾	cup water
2	cups diced yellow squash
½	cup dark raisins
¼	cup finely chopped fresh parsley leaves
	Generous 1 teaspoon ground cumin
1	teaspoon dried thyme leaves
	Generous ¼ teaspoon ground cinnamon
⅛	teaspoon ground black pepper, or to taste
	Salt (optional)
¾	cup chopped tomatoes or quartered cherry tomatoes (optional)
7	pita breads, halved
	Sweet red pepper slices (garnish)
	Yellow squash slivers (garnish)

In a Dutch oven or other large heavy pot, combine the onions, celery, garlic and oil. Cook over medium heat, stirring frequently, for 5 to 6 minutes, or until the onions are tender. Stir in the bulgur.

Add the canned tomatoes (with juice) and break them up with a spoon. Add the beans, water, squash, raisins, parsley, cumin, thyme, cinnamon, pepper and salt (if using). Stir to mix well.

Bring to a boil, then reduce the heat. Simmer, stirring occasionally, for 15 minutes, or until the bulgur and vegetables are tender and most of the liquid has been absorbed. Add the cut tomatoes (if using). Cook for an additional 2 minutes. Stir well before serving.

Divide the mixture among the pitas, being careful not to overfill them. Garnish with peppers and squash slivers.

Makes 7 servings.

Per serving: 173 calories, 2.5 g. total fat (12% of calories), 0.4 g. saturated fat, 0 mg. cholesterol

Spanish-Style Scrambled Eggs

In some recipes, you can come pretty close to fooling Mother Nature with liquid egg substitute. It cooks up much like scrambled eggs, as this zesty Spanish-style breakfast or brunch entrée proves.

⅓   **cup finely chopped onions**
⅓   **cup chopped green and/or sweet red peppers**
1   **small garlic clove, minced**
½   **cup liquid egg substitute**
2   **tablespoons 1% fat milk**
⅛   **teaspoon ground black pepper, or to taste**
3   **drops hot-pepper sauce (optional)**
⅛   **teaspoon salt (optional)**
¼   **cup mild or medium picante sauce**

Coat an 8" nonstick skillet with nonstick spray. Add the onions, green peppers and garlic. Cook, stirring frequently, over medium heat, for 6 minutes, or until the onions are tender.

In a small bowl, stir together the egg substitute, milk, black pepper, hot-pepper sauce (if using) and salt (if using). Pour into the skillet over the onion mixture. Cook without stirring until the egg mixture begins to set, then stir slightly so the uncooked portion flows to the bottom of the skillet. Continue cooking until the desired degree of doneness is reached.

Serve with the picante sauce.

Makes 2 servings.

Per serving: 54 calories, 0.6 g. total fat (9% of calories), 0 g. saturated fat, 0 mg. cholesterol

Chapter 17

FABULOUS FISH AND SHELLFISH

Many fish and most shellfish are light on fat, so they fit beautifully into reduced-fat menus. Some varieties of fish, such as salmon, herring and other coldwater fish, are fatty, but they're also great sources of omega-3 fatty acids (which help reduce the risk of heart disease). Include these in your regular diet, but remember to make allowances to keep total fat consumption low.

Fresh fish and shellfish should have a pleasant, briny aroma, not a strong "fishy" smell. And you should never overcook it. Heat fish and shellfish only until cooked through and tender.

The dishes in this chapter range from extremely quick and simple, like Quick-Baked Seasoned Fish, to fancier fare like Shrimp and Artichoke Stuffed Fish. There's also a variety of ethnic dishes, like Jambalaya.

Fish with Spicy Onion and Pepper Sauce

We love the way this spicy sauce adds character to mild fish fillets. And there are a number of different options for serving. Sometimes we arrange the fish on a bed of rice or pasta and top it with the sauce. Sometimes we make barbecue-style fish sandwiches with toasted rolls. And sometimes we simply serve the fish and sauce with a green vegetable and baked potatoes. You may use any type of lean, mild white fish fillets—flounder, turbot and haddock are good choices.

FISH

1	pound skinless mild white fish fillets
¼	teaspoon chili powder
¼	teaspoon salt
⅛	teaspoon ground black pepper

SAUCE

1	medium onion, chopped
1	small green pepper, seeded and chopped
1	small garlic clove, minced
2	teaspoons olive oil
½	cup ketchup
½	cup water
2	tablespoons Worcestershire sauce
½	teaspoon granulated sugar

To prepare the fish: Preheat the oven to 200°.

Sprinkle the fish with the chili powder, salt and pepper. Coat a 12" nonstick skillet with nonstick spray. Working in batches, if necessary, transfer the fish to the skillet. Cook over medium heat, for 3 to 6 minutes per side, or until cooked through.

Remove the fish to an ovenproof dish and keep warm in the oven.

To prepare the sauce: If any moisture remains in the skillet, blot it away with a paper towel. Place the onions, peppers, garlic and oil in the pan. Cook over medium heat, stirring frequently, for 5 to 6 minutes, or until the onions are tender. Stir in the ketchup, water, Worcestershire sauce and sugar. Cook, stirring occasionally, for 5 minutes to blend the flavors.

Transfer the fish to a platter or individual plates. Serve the sauce over the fish.

Makes 4 servings.

Per serving: 209 calories, 4.2 g. total fat (18% of calories), 0.7 g. saturated fat, 77 mg. cholesterol

Mediterranean-Style Fish

One of the quickest ways to cook fish is in a nonstick skillet on the stovetop. This dish features fish and vegetables in a flavorful toma-to sauce over rice. Use your choice of lean white fish, such as floun-der, sole, halibut or turbot. Another possibility is orange roughy, but be aware that it's considerably higher in fat than the other choices.

RICE AND VEGETABLES

1	cup uncooked long-grain white rice
12	ounces untrimmed leeks
1	garlic clove, minced
2	teaspoons olive oil
1	can (16 ounces) tomatoes, with juice
½	large green pepper, seeded and chopped
1	cup thinly sliced zucchini
2	cups small broccoli or cauliflower florets
2	tablespoons finely chopped fresh parsley leaves
½	teaspoon dried basil leaves
½	teaspoon dried thyme leaves
¼	teaspoon dried oregano leaves
¼	teaspoon salt (optional)
⅛	teaspoon ground black pepper

FISH

1	pound skinless mild white fish fillets
½	teaspoon dried basil leaves
¼	teaspoon salt
⅛	teaspoon ground black pepper

To prepare the rice and vegetables: Cook the rice according to the package directions. Set aside and keep warm.

Preheat the oven to 200°.

Trim off and discard the root end of the leeks and all but about 1" of the green tops. Peel off and discard 1 or 2 layers of the tough outer leaves. Beginning at the green end, slice down about 1" into the leeks. Put the leeks in a colander. Wash them thoroughly under cool running water, separating the layers to remove any grit trapped between them. Wash again to remove all traces of grit. Drain well and cut into ½" pieces.

In a 12" nonstick skillet, combine the leeks, garlic and oil. Cook over medium heat, stirring frequently, for 10 to 12 minutes, or until the leeks are tender.

Coarsely chop the tomatoes and add them (with juice) to the pan. Add the green peppers, zucchini, broccoli or cauliflower, parsley, basil, thyme, oregano, salt (if using) and black pepper.

Stir to combine well. Bring to a boil.

Cover, reduce the heat and cook, stirring occasionally, for 10 to 15 minutes, or until the vegetables are tender. Transfer to an oven-proof dish and keep warm in the oven.

To prepare the fish: Rinse out and dry the skillet. Coat it with non-stick spray. Sprinkle the fish with the basil, salt and pepper. Working in batches, if necessary, transfer the fish to the skillet. Cook over medium heat for 3 to 6 minutes per side, or until cooked through.

Arrange the rice on a large serving platter or on individual plates. Top with the vegetable mixture, then the fish.

Makes 5 servings.

Per serving: 333 calories, 4 g. total fat (11% of calories), 0.7 g. saturated fat, 61 mg. cholesterol

Quick-Baked Seasoned Fish

This makes an easy low-fat entrée that can be on the table in less than 15 minutes.

1	pound skinless mild white fish fillets
2	teaspoons nondiet tub-style canola or corn-oil margarine or butter, melted and divided
2½	tablespoons all-purpose or unbleached white flour
1	teaspoon mild curry powder
1	teaspoon chili powder
¼	teaspoon celery salt
1	medium lemon, quartered (garnish)

Preheat the oven to 425°. Line a jelly-roll pan with foil. Coat the foil with nonstick spray. Pat the fish dry with paper towels. Lay the fillets, slightly separated, on the foil. Brush the tops of the fillets with 1 teaspoon of the margarine or butter.

In a small bowl, stir together the flour, curry powder, chili powder and celery salt. Sprinkle half of the seasoning mixture over the fish.

Turn over the fish. Brush with the remaining 1 teaspoon margarine or butter. Sprinkle with the remaining seasoning mixture.

Bake on the upper oven rack for 7 to 9 minutes, or until the fillets are opaque and flake when touched with a fork. Immediately remove from the oven. Using a wide spatula, transfer the fish to a platter or individual plates. Serve with the lemon wedges.

Makes 4 servings.

Per serving: 139 calories, 3.1 g. total fat (21% of calories), 0.3 g. saturated fat, 49 mg. cholesterol

Shrimp and Artichoke Stuffed Fish

This savory and unusual main dish features a low-fat artichoke-shrimp stuffing. Be sure to choose a crumb-style stuffing mix.

STUFFING

1	medium onion, thinly sliced
1	garlic clove, minced
2	tablespoons dry sherry or water
1	teaspoon olive oil
1	can (16 ounces) tomatoes, well drained and coarsely chopped
1	jar (14 ounces) water-packed artichoke hearts, well drained and coarsely chopped
6	ounces small cooked and peeled shrimp
2	tablespoons finely chopped fresh parsley leaves
½	teaspoon dried basil leaves
¼	teaspoon salt (optional)
⅛	teaspoon ground black pepper
1½	cups seasoned crumb-style stuffing mix

FISH

1	pound skinless mild white fish fillets
¼	teaspoon salt
⅛	teaspoon ground black pepper
	Parsley sprigs (garnish)

To prepare the stuffing: Preheat the oven to 200°.

In a 12" nonstick skillet, combine the onions, garlic, sherry or water and oil. Cook over medium heat, stirring frequently, for 5 to 6 minutes, or until the onions are tender. Add the tomatoes, artichokes, shrimp, parsley, basil, salt (if using) and black pepper. Stir to combine well.

Bring to a boil. Cook for 3 to 4 minutes, or until the liquid has thickened and only about ¼ cup remains. Stir in the stuffing mix. Reduce the heat and cook, stirring frequently, for an additional 2 minutes. Transfer to a baking dish and keep warm in the oven.

To prepare the fish: Rinse out and dry the skillet. Coat the pan with nonstick spray.

Sprinkle the fish with salt and pepper. Working in batches, transfer the fish to the skillet. Cook over medium heat for 3 to 6 minutes per side, or until cooked through. Arrange the stuffing on a platter or on individual plates. Top with the fish. Garnish with the parsley.

Makes 5 servings.

Per serving: 231 calories, 3.3 g. total fat (12% of calories), 0.5 g. saturated fat, 74 mg. cholesterol

Fish Creole

Like traditional shrimp Creole, this dish features a bold, savory blend of herbs and vegetables complementing the seafood. Grouper is a good choice because it holds its shape and absorbs the spiciness of the other ingredients. This dish can also be made with catfish, but it won't be quite as lean.

⅓ cup chopped onions
⅓ cup chopped scallions, including tops
⅓ cup chopped celery, including leaves
½ cup chopped sweet red peppers
1 large garlic clove, minced
½ tablespoon canola or safflower oil
1 bottle (8 ounces) clam juice
½ teaspoon dried thyme leaves
½ teaspoon dried marjoram leaves
   Generous ¼ teaspoon dried oregano leaves
⅛ teaspoon ground black pepper
⅛ teaspoon ground white pepper
   Pinch of ground red pepper (optional)
¾ cup peeled and diced tomatoes
½ tablespoon nondiet tub-style canola or corn-oil margarine or butter
⅛ teaspoon salt (optional)
1 pound skinless grouper fillets, cut into 4 equal pieces
2 cups hot cooked long-grain white rice

In a 12" nonstick skillet, combine the onions, scallions, celery, chopped red peppers, garlic and oil. Cook over medium heat, stirring frequently, for 6 minutes, or until the onions are tender and beginning to brown.

Stir in the clam juice, thyme, marjoram, oregano, black pepper, white pepper and ground red pepper (if using). Bring the mixture to a simmer and cook for 10 minutes, or until almost all of the liquid evaporates from the pan.

Add the tomatoes, margarine or butter and salt (if using); stir until the margarine or butter melts.

Add the fish to the pan. Bring to a simmer. Cover and cook for 5 to 7 minutes, or until the fish pieces are opaque and just cooked through.

Place the rice onto a platter; top with the fish pieces. Spoon the vegetable mixture over and around the fish.

Makes 4 servings.

Per serving: 285 calories, 4.7 g. total fat (15% of calories), 0.7 g. saturated fat, 42 mg. cholesterol

Red Snapper and Shrimp Étouffée

Étouffée is a spicy Louisiana seafood or meat stew. It starts with a brown roux, which is normally made by mixing and browning equal amounts of flour and fat. But we've come up with a way to reduce the fat dramatically and still create the appealing flavor a brown roux gives the stew. Though not at all hot by Louisiana standards, this étouffée is a bit peppery. If you like, you may omit or decrease the red pepper. The stew makes a great one-dish meal. It may be made ahead and reheated. But for authentic presentation, use freshly cooked rice.

2	cups bottled clam juice
¼	cup all-purpose white or unbleached flour
1	tablespoon canola or safflower oil, divided
1	cup chopped onions
¾	cup chopped celery, including leaves
¾	cup chopped green peppers
1	large garlic clove, minced
½	teaspoon dried thyme leaves
½	teaspoon dried marjoram leaves
	Generous ¼ teaspoon dried oregano leaves
¼	teaspoon ground black pepper
¼	teaspoon ground white pepper
⅛	teaspoon ground red pepper (optional)
2	teaspoons nondiet tub-style canola or corn-oil margarine or butter
1	pound red snapper fillets, cut into large pieces
12	ounces medium shrimp, peeled and deveined
¼	cup chopped scallions, including tops
3	tablespoons finely chopped fresh parsley leaves
3½	cups hot cooked long-grain white rice

Put the clam juice in a blender or food processor. Set aside.

In a Dutch oven or other large heavy pot, combine the flour and ½ tablespoon of the oil. Cook over medium heat, stirring constantly, just until the flour turns a rich brown color. Immediately remove the flour from the pot and add it to the clam juice. Process until the mixture is completely smooth.

Add the remaining ½ tablespoon oil to the pot. Stir in the onions, celery, green peppers and garlic. Cook over medium heat, stirring frequently, for 5 minutes, or until the onions are tender.

Stir the clam juice mixture into the vegetables. Add the thyme, marjoram, oregano, black pepper, white pepper and red pepper (if using). Bring to a simmer and cook for 10 minutes. Add the margarine or butter and stir until it melts.

Add the fish, shrimp and scallions. Bring to a simmer. Cover and cook for 7 minutes, or until the fish and shrimp are just cooked. Sprinkle with the parsley.

To serve, mound a generous ½ cup rice in the center of individual soup plates. Spoon the seafood mixture over the rice.

Makes 6 servings.

Per serving: 345 calories, 5.5 g. total fat (15% of calories), 0.8 g. saturated fat, 115 mg. cholesterol

Grilled Fresh Salmon with Dill

When preparing this recipe, we prefer a boneless fillet since it can easily be cut into serving pieces after cooking. In addition, there is no need to marinate the side of the fish with the skin. If you can get only salmon steaks, you will need to coat them with a bit more oil and chicken broth when you invert the pieces. Dill goes beautifully with broiled salmon. But you could also substitute thyme or basil.

1	teaspoon olive oil
1	teaspoon defatted chicken broth
¾	teaspoon chopped fresh dill leaves or generous ¼ teaspoon dried dillweed
½	teaspoon lemon juice
⅛	teaspoon ground black pepper
⅛	teaspoon salt (optional)
1	pound boneless salmon fillet
	Dill sprigs (garnish)

In a cup, stir together the oil, broth, dill, lemon juice, pepper and salt (if using).

Coat a nonstick broiler pan with nonstick spray. Place the fish, skin side down, on the pan. Drizzle the marinade over the fish and spread it evenly with the back of a spoon. Allow to stand at room temperature for 8 to 10 minutes.

Preheat the broiler. Broil the fish about 5" from the heat for 10 minutes. Gently turn over the fish using a broad spatula under the thickest part. Broil for another 6 to 10 minutes, or until the flesh has turned pink and flakes easily with a fork.

Serve garnished with dill sprigs.

Makes 4 servings.

Per serving: 114 calories, 5 g. total fat (41% of calories), 1 g. saturated fat, 20 mg. cholesterol

Jambalaya

Jambalaya is a spicy Cajun grab-bag of a dish. There are many variations, depending on what the cook has in the larder and which meats and seafood are available. The small amount of country ham we use adds an extra dimension to the seasonings. You can easily double the recipe to feed a crowd. (But don't double the oil—one tablespoon is sufficient.)

1	large onion, coarsely chopped
1	large garlic clove, minced
2	teaspoons olive oil
2	cups defatted chicken broth, divided
2	large celery stalks, diced
1	large carrot, peeled and diced
1	large green pepper, seeded and chopped
1	can (28 ounces) Italian (plum) tomatoes, with juice
4	ounces country ham, trimmed of all visible fat and cut into bite-size pieces
1	large bay leaf
1½	teaspoons dried thyme leaves
1	teaspoon dried marjoram leaves
¼	teaspoon ground black pepper
	Pinch of ground red pepper
1½	cups uncooked long-grain white rice
1	package (5 ounces) frozen cooked shrimp, thawed
1½	cups frozen peas

In a Dutch oven or other large heavy pot, combine the onions, garlic, oil and 3 tablespoons of the broth. Cook over medium heat, stirring frequently, for 5 to 6 minutes, or until the onions are tender. Add the celery, carrots, green peppers and the remaining broth.

Add the tomatoes (with juice) and break them up with a spoon. Add the ham, bay leaf, thyme, marjoram, black pepper and red pepper. Bring to a boil.

Reduce the heat. Cover and simmer for 15 minutes. Bring the liquid back to a boil. Add the rice, shrimp and peas.

Reduce the heat. Cover and simmer for 20 minutes, or until the rice is tender. Remove and discard the bay leaf. Stir the jambalaya before serving.

Makes 8 servings.

Per serving: 236 calories, 2.8 g. total fat (11% of calories), 0.6 g. saturated fat, 42 mg. cholesterol

Spicy Crab Cakes

Because we both grew up in the Tidewater region, crabs from the Chesapeake Bay were a favorite summertime treat. Down at the shore, one restaurant specialized in plump spicy crab cakes served the traditional way: between two saltine crackers. The cakes were fried. Our version is broiled, but it harks back to that childhood memory. Serve as a main dish or make smaller, appetizer-size versions to serve on crackers. For best results, make your own bread crumbs from day-old whole wheat or white bread. Commercial crumbs will be too dry.

⅓   **cup dry home-made bread crumbs**
¼   **cup finely chopped scallions**
2   **tablespoons liquid egg substitute**
2   **tablespoons reduced-fat mayonnaise**
2   **teaspoons Worcestershire sauce**
½   **teaspoon Dijon mustard**
⅛   **teaspoon garlic powder**
⅛   **teaspoon ground white pepper**
2   **drops hot-pepper sauce (optional)**
8   **ounces fresh backfin or mixed crab meat, cartilage and shells removed**

Preheat the broiler.

In a medium bowl, combine the bread crumbs, scallions, egg substitute, mayonnaise, Worcestershire sauce, mustard, garlic powder, white pepper and hot-pepper sauce (if using). Stir to mix well.

Fold in the crab. Gently form into four 3½" patties.

Coat a baking sheet with nonstick spray. Place the patties on the sheet. Broil 5" from the heat for 5 to 6 minutes. Carefully turn with a large spatula. If necessary, reshape the patties. Broil for an additional 4 to 5 minutes, or until the patties are lightly browned.

Makes 4 servings.

Per serving: 73 calories, 2.3 g. total fat (29% of calories), 0.4 g. saturated fat, 9 mg. cholesterol

Tuna Steaks with Mango-Pepper Salsa

Use only firm, top-quality tuna steaks and ripe, fragrant mangoes for this colorful recipe. The sweet mango-pepper salsa complements the meaty taste of the tuna beautifully.

TUNA

¾	cup orange juice
⅔	cup chopped scallions, including tops
⅛	teaspoon grated lemon zest
1	tablespoon lemon juice
½	tablespoon balsamic vinegar
4	tuna steaks (5–6 ounces each)
2	teaspoons peanut oil
⅛	teaspoon salt
	Pinch of ground black pepper

SALSA

1½	cups peeled and diced ripe mangoes
⅓	cup diced sweet red peppers
1	tablespoon lemon juice
¼	teaspoon peeled and finely chopped ginger root
2	teaspoons balsamic vinegar
	Pinch of salt (optional)
	Pinch of ground black pepper

To prepare the tuna: In a nonreactive baking dish large enough to hold the fish in a single layer, stir together the orange juice, scallions, lemon zest, lemon juice and vinegar. Add the fish and press the pieces down to crush the scallions slightly. Turn over the pieces and press down again. Cover and refrigerate for at least 20 minutes and up to 2 hours. Turn over the pieces occasionally.

Preheat the broiler. Coat a large heavy ovenproof skillet or ridged cast-iron frying pan with nonstick spray. Place about 4" from the heat until a drop of water sprinkled into the pan or dish sizzles upon contact.

Brush the fish on both sides with the oil. Arrange the pieces, not touching, in the pan or dish. Broil for 2 minutes. Turn over the pieces and broil for 2 to 3 minutes longer, or until the fish is just barely opaque in the center when tested with a knife.

Transfer to a serving platter or individual plates. Sprinkle with the salt and pepper.

To prepare the salsa: Up to 30 minutes before serving, in a small nonreactive bowl, stir together the mangoes, red peppers, lemon juice, ginger, vinegar, salt (if using) and black pepper. Set aside at room temperature. To serve, spoon over the fish.

Makes 4 servings.

Per serving: 238 calories, 3.9 g. total fat (15% of calories), 0.8 g. saturated fat, 64 mg. cholesterol

Crab 'n' Pasta

Here's pasta topped with a tangy crab sauce that's so quick and easy you can have it on the table in about 20 minutes. We like to serve it as a luncheon or dinner entrée.

1	medium onion, finely chopped
1	large celery stalk, finely chopped
1	green pepper, seeded and chopped
1	large garlic clove, minced
2	teaspoons olive oil
1	can (15 ounces) tomato sauce, divided
1	teaspoon dried thyme leaves
1	teaspoon dried basil leaves
½	teaspoon Dijon mustard
¼	teaspoon salt
⅛	teaspoon ground white pepper
8	ounces fresh crab meat, cartilage and shells removed
8	ounces thin spaghetti

In a large saucepan, combine the onions, celery, green peppers, garlic, oil and 3 tablespoons of the tomato sauce. Cook over medium heat, stirring frequently, for 8 minutes, or until the onions have softened.

Add the thyme, basil, mustard, salt, white pepper and the remaining tomato sauce. Stir to mix well. Stir in the crab. Bring to a boil. Cover, reduce the heat and simmer for 8 minutes, or until the flavors are well blended.

Meanwhile, cook the spaghetti according to the package directions. Drain.

To serve, arrange the spaghetti on a platter or on individual plates. Top with the sauce.

Makes 4 servings.

Per serving: 352 calories, 4.5 g. total fat (12% of calories), 0.6 g. saturated fat, 30 mg. cholesterol

Seafood Risotto

This easy main-dish risotto combines the appealing creaminess of Arborio rice with ham and succulent seafood. Since the rice is cooked in the microwave instead of on the stove, there is no need for the constant stirring risotto usually demands. This is an eye-catching dish, with turmeric-tinted rice brightened by red peppers, green peas and shrimp.

⅔	cup chopped onions
⅓	cup diced sweet red peppers
2	teaspoons olive oil, preferably extra-virgin
1	cup uncooked Arborio rice
2	cups defatted chicken broth
⅛	teaspoon turmeric
1¼	cups bottled clam juice, divided
1	cup well-drained chopped canned tomatoes
¼	cup well-trimmed and finely diced country ham
½	cup frozen green peas
1	teaspoon nondiet tub-style canola or corn-oil margarine or butter
8	ounces medium shrimp, peeled and deveined
2	tablespoons chopped fresh parsley leaves
½	teaspoon chili powder
¼	teaspoon dried thyme leaves
⅛	teaspoon ground white pepper
	Salt, to taste
6	ounces bay scallops or quartered sea scallops

In a 2-quart round microwave-safe casserole, combine the onions, red peppers and oil. Microwave on high power for 1½ to 2 minutes, or until the onions are limp. Stir in the rice. Microwave on high power for 1½ minutes longer.

Stir in the broth, turmeric and 1 cup of the clam juice. Loosely cover with wax paper and microwave on high power for 10 minutes. Stir the mixture well and rotate the casserole a quarter turn.

Continue microwaving, uncovered, for 7 to 9 minutes longer, or until the rice is almost tender and most of the liquid has been absorbed. Stir in the tomatoes, ham and peas.

Microwave on medium power (50%) for 2 minutes. Cover lightly with wax paper and let stand for 5 minutes.

Meanwhile, in a 12" nonstick skillet over medium-high heat, melt the margarine or butter. Stir in the shrimp, parsley, chili powder, thyme, white pepper, salt and 2 tablespoons of the remaining clam juice. Cook, stirring, for 2 minutes; if the skillet starts to boil dry, add the remaining 2 tablespoons of clam juice.

Add the scallops and cook for 1 to 2 minutes longer, or until the shrimp is pink and curled and the scallops are cooked through. Stir the seafood into the rice.

Makes 5 servings.

Per serving: 287 calories, 4 g. total fat (13% of calories), 0.7 g. saturated fat, 92 mg. cholesterol

Shrimp in Curried Tomato Sauce

This zesty shrimp dish is very easy. Once the shrimp has marinated, it can be cooked and ready to serve in about ten minutes.

⅓	cup tomato sauce
⅓	cup water
3	tablespoons ketchup
1	teaspoon packed light brown sugar
½	tablespoon lemon juice
1½	teaspoons mild or hot curry powder
½	teaspoon chili powder
1	pound medium shrimp, peeled and deveined
1	cup thinly sliced scallions
1	small garlic clove, minced
1½	teaspoons peanut oil
2½	cups hot cooked long-grain white or brown rice
1	tablespoon finely chopped scallion tops (garnish)

In a nonreactive medium bowl, thoroughly mix the tomato sauce, water, ketchup, sugar, lemon juice, curry powder and chili powder. Stir in the shrimp. Cover with plastic wrap and marinate in the refrigerator for at least 2 hours and up to 6 hours.

In a 12" nonstick skillet, combine the scallions, garlic and oil. Cook over medium heat, stirring frequently, for 4 minutes, or until the scallions are just soft.

Add the shrimp and the marinade. Cook for 3 to 4 minutes, or until the sauce bubbles and the shrimp turns pink and curls.

Place the rice on a platter or individual plates. Spoon the shrimp mixture over the rice. Garnish with the scallion tops.

Makes 4 servings.

Per serving: 296 calories, 3.1 g. total fat (10% of calories), 0.7 g. saturated fat, 174 mg. cholesterol

S a v o r y   M u s s e l   S t e w

A wonderful one-dish meal, this goes well with a simple salad and crusty bread. You can make the stew up to 24 hours ahead and reheat it at serving time. When serving this stew, furnish some extra bowls for discarding the mussel shells.

2	pounds fresh mussels
2	large onions, chopped
2	large carrots, peeled and finely chopped
1	small celery stalk, finely chopped
½	cup coarsely diced sweet red peppers
⅓	cup finely chopped fresh parsley leaves
2	large garlic cloves, minced
1	tablespoon olive oil, preferably extra-virgin
1½	cups defatted chicken broth
1	bottle (8 ounces) clam juice
4	large boiling potatoes, peeled and cut into 1" cubes
1	can (28 ounces) Italian (plum) tomatoes, with juice
½	cup dry white wine
1	teaspoon granulated sugar
1	large bay leaf
1½	teaspoons paprika
1½	teaspoons chili powder
¼	teaspoon celery seeds
¼	teaspoon ground black pepper
¼	teaspoon dried thyme leaves
⅛	teaspoon fennel seeds
	Generous ⅛ teaspoon saffron threads, very finely crumbled (optional)
	Generous pinch of crushed red pepper flakes
¾	teaspoon salt, or to taste
	Finely chopped fresh parsley leaves (garnish)

Rinse and drain the mussels. Wash them in several changes of water, scrubbing the shells with a vegetable brush. Trim off any dark rootlike debris using kitchen shears or a sharp knife. Continue changing the water until it is clear and no sand remains. Then soak the mussels in enough cold water to cover them for at least 2 to 3 hours, to allow them to disgorge anymore sand. (Alternatively, soak the mussels in cold water sprinkled with a handful of cornmeal for about 1 hour.)

In a Dutch oven or other large heavy pot, combine the onions, carrots, celery, red peppers, parsley, garlic and oil. Cook over medium heat, stirring frequently, for 4 to 5 minutes, or until the onions are limp.

Stir in the broth, clam juice and potatoes. Bring the mixture to a boil. Cover, reduce the heat and simmer, stirring occasionally, for 15 to 18 minutes, or until the potatoes are just cooked through. Add the tomatoes (with juice) and break them up with a spoon.

Stir in the wine, sugar, bay leaf, paprika, chili powder, celery seeds, black pepper, thyme, fennel seeds, saffron (if using) and pepper flakes.

Cover and continue simmering for 20 minutes, or until the mixture is slightly thickened and the flavors have blended.

Meanwhile, place the mussels in a colander and rinse well under cold running water. Discard any that are not tightly closed or that do not close when tapped.

Stir the salt into the pot. Add the mussels and simmer for 4 to 5 minutes, or until the shells open and the mussels are cooked through. Discard any mussels that have not opened. Remove and discard the bay leaf.

Ladle the stew into soup plates or large bowls and garnish with the parsley.

Makes 4 servings.

Per serving: 349 calories, 5.5 g. total fat (14% of calories), 0.5 g. saturated fat, 42 mg. cholesterol

Rice and Salmon Pilaf

Canned salmon turns this easy pilaf into a main dish. Serve it with a simple tossed salad and stir-fried zucchini slices.

1	can (6½ ounces) pink salmon, well drained
1	small onion, finely chopped
1	large celery stalk, diced
1	teaspoon nondiet tub-style canola or corn-oil margarine or butter
2	cups water
1	medium carrot, peeled and diced
2	tablespoons finely chopped fresh parsley leaves
½	teaspoon dried thyme leaves
½	teaspoon dried basil leaves
⅛	teaspoon ground white pepper
¼	teaspoon salt (optional)
1	cup uncooked long-grain white rice

If desired, remove the skin and bones from the salmon. Flake the flesh with a fork and set aside.

In a medium saucepan, combine the onions, celery and margarine or butter. Cook over medium heat, stirring frequently, until the onions are tender. Add the water, carrots, parsley, thyme, basil, pepper, salt (if using) and the salmon.

Add the rice and stir to mix well. Bring to a boil. Cover, reduce the heat and simmer for 20 minutes, or until the rice is tender and all the water is absorbed. Stir before serving.

Makes 4 servings.

Per serving: 258 calories, 4.1 g. total fat (15% of calories), 1 g. saturated fat, 20 mg. cholesterol

Chapter 18

PERFECT POULTRY

Chicken and turkey are among our favorite choices for tempting, low-fat, fuss-free entrées and lend themselves to all sorts of ethnic dishes, from Middle Eastern and Asian to Italian and Tex-Mex to good old-fashioned American.

Almost all the recipes in this chapter call for breast meat since it is by far the leanest part of the bird. We haven't included any recipes for duck or goose, because both of them are rather high in fat.

Most markets now offer fresh chicken breast meat in a variety of convenient forms, from boneless, skinless breasts to cut-up cubes for stir-frying. Turkey used to come only whole and often frozen, but it, too, now appears in many useful, ready-to-cook forms, including cutlets for skillet dishes and ground meat for meat loaves and stews. When buying ground turkey, check labels carefully. It often contains thigh meat and skin, which makes it fatty.

Chicken with Artichoke Hearts and Sweet Red Peppers

This flavorful dish makes an easy but elegant company entrée. For a tasty variation, replace the chicken with 12 ounces boneless pork tenderloin cut into ¼" strips.

1	pound boneless, skinless chicken breast halves, cut into bite-size pieces
2	teaspoons olive oil
1½	cups defatted chicken broth, divided
1	large onion, chopped
2	garlic cloves, minced
1	jar (14 ounces) water-packed artichoke heart quarters, well drained
1	teaspoon lemon juice
1	teaspoon dried tarragon leaves
½	cup thinly sliced scallion tops
1	large sweet red pepper, seeded and cut into ½" strips
	Salt and ground black pepper, to taste
1	tablespoon cornstarch
¼	cup cold water
3	cups noodles, penne rigati or other medium pasta shapes

Coat a 12" nonstick skillet with nonstick spray. Add the chicken. Cook over medium heat, turning frequently with a slotted plastic or wooden spoon, for 4 to 5 minutes, or until the pieces begin to brown. Using the spoon, transfer to a bowl and set aside.

Add the oil and 2 tablespoons of the broth to any juices left in the pan. Stir in the onions and garlic. Cook over medium heat, stirring frequently, for 5 to 6 minutes, or until the onions are tender. (Add a bit more broth if the onions begin to stick.)

Return the chicken to the pan. Add the artichokes, lemon juice, tarragon and the remaining broth. Bring to a boil.

Cover, reduce the heat and simmer for 10 minutes. Add the scallions, red peppers and salt and black pepper. Cover and cook for an additional 5 minutes, or until the flavors are well blended and the red pepper is crisp-tender.

While the vegetables and chicken are cooking, prepare the pasta according to the package directions.

In a cup, combine the cornstarch and water. Bring the liquid in the pan to a boil. Stir in the cornstarch mixture and cook, stirring, for 1 minute, or until thickened. Drain the pasta well and transfer to a platter or individual plates. Top with the chicken mixture.

Makes 5 servings.

Per serving: 389 calories, 5 g. total fat (12% of calories), 1 g. saturated fat, 37 mg. cholesterol

Italian-Style Chicken over Pasta

Capellini, tomato sauce, peppers and a mixture of herbs give this easy dish its characteristic Italian flavor.

12	ounces boneless, skinless chicken breast halves, cut into bite-size pieces
1	tablespoon olive oil, preferably extra-virgin
2	tablespoons water
1	large onion, finely chopped
1	large garlic clove, minced
1	large green pepper, seeded and diced
2	cups thinly sliced zucchini
3	tablespoons dry sherry or defatted chicken broth
1	can (15 ounces) tomato sauce
¼	cup finely chopped fresh parsley leaves
¾	teaspoon dried basil leaves
½	teaspoon dried thyme leaves
¼	teaspoon dried oregano leaves
⅛	teaspoon ground black pepper
	Salt, to taste
8	ounces capellini

In a 12" nonstick frying pan, combine the chicken and oil. Cook over medium heat, stirring frequently, for 3 to 4 minutes, or until the chicken is white on all sides. Remove with a slotted spoon and set aside.

Add the water to the pan. Stir in the onions and garlic. Cook over medium heat, stirring frequently, for 6 to 7 minutes, or until the onions are very tender. (Add more water if the onions begin to stick.)

Stir in the green peppers, zucchini, sherry or broth, tomato sauce, parsley, basil, thyme, oregano and black pepper. Add the chicken and mix well. Bring the mixture to a boil, then reduce the heat, cover and simmer for 13 to 16 minutes, or until the vegetables are just tender. Add the salt.

While the vegetables are simmering, cook the capellini according to the package directions. Drain and divide among individual dinner plates. Top with the chicken mixture.

Makes 4 servings.

Per serving: 370 calories, 6.7 g. total fat (16% of calories), 1.2 g. saturated fat, 83 mg. cholesterol

Chicken Fajitas

This favorite main dish is zesty, colorful and satisfying—nothing is missing but excess fat. The picante sauce and amount of black pepper used will determine if the fajitas are slightly spicy or fiery.

SAUCE

2	tablespoons canned chopped mild green chili peppers, well drained
2	tablespoons reduced-fat sour cream
3½	tablespoons mild or medium picante sauce
½	teaspoon chili powder
¼	teaspoon paprika

FILLING

½	tablespoon olive oil, preferably extra-virgin
1	cup coarsely diced sweet red peppers
1	cup chopped onions
3	cups sliced mushrooms
1¼	pounds boneless, skinless chicken breast halves, cubed
¼	cup mild or medium picante sauce
2	tablespoons canned chopped mild green chili peppers, well drained
1	teaspoon mild chili powder
1	cup coarsely diced tomatoes
⅓	cup coarsely sliced scallions
¼	teaspoon salt (optional)
	Pinch of ground black pepper, or to taste
2	tablespoons reduced-fat sour cream

FAJITAS

8	large (8") flour tortillas
1	ounce reduced-fat Cheddar cheese, grated or shredded (about ¼ cup)
1	cup coarsely cubed tomatoes (garnish)
¼	cup chopped fresh cilantro leaves (garnish)
	Chopped scallions, sliced jalapeño peppers or shredded lettuce (garnish)

To prepare the sauce: In a small bowl, stir together the peppers, sour cream, picante sauce, chili powder and paprika. Set aside.

To prepare the filling: Preheat the oven to 375°.

In a 12" nonstick skillet over medium-high heat, warm the oil. Add the red peppers and onions. Cook, stirring frequently, for 3 minutes, or until slightly soft. Add the mushrooms. Cook, stirring often, for 4 minutes, or until the mushrooms release their juices.

Raise the heat to high. Stir in the chicken, picante sauce, chili peppers and chili powder. Cook, stirring frequently, for 4 to 5 minutes, or until the liquid has almost completely evaporated from the skillet; be careful not to scorch the ingredients.

Stir in the tomatoes, scallions, salt (if using) and black pepper. Cook for 1 minute; remove from the heat and stir in the sour cream.

To prepare the fajitas: Divide the filling evenly among the tortillas and roll them up to enclose the filling.

Coat a 3-quart baking dish with nonstick spray. Arrange the fajitas, seam side down, in the dish. Cover with foil and bake for 10 minutes. Spoon the sauce over the fajitas. Sprinkle with the cheese. Cover the casserole with foil and bake for 10 minutes longer.

Serve garnished with the tomatoes, cilantro and scallions, peppers or lettuce.

Makes 8 servings.

Per serving: 181 calories, 5.3 g. total fat (26% of calories), 1.6 g. saturated fat, 29 mg. cholesterol

Barbecued Chicken

Tangy, flavorful and virtually fat free, the barbecue sauce in this recipe can be used with beef or pork as well as chicken. You may store the sauce for up to a week in the refrigerator.

1	cup ketchup
1	small onion, finely chopped
1	small garlic clove, minced
1	tablespoon packed light brown sugar
½	tablespoon apple cider vinegar
½	teaspoon dry mustard
¼	teaspoon dried thyme leaves
	Pinch of ground cloves
	Pinch of ground black pepper
2	drops hot-pepper sauce (optional)
5	boneless, skinless chicken breast halves (4 ounces each)

In a small bowl, mix the ketchup, onions, garlic, sugar, vinegar, mustard, thyme, cloves, pepper and hot-pepper sauce (if using). Cover and refrigerate for at least 1 hour to blend the flavors.

Place the chicken in a medium nonreactive bowl. Add about two-thirds of the sauce, reserving the rest. Stir to coat the chicken. Cover and refrigerate for 30 minutes or up to 8 hours.

Transfer the chicken to a broiler pan. Broil 5" from the heat for 11 to 13 minutes per side, or until cooked through. Warm the remaining third of the sauce and serve with the chicken.

Makes 5 servings.

Per serving: 156 calories, 2.1 g. total fat (12% of calories), 0.6 g. saturated fat, 46 mg. cholesterol

Chicken Couscous

Used extensively in Middle Eastern cooking, couscous is a mild-flavored wheat product that needs very little cooking. Like rice, it goes well with a variety of herbs, spices, meats and vegetables. This savory couscous dish is one of our favorites.

8	ounces skinless, boneless chicken breast halves, cut into bite-size pieces
1	large onion, chopped
1	large garlic clove, minced
2	teaspoons olive oil
2¼	cups defatted chicken broth, divided
1	can (15 ounces) garbanzo beans, rinsed and drained
1	large carrot, peeled and thinly sliced
1	celery stalk, diced
1	cup diced zucchini
1½	teaspoons dried thyme leaves
1	teaspoon dried marjoram leaves
1	bay leaf
⅛	teaspoon ground black pepper, or to taste
1	cup uncooked couscous
	Salt, to taste
	Parsley sprigs (garnish)

Coat a Dutch oven or other large heavy pot with nonstick spray. Add the chicken. Cook over medium heat, stirring frequently, until the pieces turn white. Using a slotted spoon, transfer to a bowl and set aside.

Add the onions, garlic, oil and 2 tablespoons of the broth to the pot. Cook over medium heat, stirring frequently, for 5 to 6 minutes, or until the onions are tender. Return the chicken to the pot. Add the beans, carrots, celery, zucchini, thyme, marjoram, bay leaf, pepper and the remaining broth. Bring to a boil.

Cover, reduce the heat and simmer for 15 to 20 minutes, or until the vegetables are tender. Add the couscous and stir to mix well. Cover and cook for 2 minutes.

Remove the pot from the heat, stir well, cover and allow the mixture to stand for 10 to 12 minutes. Remove and discard the bay leaf.

Fluff the couscous with a fork. Season with the salt. Garnish with the parsley.

Makes 4 servings.

Per serving: 372 calories, 5.3 g. total fat (13% of calories), 0.9 g. saturated fat, 22 mg. cholesterol

Easy Baked Chicken Breasts

This is a nearly fuss-free recipe. All you have to do is shake the chicken pieces in a bag to coat them with seasonings and then bake them until tender. To help round out the meal, we like to bake some white potatoes or sweet potatoes along with the chicken and also serve a simple salad and a quick vegetable or fruit dish.

2	teaspoons nondiet tub-style canola or corn-oil margarine or butter
1½	tablespoons all-purpose or unbleached white flour
1½	tablespoons yellow cornmeal
1	teaspoon chili powder
1	teaspoon dried dillweed
1	teaspoon paprika
½	teaspoon celery salt
¼	teaspoon salt (optional)
2	pounds skinless, bone-in chicken breast halves

Preheat the oven to 400°.

Put the margarine or butter in a 10" pie plate or similar baking dish. Place the plate in the oven until the margarine or butter melts. Tilt the plate from side to side to coat the surface. Set aside.

In a large sturdy paper bag, combine the flour, cornmeal, chili powder, dill, paprika, celery salt and salt (if using). Mix well.

Pat the chicken pieces dry with paper towels. Add to the bag and shake until the chicken is evenly coated. (Reserve the leftover flour mixture.)

Place the chicken pieces, bone side up, in the pie plate. Lightly press down each breast to partially coat with the margarine. Tightly cover the dish with foil. Bake for 25 minutes.

Turn over the pieces. Sprinkle the top with the leftover flour mixture. Bake, uncovered, for 20 to 25 minutes longer, or until the pieces are nicely browned and cooked through.

Makes 4 servings.

Per serving: 216 calories, 5.9 g. total fat (26% of calories), 1.4 g. saturated fat, 91 mg. cholesterol

Chicken and Savory Dumplings

Here's a dish that's homey, tempting and very satisfying. We've pared the fat from this classic entrée in several ways: by using skinless chicken breasts, by skimming the broth carefully and by adding only enough fat to the dumplings to keep them fluffy and tender.

CHICKEN

4	large skinless chicken breast halves
1⅓	cups water
1	medium onion, chopped
1¼	teaspoons dried marjoram leaves
½	teaspoon dried dillweed
⅛	teaspoon dried thyme leaves
¼	teaspoon ground black pepper, or to taste
	About 2½ cups defatted chicken broth, divided
2	medium celery stalks, chopped
½	cup chopped fresh parsley leaves
1	large carrot, peeled and diced
¼	cup cornstarch
¼	teaspoon salt (optional)

DUMPLINGS

2	cups all-purpose or unbleached white flour
1¼	teaspoons baking powder
¼	teaspoon baking soda
	Generous ¼ teaspoon salt
1½	tablespoons nondiet tub-style canola or corn-oil margarine or butter, chilled and cut into small pieces
1½	tablespoons canola or safflower oil
½	cup defatted chicken broth
⅓	cup skim milk
¼	cup finely chopped fresh parsley leaves
½	teaspoon dried dillweed

To prepare the chicken: In a Dutch oven or other large heavy pot, combine the chicken, water, onions, marjoram, dill, thyme, pepper and 1½ cups of the broth. Bring to a boil over high heat. Cover, reduce the heat and simmer for 40 to 50 minutes, or until the chicken is tender. Remove the chicken from the pot and set aside until cool enough to handle. Cut the meat into bite-size pieces, discarding the bones.

Using a fat skimmer or a large shallow spoon, skim off all the fat from the liquid. (Or refrigerate the mixture for at least 4 hours, until the fat solidifies on the surface for easy removal. Reheat the liquid.) Measure the liquid; add enough broth to measure 3 cups.

Return the liquid to the pot. Add the celery, parsley and carrots. Cover and simmer for 15 minutes.

In a cup, stir together the cornstarch and ½ cup of the remaining broth. Stir into the pot and simmer about 2 minutes, or until the liquid thickens slightly and turns clear. Remove from the heat and stir in the chicken. Add the salt (if using).

Pour the mixture into a 12" × 8" baking dish. Preheat the oven to 375°.

To prepare the dumplings: In a medium bowl, thoroughly stir together the flour, baking powder, baking soda and salt.

Using a pastry blender or forks, cut in the margarine or butter and oil until the mixture resembles coarse meal. Add the broth, milk, parsley and dill; stir only until evenly incorporated. Do not overmix.

Using a large spoon, drop tablespoonfuls of the dough over the chicken mixture, separating them as much as possible. Loosely cover the dish with foil.

Bake for 10 minutes. Remove the foil and bake for 12 to 15 minutes longer, or until the dumplings are lightly browned and a toothpick inserted in a center dumpling comes out clean.

Makes 6 servings.

Per serving: 403 calories, 10.4 g. total fat (24% of calories), 2.2 g. saturated fat, 82 mg. cholesterol

Middle-Eastern Spiced Chicken with Raisins

An unusual blend of spices, herbs and raisins lends fragrance and a wonderfully exotic flavor to this savory chicken dish. Chunks of red and green peppers and tomatoes also contribute appealing color. The recipe calls for cardamom, a spice that is sometimes difficult to find; you may omit it if absolutely necessary.

2	large onions, cut into eighths
½	medium sweet red pepper, seeded and cut into 1" pieces
1	small green pepper, seeded and cut into 1" pieces
1	large garlic clove, minced
1	tablespoon nondiet tub-style canola or corn-oil margarine or butter
1	pound boneless, skinless chicken breast halves, cut into ¾" cubes
½	cup defatted chicken broth
⅓	cup golden raisins
1	large tomato, peeled and cut into 1¼" pieces
2	teaspoons peeled and minced ginger root
¼	teaspoon dried thyme leaves
6	tablespoons finely chopped fresh cilantro leaves, divided
2½	teaspoons mild chili powder
1	teaspoon ground coriander
¼	teaspoon ground allspice
¼	teaspoon ground cloves
⅛	teaspoon ground cardamom (optional)
	Generous ¼ teaspoon salt, or to taste
1½	tablespoons lemon juice, or to taste
4	cups hot cooked long-grain white or brown rice

In a 12" nonstick skillet, combine the onions, red peppers, green peppers, garlic and margarine or butter. Cook over medium-high heat, stirring frequently, for 6 to 7 minutes, or until the vegetables are nicely browned.

Add the chicken and cook, stirring, for 2 minutes. Stir in the broth, raisins, tomatoes, ginger, thyme and 4 tablespoons of the cilantro. Reduce the heat to medium and cook for 3 minutes.

Stir in the chili powder, coriander, allspice, cloves, cardamom (if using), salt and lemon juice. Remove the skillet from the heat.

Spoon the rice onto a platter or divide among individual plates. Top with the chicken mixture. Sprinkle with the remaining 2 tablespoons cilantro.

Makes 5 servings.

Per serving: 382 calories, 4.8 g. total fat (11% of calories), 0.9 g. saturated fat, 36 mg. cholesterol

Singapore Noodle-Chicken Stir-Fry with Sesame Oil

When you need an easy, delicious, healthful entrée—and you need it in a hurry—this is a good choice.

1	teaspoon peeled and minced ginger root
½	teaspoon curry powder
2½	tablespoons reduced-sodium soy sauce, divided
1½	teaspoons oriental sesame oil, divided
1	teaspoon canola oil
8	ounces boneless, skinless chicken breast halves, cut into 2" × ⅛" strips
1	small onion, thinly sliced lengthwise
1	small celery stalk, cut into 2" × ⅛" strips
½	medium sweet red pepper, seeded and cut into 2" × ⅛" strips
½	cup Chinese pea pods, trimmed and halved lengthwise
¼	cup julienned carrots
½	cup baby corn ears
2	tablespoons defatted chicken broth
3	drops hot-pepper oil, or to taste
3	cups cooked Chinese lo mein noodles or vermicelli, cut into 2½" lengths
	Sesame seeds (garnish)

In a medium bowl, mix the ginger, curry powder, 1 tablespoon of the soy sauce and 1 teaspoon of the sesame oil. Add the chicken and mix well. Set aside to marinate for 10 to 15 minutes.

In a 12" nonstick skillet over medium-high heat, warm the canola oil until hot but not smoking. Add the onions, celery and peppers. Cook, stirring constantly, for 4 minutes, or until the onions are slightly soft.

Stir in the chicken and marinade. Cook, stirring, for 3 minutes longer, or until the chicken is almost cooked through. Add the pea pods, carrots and corn. Cook for 30 seconds.

Stir in the broth, hot-pepper oil, the remaining ½ teaspoon sesame oil and the remaining 1½ tablespoons soy sauce. Add the noodles and heat through. Sprinkle with sesame seeds.

Makes 4 servings.

Per serving: 188 calories, 4.1 g. total fat (18% of calories), 0.7 g. saturated fat, 23 mg. cholesterol

Herbed Chicken Breasts
with Lime and Tomatoes

This simple entrée has an appealing pungency and aroma. It's especially good served on a bed of rice. And it's very convenient for entertaining since most of the preparation can be done ahead.

¼	teaspoon finely grated lime zest
2	tablespoons lime juice
1	teaspoon chili powder
¼	teaspoon finely crumbled dried rosemary
¼	teaspoon salt
4	boneless, skinless chicken breast halves (4 ounces each)
1	teaspoon olive oil, preferably extra-virgin
	About ½ cup defatted chicken broth
¾	cup peeled and diced tomatoes

In a nonreactive medium bowl, stir together the lime zest, lime juice, chili powder, rosemary and salt to form a paste. Add the chicken and toss until the pieces are well coated. Cover and refrigerate at least 20 minutes and up to 2 hours.

In a 12" nonstick skillet over medium-high heat, warm the oil until hot but not smoking. Add the chicken, reserving the leftover paste. Cook, turning the chicken occasionally, for 4 minutes, or until the pieces are lightly browned. If necessary, lower the heat slightly to prevent burning.

Add ½ cup broth to the bowl with the remaining paste and stir well. Pour the mixture over the chicken. Lower the heat and simmer for 9 minutes; add a bit more broth, if necessary, to prevent the pan from boiling dry.

Add the tomatoes and simmer for 2 to 3 minutes, or until the chicken is just cooked through.

Makes 4 servings.

Per serving: 101 calories, 2.2 g. total fat (20% of calories), 0.6 g. saturated fat, 45 mg. cholesterol

Quick Honey-Mustard Chicken

When you need a tasty, nourishing main dish and you want it fast, this is a perfect choice. Preparation time is minimal, especially if you buy boneless chicken breasts. Cooking time is short, too, so the dish can be ready in about 30 minutes.

1	tablespoon finely chopped onions
1½	teaspoons canola or safflower oil
5	boneless, skinless chicken breast halves (4 ounces each)
½	cup water
¼	cup Dijon mustard
2	tablespoons dry white wine or orange juice
2	tablespoons chopped fresh chives or 1 tablespoon dried chives
1½	tablespoons mild honey, such as clover

In a 12" nonstick skillet, stir together the onions and oil. Cook over medium heat, stirring occasionally, for 3 minutes, or until the onions are limp.

Add the chicken. Cook, turning the pieces until all sides are opaque and beginning to brown.

In a small bowl, stir together the water, mustard, wine or orange juice, chives and honey. Pour over the chicken and bring the mixture to a simmer. Adjust the heat so the mixture simmers gently.

Cover and cook for 5 minutes. Uncover and continue simmering, occasionally turning chicken pieces, for 12 to 15 minutes longer, or until the pieces are cooked through but not dry. (If the sauce evaporates too rapidly and the pan looks dry, add a tablespoon or so more water to the skillet as necessary.)

Makes 5 servings.

Per serving: 137 calories, 4.1 g. total fat (27% of calories), 0.6 g. saturated fat, 46 mg. cholesterol

Turkey Scaloppine with Lemon and Parsley

In this Italian-style recipe, the turkey breast cutlets look and taste remarkably like veal but are much lower in fat. The dish is good served with our Herbed Lentils and Rice with Tomatoes. To ensure that the cutlets don't stick during browning, use a nonstick skillet with a very smooth finish. A pan with a worn or scratched surface will not work as well.

1	pound turkey breast cutlets
⅓	cup lemon juice
¼	cup all-purpose or unbleached white flour, divided
2	teaspoons olive oil, preferably extra-virgin, divided
2	teaspoons nondiet tub-style canola or corn-oil margarine or butter, divided
2	large garlic cloves, halved and crushed, divided
¼	teaspoon salt, divided
½	cup defatted chicken broth
¼	cup + 2 tablespoons chopped fresh parsley leaves, divided
	Ground black pepper, to taste
1	medium lemon, cut into 8 wedges

Lay the cutlets between sheets of plastic wrap. Using a kitchen mallet or the back of a large, heavy spoon, pound each cutlet to ⅛" thick. Transfer the cutlets to a large, flat glass dish or nonreactive platter.

Pour the lemon juice over the cutlets. Cover the dish with plastic wrap and refrigerate for at least 45 minutes and up to 2 hours, turning occasionally.

Drain the cutlets well, discarding the lemon juice. Pat the cutlets dry with paper towels. Transfer the pieces to clean paper towels. Sift about 2 tablespoons of the flour over them and pat it into the top surface. Turn over the pieces and repeat with the remaining 2 tablespoons flour.

Preheat the oven to 200°.

In a 12" nonstick skillet, combine 1 teaspoon of the oil and 1 teaspoon of the margarine or butter. Add 1 garlic clove half, pressing it into the pan. Heat the skillet over medium-high heat until hot but not smoking. Add half of the cutlets. Sprinkle with ⅛ teaspoon of the salt. Cook the cutlets for 1½ minutes, or until lightly browned. Turn over the pieces and cook for 2 minutes, or until lightly browned and just cooked through. Transfer to an oven-proof serving dish, cover and place in the oven. Discard the garlic from the skillet.

Repeat the procedure, using the remaining 1 teaspoon oil, 1 teaspoon margarine or butter, 1 of the remaining garlic clove halves, remaining turkey cutlets and ⅛ teaspoon salt. Transfer the cooked cutlets to the serving dish and keep warm; discard the garlic.

Add the broth, ¼ cup of the parsley and the remaining 2 garlic clove halves to the skillet. Cook over medium heat, stirring, for 4 minutes, or until the liquid has reduced to about 3 tablespoons.

Strain the liquid through a fine sieve and pour over the cutlets. Sprinkle with the remaining 2 tablespoons parsley. Add the pepper. Garnish with the lemon wedges.

Makes 4 servings.

Per serving: 188 calories, 6.8 g. total fat (33% of calories), 1.4 g. saturated fat, 49 mg. cholesterol

Baked Herbed Turkey Cutlets Dijonnaise

Turkey breast is so lean and healthful that we like to serve it often. The following very tasty recipe makes doing so easy, since it requires little in the way of preparation or cooking time. The turkey is good served with oven-baked or microwaved potatoes.

1	pound turkey breast cutlets
5	tablespoons Dijon mustard
2½	tablespoons lemon juice
1½	tablespoons granulated sugar
1	tablespoon dried tarragon leaves

Lay the cutlets between sheets of plastic wrap. Using a kitchen mallet or the back of a large, heavy spoon, pound each cutlet to ⅛" thick. Transfer the cutlets to a large, flat glass dish or nonreactive platter.

In a small deep bowl, thoroughly stir together the mustard, lemon juice, sugar and tarragon. Spread half of the mixture evenly over the cutlets. Turn over the cutlets and cover them evenly with the remainder of the mixture.

Cover the dish with plastic wrap and refrigerate for at least 20 minutes and up to several hours.

Preheat the oven to 450°. Cover a large jelly-roll pan with foil and place the turkey cutlets, slightly separated, in the pan. Bake on the upper oven rack for 8 minutes, or until cooked through. Serve immediately.

Makes 4 servings.

Per serving: 147 calories, 3.5 g. total fat (22% of calories), 0.7 g. saturated fat, 49 mg. cholesterol

Tandoori Spice Turkey Cutlets

For this recipe we've adapted the basic idea of a popular Indian dish, Tandoori chicken, to turkey breast cutlets. In the classic recipe, chicken pieces are marinated in a distinctive blend of spices and yogurt before being cooked in a special oven. Here, we marinate turkey cutlets and then bake them quickly.

1	pound turkey breast cutlets
¾	cup plain nonfat yogurt
½	tablespoon white vinegar
1	small garlic clove, minced
1¼	teaspoons chili powder
1	teaspoon ground coriander
1	teaspoon paprika
½	teaspoon ground ginger
¼	teaspoon ground turmeric
¼	teaspoon ground cumin
¼	teaspoon dry mustard
⅛	teaspoon ground cloves
⅛	teaspoon ground cardamom (optional)
⅛	teaspoon salt, or to taste (optional)

Lay the cutlets between sheets of plastic wrap. Using a kitchen mallet or the back of a large, heavy spoon, pound each cutlet to ⅛" thick. Transfer the cutlets to a large, flat glass dish or nonreactive platter.

In a small deep bowl, thoroughly stir together the yogurt, vinegar, garlic, chili powder, coriander, paprika, ginger, turmeric, cumin, mustard, cloves and cardamom (if using). Spread half the mixture over the cutlets. Turn over the cutlets and cover them evenly with the remainder of the mixture.

Cover the dish with plastic wrap and refrigerate for at least 6 hours and up to 24 hours.

Preheat the oven to 450°. Cover a large jelly-roll pan with foil and place the turkey cutlets, slightly separated, in the pan. Bake on the upper oven rack for 8 minutes, or until cooked through. Sprinkle with the salt (if using). Using tongs, transfer the cutlets to a serving platter; discard any juices from the baking pan.

Makes 4 servings.

Per serving: 136 calories, 2.4 g. total fat (16% of calories), 0.8 g. saturated fat, 50 mg. cholesterol

Turkey Sloppy Joes

While turkey breast is one of the leanest meats you can serve, ground turkey isn't necessarily lower in fat than extra-lean ground beef. That's because ground turkey often contains dark meat and even skin. So if you like to use ground turkey, check package labels or ask your butcher about the fat content before you buy. Ground turkey has a less meaty flavor than ground beef and works best in spicy recipes that feature flavorful ingredients, like this one. Incidentally, this filling tastes as good on baked potatoes as it does in a sandwich bun.

1	pound lean ground turkey
1	large onion, chopped
1	celery stalk, thinly sliced
1	large garlic clove, minced
1	cup ketchup
1	large carrot, peeled and grated or shredded
1	tablespoon apple cider vinegar
2	teaspoons granulated sugar
½	teaspoon dried thyme leaves
¼	teaspoon ground black pepper
⅛	teaspoon dry mustard
3	drops hot-pepper sauce
5	hamburger buns

In a very large saucepan or small Dutch oven, combine the turkey, onions, celery and garlic. Cook over medium heat, stirring frequently, for 5 minutes, or until the turkey has changed color and the onions are soft.

Add the ketchup, carrots, vinegar, sugar, thyme, pepper, mustard and hot-pepper sauce. Stir to mix well. Bring to a boil. Cover, reduce the heat and simmer for 15 to 20 minutes, or until the flavors are well blended.

Serve in the buns.

Makes 5 servings.

Per serving: 303 calories, 9.1 g. total fat (27% of calories), 2.3 g. saturated fat, 34 mg. cholesterol

Turkey Breast Cutlets with Marsala Wine and Mushroom Sauce

Classic veal Marsala was the inspiration for this lean but succulent turkey variation. Marsala wine and mushrooms dress up the turkey so effectively many people don't even realize they aren't eating veal.

1	pound turkey breast cutlets
½	cup Marsala wine
1	teaspoon reduced-sodium soy sauce
4	tablespoons all-purpose or unbleached flour, divided
2	teaspoons canola or safflower oil, divided
2	teaspoons nondiet tub-style canola or corn-oil margarine or butter, divided
¼	teaspoon salt, divided
2½	cups sliced mushrooms
1	tablespoon finely chopped onions
1	small garlic clove, minced
½	cup defatted chicken broth
	Pinch of ground black pepper, or to taste
1	tablespoon finely chopped fresh parsley leaves (optional)

Lay the cutlets between sheets of plastic wrap. Using a kitchen mallet or the back of a large, heavy spoon, pound each cutlet to ⅛" thick. Transfer the cutlets to a large, flat glass dish or nonreactive platter.

In a small cup, stir together the wine and soy sauce. Pour over the cutlets. Cover the dish with plastic wrap and refrigerate for at least 45 minutes and up to 2 hours, turning occasionally.

Drain the cutlets well, reserving the marinade. Pat the cutlets dry with paper towels. Transfer the pieces to clean paper towels. Sift about 1½ tablespoons of the flour over them and pat it into the top surface. Turn over the pieces and repeat with 1½ tablespoons of the remaining flour.

Preheat the oven to 200°.

In a 12" nonstick skillet over medium-high heat, warm ½ teaspoon of the oil and ½ teaspoon of the margarine or butter until hot but not smoking. Add half of the cutlets. Sprinkle with ⅛ teaspoon of the salt. Cook the cutlets for 1½ minutes, or until lightly browned. Turn over the pieces and cook for 2 minutes, or until lightly browned and just cooked through. Transfer to an oven-proof serving dish, cover and place in the oven.

Repeat the procedure, using ½ teaspoon of the remaining oil, ½ teaspoon of the remaining margarine or butter, the remaining turkey cutlets and the remaining ⅛ teaspoon salt. Transfer the cooked cutlets to the serving dish and keep warm.

Add the remaining 1 teaspoon oil and 1 teaspoon margarine or butter to the skillet. Add the mushrooms, onions and garlic. Cook over medium heat, stirring frequently, for 4 minutes, or until the mushrooms have browned and most of the liquid they've given off has evaporated from the pan.

Stir in the remaining 1 tablespoon flour. Cook, stirring constantly, for 30 seconds. Add the broth and the reserved marinade. Cook, stirring, until the mixture thickens and boils. Remove from the heat. Add the pepper. Spoon the mixture over the cutlets. Sprinkle with the parsley (if using).

Makes 4 servings.

Per serving: 215 calories, 6.9 g. total fat (29% of calories), 1.3 g. saturated fat, 49 mg. cholesterol

Chapter 19

THE BEST BEEF, PORK AND LAMB

Here's the meat of this book: recipes like Beef Burgundy, Pork Tenderloin with Glazed Apples, Chili con Carne, Lamb Shish Kebab.

Many of the dishes in this chapter are one-pot meals and skillet dinners that combine meat, vegetables, grains and other filling ingredients with a flavorful blend of herbs and spices. These types of recipes do double duty. Mixing the meat with carbohydrates and vegetables lowers the overall fat content. This technique also makes getting dinner on the table a snap. Just add a salad and bread, and you have a complete meal.

Please notice that we've selected our cuts of meat carefully. We emphasize lean ground round of beef, flank steak, lean stew beef, pork tenderloin and Canadian bacon precisely because they're easy on your fat budget.

Chili con Carne

When we first began experimenting with trimming the fat from our meals by using less meat in favorite family dishes, we found that we could replace some of the ground beef with finely ground vegetables. In this chili, the vegetables not only add volume but also give the sauce extra flavor. If you'd like, you may replace the broccoli with celery. The mixture will keep for three to four days.

12	ounces extra-lean ground round of beef
1	large onion, finely chopped
2	large garlic cloves, minced
1	large carrot, peeled and cut into 2" sections
1	small broccoli stalk, peeled and cut into 2" sections
2	cans (16 ounces each) tomatoes, with juice
3	cans (16 ounces each) kidney beans, rinsed and drained
1	can (15 ounces) tomato sauce
2½	tablespoons chili powder, or to taste
¼	teaspoon ground black pepper
1½	teaspoons granulated sugar (optional)
	Salt, to taste (optional)
1½	cups uncooked long-grain white rice

In a Dutch oven or other large heavy pot, combine the beef, onions and garlic. Cook over medium heat, stirring frequently and breaking up the meat with a spoon, until browned. Transfer the mixture to a plate lined with paper towels. When the fat has been absorbed by the towels, return the mixture to the pot.

Meanwhile, combine the carrots and broccoli in a food processor. Remove the tomatoes from the cans with a fork, reserving the juice. Add the tomatoes to the processor and process with on/off pulses until the vegetables are finely chopped. Add to the meat. Stir in the beans, tomato sauce, chili powder, pepper and the reserved tomato juice.

Taste the chili. If the tomatoes are acid, add some sugar. Add the salt (if using). Bring to a boil. Cover, reduce the heat and simmer, stirring occasionally, for 1½ hours, or until the flavors are well blended. Skim any fat from the top of the chili with a large shallow spoon.

About 25 minutes before the chili is done, cook the rice according to the package directions. Serve the chili over the rice.

Makes 8 servings.

Per serving: 386 calories, 5.5 g. total fat (13% of calories), 2.1 g. saturated fat, 26 mg. cholesterol

Quick and Easy Lasagna

*Nonfat cheeses work particularly well in this hearty recipe.
"No-boil" noodles make preparation a snap.*

8	ounces extra-lean ground round of beef
1	medium onion, diced
1	garlic clove, chopped
1	can (29 ounces) tomato sauce
½	medium green pepper, seeded and diced
¾	cup diced zucchini
1	teaspoon dried thyme leaves
1	teaspoon dried oregano leaves
	Pinch of ground black pepper
9	ounces no-boil lasagna noodles, divided
1½	cups nonfat ricotta cheese, divided
6	ounces nonfat mozzarella cheese, shredded and divided (about 1½ cups)

In a large saucepan, combine the beef, onions and garlic. Cook over medium heat, stirring frequently and breaking up the meat with a spoon, until browned. Transfer the mixture to a plate lined with paper towels to absorb the fat; return the mixture to the pan.

Add the tomato sauce, green peppers, zucchini, thyme, oregano and black pepper. Bring to a boil. Reduce the heat and simmer for 10 minutes, or until the vegetables are partially cooked.

Spread a thin layer of sauce in the bottom of a 12" × 8" glass baking dish with the back of a large spoon. Arrange a layer of noodles over the sauce. Top with half of the ricotta, spreading it out evenly with the spoon. Sprinkle with one-third of the mozzarella.

Repeat to make another layer of sauce, noodles, ricotta and mozzarella. Finish with a final layer of noodles and the rest of the sauce.

Preheat the oven to 350°. Cover the dish with foil and bake for 30 minutes. Remove the foil and bake for an additional 25 minutes, or until the noodles are tender. Sprinkle with the remaining mozzarella and bake for 5 minutes.

Let stand for 5 minutes before cutting.

Makes 8 servings.

Microwave option: After assembling the lasagna, cover with wax paper. Microwave on high power for 12 to 15 minutes; halfway through the cooking time, give the dish a quarter turn. Top the lasagna with the remaining mozzarella. Cover with another sheet of wax paper; cook on high power for 3 to 5 minutes more, or until the noodles are tender.

Per serving: 277 calories, 5.5 g. total fat (18% of calories), 2.6 g. saturated fat, 50 mg. cholesterol

Sweet-and-Sour Ground Beef and Cabbage

Since ground meat combines so well with vegetables and grains, we need to use only a small amount of meat per serving in this hearty one-dish combo.

12	ounces extra-lean ground round of beef
1	large onion, chopped
1	garlic clove, minced
1	can (16 ounces) tomatoes, with juice
1½	cups defatted chicken broth
2	teaspoons apple cider vinegar
1	tablespoon mild honey, such as clover
1	teaspoon dried thyme leaves
1	bay leaf
⅛	teaspoon ground cinnamon
⅛	teaspoon ground black pepper
	Pinch of ground cloves
3	drops hot-pepper sauce (optional)
3	cups thinly sliced cabbage
1	cup uncooked long-grain white rice
1	medium sweet yellow or red pepper, seeded and diced
	Salt, to taste (optional)

In a Dutch oven or other large heavy pot, combine the beef, onions and garlic. Cook over medium heat, stirring frequently and breaking up the meat with a spoon, until browned. Transfer the mixture to a plate lined with paper towels. When the fat has been absorbed by the towels, return the mixture to the pot.

Add the tomatoes (with juice), breaking up the tomatoes with a spoon. Add the broth, vinegar, honey, thyme, bay leaf, cinnamon, black pepper, cloves and hot-pepper sauce (if using). Stir to mix well.

Stir in the cabbage and bring to a boil. Cover, reduce the heat and simmer for 5 minutes, or until the cabbage has lost some of its crispness. Stir in the rice, yellow or red peppers and salt (if using).

Bring to a boil. Cover, reduce the heat and simmer for an additional 20 minutes, or until the rice is tender and most of the liquid has been absorbed. Remove and discard the bay leaf.

Makes 5 servings.

Per serving: 329 calories, 8.8 g. total fat (24% of calories), 3.3 g. saturated fat, 42 mg. cholesterol

Spaghetti and Sauce

Here's another recipe in which ground vegetables replace some of the beef. For variety, you may replace the broccoli with celery.

12	ounces extra-lean ground round of beef
1	large onion, chopped
2	garlic cloves, minced
1	large carrot, peeled and grated or shredded
1	large broccoli stalk, peeled and grated or shredded
1	can (14½ ounces) Italian (plum) tomatoes, with juice
2	cans (15 ounces each) tomato sauce
1	can (6 ounces) tomato paste
½	large green pepper, seeded and chopped
1	teaspoon dried thyme leaves
1	teaspoon dried basil leaves
1	teaspoon dried oregano
1	bay leaf
	Salt and ground black pepper, to taste (optional)
2½	teaspoons granulated sugar (optional)
1	box (16 ounces) thin spaghetti

In a Dutch oven or other large heavy pot, combine the beef, onions and garlic. Cook over medium heat, stirring frequently and breaking up the meat with a spoon, until browned. Transfer the mixture to a plate lined with paper towels. When the fat has been absorbed by the towels, return the mixture to the pot.

Meanwhile, combine the carrots, broccoli and tomatoes (with juice) in a food processor. Process with on/off pulses until the vegetables are finely chopped. Add to the meat mixture.

Stir in the tomato sauce, tomato paste, green peppers, thyme, basil, oregano, bay leaf and salt and black pepper (if using). Taste the sauce. If the tomatoes are acid, add some sugar.

Bring the mixture to a boil. Cover, reduce the heat and simmer, stirring occasionally, for 40 to 50 minutes, or until the flavors are well blended.

While the sauce is simmering, cook the spaghetti according to the package directions. Drain and divide among individual plates or wide shallow bowls.

Remove and discard the bay leaf from the sauce. Then stir to distribute the meat and vegetables evenly. Spoon over the spaghetti.

Makes 6 servings.

Per serving: 513 calories, 9.1 g. total fat (16% of calories), 3 g. saturated fat, 35 mg. cholesterol

Savory Mussel Stew (page 216)

Seafood Risotto (page 214)

Singapore Noodle-Chicken Stir-Fry with Sesame Oil (page 229)

Chicken with Artichoke Hearts and Sweet Red Peppers (page 220)

Barbecued Chicken (page 223); Savory Cabbage Slaw (page 133); Potato Salad (page 100) **247**

2 4 8   Tandoori Spice Turkey Cutlets (page 234); Potatoes and Spinach, Indian-Style (page 189)

Chicken Fajitas (page 222)

Chicken and Savory Dumplings (page 226)

Turkey Scaloppine with Lemon and Parsley (page 232); Rice and Vegetable Pilaf (page 180)

Lamb Shanks with Couscous (page 272)

Lamb Shish Kebab (page 273); Bulgur-Parsley Salad (page 135)

Marinated Thin-Sliced Steak (page 263); Potato Slices (page 186)

Smoked Pork and Winter-Vegetable Stew (page 267)

Scalloped Potatoes with Canadian Bacon (page 271)

Beef Burgundy (page 260)

Easy Honey-Oat Yeast Bread (page 286)

Stuffed Peppers, South-of-the-Border-Style

Cooking the filling mixture separately means you can easily remove the excess fat from this dish. Be sure to cook the peppers to the desired degree of doneness before adding the filling since they won't really be cooked further later on.

8	ounces ground round of beef
1	large onion, chopped
1	garlic clove, minced
1	can (15 ounces) tomato sauce
1	can (16 ounces) kidney beans, rinsed and drained
1	cup loose-pack frozen corn kernels
½	cup chopped sweet red peppers
2	tablespoons uncooked long-grain white rice
2	teaspoons chili powder, or to taste
1	teaspoon ground cumin
⅛	teaspoon ground black pepper
3	drops hot-pepper sauce (optional)
	Salt (optional)
4	large green peppers, halved lengthwise and seeded

In a Dutch oven or other large pot, combine the beef, onions and garlic. Cook over medium heat, stirring frequently and breaking up the meat with a spoon, until browned. Transfer to a plate lined with paper towels to absorb the fat; return the mixture to the pot.

Add the tomato sauce, beans, corn, red peppers, rice, chili powder, cumin, black pepper, hot-pepper sauce and salt (if using). Mix well. Bring to a boil over high heat. Cover, reduce the heat and simmer gently, stirring occasionally, for 20 minutes, or until the rice is cooked.

Meanwhile, bring a large pot of water to a boil over high heat. Add the peppers. Cover and reduce the heat. Boil for 6 to 8 minutes, or until as tender as desired. Drain in a colander and set aside until cool enough to handle.

Arrange peppers, cut side up, in a shallow microwave-safe baking dish. Using a large spoon, divide the meat mixture equally among the peppers. Microwave on high power for 8 to 10 minutes, or until the peppers are heated through; halfway through the cooking time, give the dish a quarter turn. Or, bake the peppers at 350° for 20 minutes.

Makes 4 servings.

Per serving: 324 calories, 7.7 g. total fat (21% of calories), 2.8 g. saturated fat, 35 mg. cholesterol

Beef Burgundy

Here's a main dish we love to serve on special occasions. We've not only streamlined the recipe to reduce preparation time but also removed a good deal of the fat—without compromising the subtle marriage of flavors that makes this traditional French dish so distinctive. One of our fat-busting techniques calls for coating the beef cubes with flour and browning them under the broiler. That both simplifies preparation and eliminates the oil that would ordinarily be used for browning.

2	ounces country ham, trimmed of all visible fat and cut into thin ¾" strips
1	large onion, finely chopped
2	large garlic cloves, minced
2	teaspoons olive oil
1½	cups defatted beef broth, divided
8	ounces mushrooms, sliced
1	pound very lean stew beef, trimmed of all visible fat and cut into bite-size pieces
2½	tablespoons all-purpose or unbleached white flour, divided
1¼	cups red burgundy wine
1	large carrot, peeled and ground or grated
1	large celery stalk, ground or grated
1	large broccoli stem, peeled and ground or grated
2	tablespoons tomato paste
1	teaspoon dried thyme leaves
1	large bay leaf
¼	teaspoon ground black pepper
16	small (1" diameter) white onions
¼	cup cold water
1½	cups uncooked long-grain white rice

In Dutch oven or other large heavy pot, combine the ham, chopped onions, garlic, oil and 3 tablespoons of the broth. Cook over medium heat, stirring frequently, for 6 to 7 minutes, or until the onions are tender. If the liquid begins to evaporate, add a bit more broth.

Remove the onions, garlic and ham with a slotted spoon; set aside. Add 3 tablespoons of the remaining broth to the pot. Then add the mushrooms. Cook, stirring, for 5 minutes, or until they change color; add more broth, if needed, to keep them from sticking.

Add the remaining broth and stir in the reserved ham mixture. Remove the pot from the burner and set aside briefly.

Preheat the broiler. Adjust the rack so it's about 3" from the heating element.

Place the meat in a shallow baking pan. Sprinkle with 1½ tablespoons of the flour. Stir to coat the meat with flour. Spread out the pieces so they are separated from one another. Broil, stirring occasionally, for 7 to 8 minutes, or until the meat is browned on all sides.

Return the pot with the mushrooms to the stove. Using a slotted spoon, add the beef. Add the wine, carrots, celery, broccoli, tomato paste, thyme, bay leaf and pepper. Bring to a boil. Cover, reduce the heat and simmer for 1¾ hours. Remove and discard the bay leaf.

Meanwhile, bring a medium saucepan of water to a boil. Add the white onions and boil for 1 minute. Drain and cool under cold running water. Trim the root ends and remove the skins.

Add the onions to the beef. Bring to a boil.

In a cup, stir together the water and the remaining 1 tablespoon flour. Add to the pot and stir to mix well. Reduce the heat, cover and cook for 25 to 30 minutes, or until the onions are tender.

During this time, cook the rice according to the package directions. Divide among individual plates. Top with the beef mixture.

Makes 5 servings.

Per serving: 493 calories, 8.1 g. total fat (15% of calories), 2.2 g. saturated fat, 62 mg. cholesterol

Ginger Beef with Saffron

The saffron is an essential component in this colorful stir-fry, so do not omit it or substitute turmeric, which gives the same color but not the same flavor. For best results, cut the steak into very thin strips. This is easier to do if you partially freeze the meat first. In addition, cut the steak across the grain for more tender strips.

BEEF

- 12 ounces beef top round steak, trimmed of all visible fat
- 1½ tablespoons reduced-sodium soy sauce
- 1½ tablespoons orange juice
- 1 tablespoon peeled and minced ginger root
- 1 small garlic clove, minced

SAUCE

- 3 tablespoons hot water
- 1 teaspoon chili powder
   Generous pinch of saffron threads
- 2½ teaspoons cornstarch
- 1½ tablespoons reduced-sodium soy sauce
- 3 tablespoons cold water

VEGETABLES AND RICE

- 2 medium celery stalks, cut diagonally into ⅛" thick slices
- 1 cup cut (1" long) scallion pieces
- 1 cup julienned sweet red peppers
- 2 teaspoons peanut oil, divided
- 1 cup Chinese pea pods, trimmed
- 3½ cups hot cooked long-grain white or brown rice

To prepare the beef: Cut the meat across the grain into 2½" × ⅛" strips. Place in a medium bowl. Add the soy sauce, orange juice, ginger and garlic. Marinate for at least 10 and up to 30 minutes.

To prepare the sauce: In a small bowl or cup, stir together the hot water, chili powder and saffron. Let stand for 5 minutes, or until the water cools completely. Add the cornstarch and stir until smooth. Stir in the soy sauce and cold water. Set aside.

To prepare the vegetables and rice: In a medium bowl, combine the celery, scallions and peppers.

In a 12" nonstick skillet over medium-high heat, warm 1 teaspoon of the oil until hot but not smoking. Using a slotted spoon, transfer the beef to the pan, reserving the marinade. Cook, stirring constantly, for 2 minutes. If necessary, lower the heat slightly to prevent the mixture from burning.

Add the remaining 1 teaspoon oil and the celery mixture. Cook, stirring, for 1½ minutes longer. Add the pea pods.

Stir the saffron sauce and add it to the skillet, along with the reserved marinade. Cook, stirring, for 1 minute longer, or until the mixture is slightly thickened and smooth. (If the sauce seems too thick, thin it with a little water.)

Immediately remove the pan from the heat. Serve the mixture over the rice.

Makes 4 servings.

Per serving: 407 calories, 6.5 g. total fat (15% of calories), 1.8 g. saturated fat, 48 mg. cholesterol

Marinated Thin-Sliced Steak

This recipe proves it's not necessary to give up steak on a low-fat diet. Use leftovers in sandwiches.

	No-Fat Ginger-Soy Marinade (page 140), divided
1½	**pounds round steak or flank steak, trimmed of all visible fat**
1	**teaspoon cornstarch**
5	**tablespoons water**
2	**drops hot-pepper sauce**

Measure out and reserve ⅓ cup of the marinade to use as a sauce for the steak. Pour half of the remaining marinade in a shallow glass baking dish large enough to hold the steak. Add the steak and pour the remaining marinade over the top. Cover and refrigerate for at least 6 hours and up to 24 hours.

Adjust the oven rack so the broiler pan is about 5" from the heat. Preheat the broiler.

Drain off and discard the marinade from the steak. Lay the steak on the broiler pan and broil for about 6 minutes. Turn over and broil for 4 to 8 minutes longer, to the desired degree of doneness; the exact time will vary depending on the thickness of the steak. Transfer to a cutting board and let stand for 10 minutes.

Meanwhile, in a small saucepan, stir together the cornstarch and water. Strain the reserved ⅓ cup marinade into the pan and stir well. Add the hot-pepper sauce. Bring the mixture to a simmer over medium heat. Cook, stirring, for 2 minutes, or until the mixture thickens and clears. Transfer to a sauce boat.

Cut the meat across the grain into scant ⅛" thick slices, using an electric knife or sharp chef's knife. Arrange the slices on a serving platter and serve with the sauce.

Makes 5 servings.

Per serving: 220 calories, 6.4 g. total fat (26% of calories), 2.2 g. saturated fat, 86 mg. cholesterol

Easy Barbecued Beef Stew

Here's a great recipe for a busy day since this flavorful stew cooks itself. And there's no added fat, because the vegetables need no sautéing. One note about Crockpot cooking: Vegetables take longer to cook than meat, so cut them into small pieces and add them to the pot first.

1	large onion, finely chopped
1	pound boiling potatoes, cut into ¾" cubes
1½	cups cut (1¼") green beans or 2 cups coarsely shredded cabbage
1	large carrot, sliced
1	large celery stalk, sliced
1	large garlic clove, minced
1	pound very lean stew beef, trimmed of all visible fat and cut into bite-size pieces
1	cup defatted beef broth
1	can (8 ounces) tomato sauce
½	cup ketchup
2	tablespoons packed light brown sugar
1	tablespoon apple cider vinegar
1	teaspoon dried thyme leaves
1	teaspoon Dijon mustard
¼	teaspoon ground allspice
¼	teaspoon ground black pepper

In a large Crockpot or other slow cooker, combine the onions, potatoes, beans or cabbage, carrots, celery and garlic. Mix well. Top with the meat.

In a medium bowl, stir together the broth, tomato sauce, ketchup, sugar, vinegar, thyme, mustard, allspice and pepper. Pour the mixture over the meat and vegetables.

Cover the slow cooker. Cook on high for 4 to 4½ hours, or until the meat and vegetables are tender; stir well after the first 3 hours.

Makes 5 servings.

Per serving: 311 calories, 6.1 g. total fat (16% of calories), 1 g. saturated fat, 58 mg. cholesterol

Note: An alternate slow-cooker method is to cook the vegetables and meat on high for 1 hour, then reduce the temperature to low and cook for an additional 6 or 7 hours.

Pork Tenderloin with Glazed Apples

Pork tenderloin is flavorful and sumptuous, yet it's low in fat. In this recipe we pair it—with great success—with apple cider and Golden Delicious apples. We like these particular apples because they're fragrant and sweet. Also, they hold their shape and turn a rich, tawny brown as they cook.

- 1 pound lean pork tenderloin, trimmed of all visible fat
- 1 tablespoon finely chopped onions
- 1 teaspoon peanut or canola oil
- 1¾ cups apple cider, divided
- 3 large Golden Delicious apples, peeled, cored and cut into eighths
- ½ tablespoon reduced-sodium soy sauce
- 1 teaspoon balsamic or apple cider vinegar
  Pinch of ground black pepper, or to taste

Cut the pork on the diagonal into 8 slices. Lay the slices, separated by several inches, between sheets of plastic wrap. Using a kitchen mallet or the back of a large heavy spoon, pound the slices until they are a scant ¼" thick. Set aside.

In a 12" nonstick skillet, combine the onions and oil. Cook over medium-high heat, stirring, for 3 minutes, or until the onions are limp. Add the pork and cook for 3 minutes, or until it's nicely browned on one side. Turn over the slices and cook for 3 minutes longer, or until browned. Remove the pork and onions from the pan and set aside.

Add 1 cup of the cider to the pan. Raise the heat to high and cook until the liquid is reduced by about half. Add the apples and cook, stirring frequently, for 3 minutes, or until all the liquid has evaporated. Remove the apples from the pan and set them aside.

Add the soy sauce, vinegar, pepper and the remaining ¾ cup cider to the pan. Cook until the cider mixture has reduced by half. Return the pork and onions to the pan. Cook until heated through. Add the apples and heat briefly.

Place the pork slices in the center of a platter or individual plates and arrange the apple slices around them.

Makes 4 servings.

Per serving: 266 calories, 5.7 g. total fat (19% of calories), 1.7 g. saturated fat, 81 mg. cholesterol

Pork Loin, Caribbean-Style

This is a spicy island-style entrée. And it's a great way to use both sweet potatoes and pineapple in a main dish. Thinly sliced pork loin (often labeled "quick-fry" in the store) works best in this dish. If it is unavailable where you shop, substitute a thicker piece and cut it into bite-size pieces.

1	pound thinly sliced pork loin, trimmed of all visible fat
1	medium onion, chopped
1	garlic clove, minced
2	teaspoons canola or safflower oil
	About ¼ cup cold water, divided
1	can (8 ounces) juice-packed pineapple chunks, divided
1½	cups orange juice
1	tablespoon light brown sugar
½	teaspoon dried thyme leaves
¼	teaspoon ground ginger
⅛	teaspoon ground cloves
⅛	teaspoon ground white pepper
	Salt, to taste (optional)
1	large sweet potato
1⅓	cups uncooked long-grain white rice
1	large green pepper, seeded and diced
1	tablespoon cornstarch

Coat a Dutch oven or other large heavy pot with nonstick spray. Place over medium heat. Add the pork and cook the pieces just until white on each side. Remove and reserve.

Add the onions, garlic, oil and 2 tablespoons of the water to the pot. Cook, stirring frequently, for 5 to 6 minutes, or until the onions are tender. If the onions begin to stick to the bottom of the pot, add a bit more water.

Drain the juice from the pineapple and add it to the pan, reserving the chunks. Stir in the orange juice, sugar, thyme, ginger, cloves, white pepper and salt (if using).

Peel and cut the sweet potato into ¼" rounds; then cut the rounds into quarters and add them to the pan. Stir to mix well. Bring to a boil. Cover, reduce the heat and cook, stirring occasionally, for 25 minutes.

Meanwhile, in a medium saucepan, start to cook the rice according to the package directions.

Add the reserved pork, green peppers and the reserved pineapple chunks to the pot with the pork. Simmer for 8 to 10 minutes longer, or until the sweet potatoes are tender and the pork is cooked through.

In a small bowl or cup, stir together the cornstarch and the remaining 2 tablespoons water. Add to the pork. Cook, stirring, until the sauce is clear and slightly thickened.

Serve over the cooked rice.

Makes 5 servings.

Per serving: 432 calories, 8.3 g. total fat (17% of calories), 2.3 g. saturated fat, 41 mg. cholesterol

Smoked Pork and Winter-Vegetable Stew

A nice change of pace from beef stew, this easy one-dish meal features an array of winter vegetables and boneless smoked pork loin. Since the pork doesn't require long cooking, you can serve the stew as soon as the vegetables are tender.

2¾	cups defatted chicken broth
1½	cups water
4	medium carrots, peeled and cut into 1" pieces
3	medium onions, quartered
1	medium rutabaga, peeled and cut into 1" cubes
½	cup chopped fresh parsley leaves
2	bay leaves
¼	teaspoon dried marjoram leaves
¼	teaspoon ground black pepper, or to taste
6	large all-purpose potatoes, peeled and cut into 1¼" cubes
2	cups cut (1¼") green beans
12	ounces boneless smoked center-cut loin pork chops, trimmed of all visible fat and cut into ½" cubes

In a Dutch oven or other large heavy pot, combine the broth, water, carrots, onions, rutabagas, parsley, bay leaves, marjoram and pepper. Bring to a boil over high heat. Cover, reduce the heat and simmer for 20 minutes.

Add the potatoes, beans and pork. Raise the heat to high until the mixture returns to a simmer. Then adjust the heat so the mixture simmers gently and continue cooking, stirring occasionally, for 20 to 25 minutes, or until the potatoes and beans are tender. Remove and discard the bay leaves before serving.

Makes 5 servings.

Per serving: 323 calories, 4.3 g. total fat (12% of calories), 0.8 g. saturated fat, 30 mg. cholesterol

Potato, Pepper and Ham Frittata

Many breakfast, brunch and luncheon dishes tend to be fatty. But this tasty frittata isn't. It contains enough cheese and ham to be satisfying, yet it fits comfortably into a healthful diet. If desired, you may prepare the vegetable mixture and the egg mixture ahead. Store them separately for up to 12 hours. However, since this frittata tastes best fresh from the oven, assemble and bake it at the last minute.

⅔	cup finely chopped onions
⅔	cup finely chopped sweet red or green peppers
2	teaspoons nondiet tub-style canola or corn-oil margarine or butter
	About 1 cup defatted chicken broth
1⅔	cups finely diced potatoes
½	cup finely diced well-trimmed country ham or baked ham
½	cup dry bread crumbs
1¼	cups liquid egg substitute
3	tablespoons 2% fat milk
3	tablespoons chopped fresh parsley leaves
½	teaspoon Worcestershire sauce
½	teaspoon dry mustard
¼	teaspoon salt (optional)
¼	teaspoon ground black pepper
⅛	teaspoon dried marjoram leaves
4	tablespoons grated Parmesan cheese, divided

Preheat the oven to 375°.

In a 12" nonstick skillet, combine the onions, peppers and margarine or butter. Cook over medium heat, stirring frequently, for 5 minutes, or until the onions are tender.

Stir in the broth, potatoes and ham. Continue cooking, stirring frequently, until the potatoes are just tender and almost all the liquid has evaporated from the pan. If the skillet begins to boil dry before the potatoes are tender, add a few more tablespoons of broth.

Sprinkle the bread crumbs evenly in an 8" × 8" baking dish. Top with the vegetables.

In a medium bowl, stir together the egg substitute, milk, parsley, Worcestershire sauce, mustard, salt (if using), black pepper, marjoram and 2 tablespoons of the Parmesan. Pour the mixture over the vegetables.

Bake in the upper third of the oven for 15 minutes. Sprinkle with the remaining 2 tablespoons Parmesan. Bake for 5 minutes longer, or until the frittata is just set in the center when the dish is jiggled.

Remove from the oven and let stand for 5 minutes. Cut into squares and serve using a wide-bladed spatula.

Makes 4 servings.

Per serving: 255 calories, 7.6 g. total fat (27% of calories), 2.2 g. saturated fat, 16 mg. cholesterol

Red Beans and Rice with Ham

The smoky flavor of ham is a savory addition to this southern dish. If you prefer, you may replace the ham with six ounces of Canadian bacon.

- 1   large onion, finely chopped
- 1   large garlic clove, minced
- 2   teaspoons olive oil
- 1¼   cups defatted chicken broth, divided
- 3   cans (16 ounces each) kidney beans, rinsed and drained
- 1   can (15 ounces) tomato sauce
- 12   ounces fully cooked thick-cut boneless ham, trimmed of all visible fat and cut into bite-size pieces
- ½   green pepper, seeded and chopped
- 1½   teaspoons dried thyme leaves
- 1   bay leaf
- 3   drops hot-pepper sauce
  Salt and ground black pepper, to taste (optional)
- 1½   cups uncooked long-grain white rice

In a Dutch oven or other large heavy pot, combine the onions, garlic, oil and 2 tablespoons of the broth. Cook over medium heat, stirring frequently, for 5 to 6 minutes, or until the onions are tender. If the onions begin to stick, add a little more broth.

Stir in the beans, tomato sauce, ham, green peppers, thyme, bay leaf, hot-pepper sauce, salt and black pepper (if using) and the remaining broth. Bring to a boil. Reduce the heat, cover and simmer for 45 to 50 minutes, or until the flavors are well blended. Remove and discard the bay leaf.

While the beans are simmering, in a medium saucepan, cook the rice according to the package directions. Transfer to a platter or individual plates.

Stir the beans before serving. Spoon over the rice.

Makes 8 servings.

Per serving: 339 calories, 4 g. total fat (11% of calories), 0.8 g. saturated fat, 11 mg. cholesterol

Pasta with Bacon and Vegetables in Creamy Tomato Sauce

We love everything about pasta carbonara-style, except the fat. So we've designed this tasty dish with some of the same basic flavors but trimmed away excess fat by using lean Canadian bacon and a creamy sauce that blends tomatoes and nonfat ricotta cheese.

4	ounces Canadian bacon, trimmed of all visible fat and cut into thin 1" strips
1	large onion, chopped
1	garlic clove, minced
2	teaspoons olive oil
½	cup defatted chicken broth, divided
1½	cups diced zucchini
1½	cups sliced cauliflower florets
½	large green pepper, seeded and diced
2	tablespoons finely chopped fresh parsley leaves
1½	teaspoons dried basil leaves
1	teaspoon dried thyme leaves
1	can (14½ ounces) Italian (plum) tomatoes, with juice
	Salt and ground black pepper, to taste
⅓	cup nonfat ricotta cheese
1½	cups cut fusilli or other medium pasta
	Parsley sprigs (garnish)

In a 12" nonstick skillet, combine the Canadian bacon, onions, garlic, oil and 1 tablespoon of the broth. Cook over medium heat, stirring frequently, for 5 to 6 minutes, or until the onions are tender. If the onions begin to stick, add a bit more broth.

Add the zucchini, cauliflower, green peppers, chopped parsley, basil and thyme. Cook, stirring frequently, for an additional 5 to 6 minutes, or until the vegetables are almost tender.

Add the tomatoes (with juice), breaking them up with a spoon. Stir in the salt and black pepper and the remaining broth. Bring to a boil. Cover, reduce the heat and simmer for 3 to 4 minutes, or until the vegetables are tender and the flavors have blended.

Lower the heat so the mixture stays hot but does not boil. Stir in the ricotta and mix well.

While the vegetables cook, cook the pasta according to the package directions. Drain well and transfer to a serving platter. Top with the tomato sauce. Garnish with the parsley.

Makes 4 servings.

Per serving: 280 calories, 7 g. total fat (22% of calories), 1.4 g. saturated fat, 53 mg. cholesterol

Scalloped Potatoes with Canadian Bacon

This hearty casserole gets its smokey flavor from Canadian bacon, which is far lower in fat than bacon. Plus, it tastes so robust that a little goes a long way. To speed preparation, we've done part of the cooking in the microwave. However, to prepare the casserole entirely in the oven, bake it for about 1 hour and 35 minutes at 350°.

7	cups thinly sliced new red potatoes
1	medium onion, chopped
1	small garlic clove, minced
6	ounces Canadian bacon, trimmed of all visible fat and cut into thin ¾" strips
2	tablespoons cornstarch
2	cups 2% fat milk
1	large bay leaf
1	teaspoon dried thyme leaves
½	teaspoon dried basil leaves
½	teaspoon dry mustard
⅛	teaspoon ground white pepper
⅛	teaspoon salt, or to taste (optional)

Preheat the oven to 350°. Coat a 2½-quart ovenproof and microwave-safe casserole with nonstick spray.

Combine the potatoes, onions and garlic in the casserole. Stir to mix well. Cover with wax paper and microwave on high power for 10 to 13 minutes, or until the potatoes are partially cooked; twice during the cooking time, give the casserole a quarter turn and stir the potatoes. Add the Canadian bacon and mix well.

While the vegetables are cooking, place the cornstarch in a medium saucepan. Gradually add the milk, stirring vigorously until smooth. Stir in the bay leaf, thyme, basil, mustard, pepper and salt (if using). Bring to a simmer over medium heat, stirring frequently. Reduce the heat and cook, stirring, until the mixture thickens. Reduce the heat to low. Cook, stirring, for 1 minute longer.

Pour the sauce over the potato mixture and stir well. Cover and bake for 20 minutes. Stir well and make sure the bay leaf is visible for easy removal later. Cover and bake for another 10 to 20 minutes, or until the potatoes are tender. If a crusty top is desired, do not re-cover after stirring.

Remove and discard the bay leaf. Allow the casserole to stand for about 5 minutes before serving.

Makes 5 servings.

Per serving: 369 calories, 5 g. total fat (12% of calories), 2.2 g. saturated fat, 27 mg. cholesterol

Lamb Shanks with Couscous

This hearty, Middle-Eastern-style dish is a good way to take advantage of lamb shanks, an inexpensive but very flavorful cut from the bony portion of the leg. Since lamb does tend to be more fatty than beef, we like to do most of the cooking a day ahead and refrigerate the lamb and broth overnight. Then it's easy to remove solidified fat from the surface before reheating the mixture and adding the couscous.

3	pounds lamb shanks
1	tablespoon all-purpose or unbleached white flour
2	cups chopped onions
2	garlic cloves, minced
2	teaspoons olive oil
3	cups defatted beef broth, divided
2	large carrots, peeled and sliced
2	celery stalks, sliced
¼	cup chopped fresh parsley leaves
2	bay leaves
2	teaspoons dried thyme leaves
2	teaspoons dried mint leaves
⅛	teaspoon ground black pepper
1¼	cups uncooked couscous

Preheat the broiler. Adjust the rack so it is about 3" from the heating element.

Place the lamb in a shallow baking pan. Sprinkle it with the flour and mix well to coat the pieces. Spread out the pieces so they are separated. Broil for 10 to 14 minutes, turning the pieces occasionally, until the shanks are browned on all sides. Remove from the pan with a slotted spoon.

Meanwhile, in a Dutch oven or other large heavy pot, combine the onions, garlic, oil and 3 tablespoons of the broth. Cook over medium heat, stirring frequently, for 6 to 7 minutes, or until the onions are tender. If the liquid begins to evaporate, add a bit more broth.

Add the lamb to the pan along with the carrots, celery, parsley, bay leaves, thyme, mint, pepper and the remaining broth. Stir to mix well. Bring to a boil. Cover, reduce the heat and simmer for 1½ to 2 hours, or until the lamb is tender.

Remove and discard the bay leaves. Remove and reserve the lamb. When it's cool enough to handle, cut off the lean meat and return it to the pot. Discard the bones and fat.

At this point, refrigerate the dish overnight or until the fat solidifies, then lift it off and discard it. Alternatively, skim off the fat with a large shallow spoon.

Bring the lamb mixture to a boil. Stir in the couscous. Cover and boil, stirring occasionally, for 1½ minutes. Remove the pot from the burner, cover and allow to stand for 10 minutes. Fluff the couscous with a fork before serving.

Makes 6 servings.

Per serving: 224 calories, 4.9 g. total fat (20% of calories), 1.7 g. saturated fat, 69 mg. cholesterol

Lamb Shish Kebab

Over the years, we've found shish kebab to be an easy meal to prepare for company. What's more, it has both great eye appeal and taste appeal. While we've tried many marinades for lamb, this is one of our very favorites. To make sure the meat and vegetables are done at the same time, we parboil some of the vegetables before threading them onto the skewers. And we grill the cherry tomatoes separately because they cook more rapidly than the other items. If small white onions are unavailable, substitute very small yellow onions or cut larger onions into quarters. This marinade is also good on chicken; use two pounds of boneless, skinless breast meat and cut it into 1¼" cubes.

¼	cup lemon juice
3	tablespoons defatted chicken broth
2	tablespoons canola or safflower oil
1	medium onion, coarsely chopped
¼	cup coarsely chopped fresh parsley leaves
1	large garlic clove, minced
1½	teaspoons dried marjoram leaves
1½	teaspoons dried thyme leaves
½	teaspoon salt
2	pounds lean boneless lamb (from the leg or shoulder), trimmed of all visible fat and cut into 1¼" cubes
12	small (1½" diameter) white onions or 3 medium onions, quartered
2	large green peppers, seeded and cut into 1½" pieces
1	large sweet red pepper, seeded and cut into 1½" pieces
1	large zucchini, cut into ½" thick rounds
12	cherry tomatoes

In a medium bowl, combine the lemon juice, broth, oil, chopped onions, parsley, garlic, marjoram, thyme and salt. Stir to mix well.

Add the lamb and stir to coat well. Cover and refrigerate for at least 12 hours (preferably 24 hours); stir occasionally.

Bring a medium saucepan of water to a boil. Add the small or quartered onions, green peppers and red peppers. Boil over medium heat for 3 to 4 minutes. Drain in a colander. Trim and peel the onions.

Using a slotted spoon, remove the lamb from the marinade. Divide the pieces among large skewers, alternating them with the peppers, onions and zucchini. (Pack the skewers tightly to help keep the vegetables from shifting as the skewers are turned during grilling.)

Thread the tomatoes onto a separate skewer and set aside.

To grill, place the meat-and-vegetable skewers on a grill and cook for 20 to 30 minutes, depending on the heat and the degree of doneness desired. Turn frequently so that the meat and vegetables cook evenly. (Alternatively, broil the skewers: Rest the ends of the skewers on the rim of a 13" × 9" baking pan so that any fat from the meat can drip into the pan during broiling. Broil about 5" from the heat for 25 to 30 minutes.)

During the last 5 minutes of cooking, add the tomatoes to the grill or broiling pan. Cook, turning them frequently.

To serve, use a fork to slide the meat and vegetables off the skewers onto a large serving platter.

Makes 6 servings.

Per serving: 207 calories, 8.1 g. total fat (36% of calories), 2.5 g. saturated fat, 76 mg. cholesterol

BEAUTIFUL BREADS AND BREAKFAST FARE

Bread has long been called the staff of life. Today, more and more nutrition experts are reaffirming its key role, recommending that bread, pasta, cereal and grain dishes be the foundation of our diets.

With that in mind, we've devised a large chapter of low-fat muffins, quick breads, yeast breads and even pancakes, French toast and granola to help you enjoy "grain foods" often. We've emphasized muffins and quick breads, since these are particularly easy to prepare. The choices range from savory breads like Spicy Cornbread and Buffins (a cross between drop biscuits and muffins) to sweet treats such as Applesauce-Streusel Muffins.

Note: *Though it is always best not to overmix quick bread batters, it's especially important with lean batters. For the most tender breads, stir the wet and dry ingredients together gently and only until evenly blended.*

Applesauce-Streusel Muffins

Spicy-sweet and very aromatic, these are good for breakfast, brunch, tea or snacking any time of day. They are a fine example of just how enticing low-fat, fiber-rich fare can be. They are best when fresh but can be stored for up to two days in an airtight container.

STREUSEL

¾	cup quick-cooking rolled oats
½	cup packed light brown sugar
1¼	teaspoons ground cinnamon
½	teaspoon ground allspice
¼	cup all-purpose or unbleached white flour
3	tablespoons canola or safflower oil

MUFFINS

1	cup all-purpose or unbleached white flour
1½	teaspoons baking powder
¾	teaspoon baking soda
⅛	teaspoon salt
⅔	cup unsweetened applesauce
½	cup plain nonfat yogurt
1	large egg white
1	tablespoon mild honey, such as clover

To prepare the streusel: In a small bowl, stir together the oats, sugar, cinnamon, allspice and flour. Stir in the oil until evenly incorporated. Set aside.

To prepare the muffins: Preheat the oven to 400°. Coat 12 standard muffin tin cups with nonstick spray.

Place the flour in a medium bowl. Add the baking powder, baking soda and salt; mix well. Using a large wooden spoon, stir in a generous three-quarters of the streusel mixture and mix well.

In a 2-cup measure, thoroughly mix the applesauce, yogurt, egg white and honey. Pour over the flour mixture and stir just until the dry ingredients are moistened; do not overmix.

Divide the batter evenly among the muffin cups. (They will be almost full.) Sprinkle with the remaining streusel. Bake on the center oven rack for 17 to 20 minutes, or until the muffins are tinged with brown and spring back when touched lightly. Transfer the pan to a wire rack and let stand for 10 minutes before removing them.

Makes 12 muffins.

Per muffin: 168 calories, 4.2 g. total fat (22% of calories), 0.4 g. saturated fat, 0 mg. cholesterol

Apricot-Orange Muffins

These tempting, golden-brown muffins are rich and satisfying, yet only 26 percent of their calories come from fat. They are especially nice for brunch or with afternoon coffee or tea. We prefer to use American dried apricots in this recipe because they have a zestier flavor and a brighter color than most brands of the imported fruit. Like most low-fat muffins, these are best when fresh. But you may reheat them (wrap in foil and warm for 10 to 15 minutes at 375°).

⅓	cup orange juice
⅓	cup finely diced dried apricots
½	teaspoon finely grated orange zest
1¼	cups all-purpose or unbleached white flour
⅔	cup whole wheat pastry flour or whole wheat flour
6½	tablespoons granulated sugar
2½	teaspoons baking powder
¾	teaspoon baking soda
¼	teaspoon salt
1	cup buttermilk
1	large egg white
3½	tablespoons canola or safflower oil
1	teaspoon vanilla extract
¼	teaspoon almond extract

Preheat the oven to 425°. Coat 12 standard muffin tin cups with nonstick spray.

In a small saucepan, combine the orange juice, apricots and orange zest. Bring to a simmer over medium-high heat. Reduce the heat and simmer, stirring occasionally, for 6 to 8 minutes, or until almost all the liquid has been absorbed. Set aside.

In a large bowl, thoroughly stir together the white and whole wheat flours, sugar, baking powder, baking soda and salt. In a 2-cup measure, stir together the buttermilk, egg white, oil, vanilla and almond extract with a fork until evenly mixed.

Gently stir the apricots and buttermilk mixture into the dry ingredients just until incorporated; do not overmix.

Divide the batter evenly among the muffin cups. (They will be full.) Bake on the center oven rack for 14 to 17 minutes, or until the muffins are tinged with gold and spring back when touched lightly. Transfer the pan to a wire rack and let stand for 5 minutes before removing the muffins.

Makes 12 muffins.

Per muffin: 153 calories, 4.4 g. total fat (26 % of calories), 0.4 g. saturated fat, 1 mg. cholesterol

Banana and Oat Bran Muffins

Back when oat bran was being touted as the cholesterol cure-all, we became interested in using the product in muffins, coffee cakes and quick breads. We don't bake with oat bran as much now, but we still find the flavor very pleasant. And it's worth including in your diet, since newer studies confirm that oat bran does indeed lower cholesterol. These light muffins are also a great way to use up a ripe banana. They taste best fresh-baked but will keep, tightly wrapped, for two to three days at room temperature.

1	cup all-purpose or unbleached white flour
1	cup oat bran
1	teaspoon baking powder
1	teaspoon baking soda
½	teaspoon ground cinnamon
¼	teaspoon ground ginger
⅛	teaspoon salt
1	large egg white
1	cup buttermilk
¼	cup packed light brown sugar
1	large ripe banana, mashed
2	tablespoons canola or safflower oil
1	tablespoon mild honey, such as clover
½	teaspoon grated orange zest

Preheat the oven to 400°. Coat 12 standard muffin tin cups with nonstick spray.

In a medium bowl, combine the flour, oat bran, baking powder, baking soda, cinnamon, ginger and salt. Mix well. Add the egg white, buttermilk, sugar, banana, oil, honey and orange zest. Stir just until the dry ingredients are moistened; do not overmix.

Divide the batter evenly among the muffin cups. Bake on the center oven rack for 14 to 17 minutes, or until the tops are light brown. Loosen the muffins by rapping the pan sharply against the edge of the counter. Remove them immediately to a wire rack. Cool for 10 to 15 minutes before serving.

Makes 12 muffins.

Per muffin: 118 calories, 3.1 g. total fat (22% of calories), 0.4 g. saturated fat, 1 mg. cholesterol

Blueberry Muffins

Blueberry muffins are among our favorites. Since these are both tempting and healthful, we serve them often. The muffins are best when fresh, but you may reheat them successfully. (Wrap them in foil and warm for 15 minutes at 375°.)

1¼	cups all-purpose or unbleached white flour
¾	cup whole wheat pastry flour or whole wheat flour
2¾	teaspoons baking powder
¼	teaspoon baking soda
¼	teaspoon salt
⅓	cup granulated sugar
¾	cup skim milk
1	large egg white
3	tablespoons mild honey, such as clover
3	tablespoons canola or safflower oil
1¼	teaspoons vanilla extract
⅛	teaspoon finely grated orange zest
1	cup fresh or partially thawed frozen blueberries (see note)

Preheat the oven to 425°. Coat 12 standard muffin tin cups with nonstick spray.

Sift the white and wheat flours, baking powder, baking soda and salt into a large bowl. Stir in the sugar until evenly distributed.

In a small bowl, beat together the milk, egg white, honey, oil, vanilla and orange zest with a fork until well mixed.

Gently stir the blueberries into the flour mixture until evenly incorporated. Add the milk mixture and stir just until the dry ingredients are moistened; do not overmix.

Divide the batter evenly among the muffin cups. Bake on the center oven rack for 13 to 16 minutes, or until the muffins are golden brown and spring back when touched lightly. Transfer the pan to a wire rack and let stand for 5 minutes. Run a knife around the muffins to loosen them before removing from the pan.

Makes 12 muffins.

Per muffin: 152 calories, 3.7 g. total fat (22% of calories), 0.3 g. saturated fat, 0 mg. cholesterol

Note: If you're using partially thawed frozen berries, rinse and drain them well, then pat away excess moisture with paper towels before adding them to the dry ingredients.

Raisin-Oat Muffins

These easy, delicious muffins are high in fiber and complex carbohydrates. They're also remarkably low in fat and light in texture. Enjoy them for breakfast, with brunch or lunch, at tea time, with supper or as a satisfying snack.

1⅓	cups old-fashioned rolled oats
1	cup skim milk
⅔	cup dark raisins
3	tablespoons mild honey, such as clover
3	tablespoons canola or safflower oil
2½	tablespoons packed light brown sugar
1	large egg white
¾	cup all-purpose or unbleached white flour
½	cup whole wheat flour
1½	teaspoons baking powder
1	teaspoon ground cinnamon
½	teaspoon baking soda
¼	teaspoon salt

Preheat the oven to 425°. Coat 12 standard muffin tin cups with nonstick spray.

In a medium bowl, thoroughly mix the oats, milk, raisins, honey, oil, sugar and egg white.

In a large bowl, thoroughly stir together the white and whole wheat flours, baking powder, cinnamon, baking soda and salt. Pour the milk mixture over the flour mixture. Stir just until the dry ingredients are moistened; do not overmix.

Divide the batter evenly among the muffin cups. (They will be almost full.) Bake on the center oven rack for 13 to 16 minutes, or until the muffins are nicely browned and spring back when touched lightly. Transfer the pan to a wire rack and let stand for 5 minutes before removing the muffins.

Makes 12 muffins.

Per muffin: 203 calories, 4.8 g. total fat (21% of calories), 0.7 g. saturated fat, 0 mg. cholesterol

Zucchini Muffins

These have a mild but enticing flavor. The zucchini makes the muffins moist, so only a small amount of fat is needed in the batter.

⅔	cup grated or very finely chopped zucchini
1	cup all-purpose or unbleached white flour
½	cup whole wheat flour
1¾	teaspoons baking powder
½	teaspoon ground cinnamon
¼	teaspoon baking soda
¼	teaspoon salt
¾	cup skim milk
½	cup wheat bran
¼	cup light corn syrup
¼	cup packed dark brown sugar
1	large egg white
2½	tablespoons canola or safflower oil

Preheat the oven to 425°. Coat 12 standard muffin tin cups with nonstick spray.

Place the zucchini in a colander and let it drain while you measure and mix the remaining ingredients.

In a large bowl, thoroughly mix the white and wheat flours, baking powder, cinnamon, baking soda and salt.

In a medium bowl, mix the milk, wheat bran, corn syrup, sugar, egg white and oil. Pour the milk mixture over the flour mixture; add the zucchini. Stir just until the dry ingredients are moistened; do not overmix.

Divide the batter evenly among the muffin cups. Bake on the center oven rack for 14 to 18 minutes, or until the muffins are nicely browned and spring back when touched lightly. Transfer the pan to a wire rack and let stand for 5 minutes before removing the muffins.

Makes 12 muffins.

Per muffin: 132 calories, 3.2 g. total fat (21% of calories), 0.3 g. saturated fat, 0 mg. cholesterol

Buffins

Quick breads are a pleasing addition to any meal, yet sometimes it's difficult to find time to bake them. That's why we wanted to develop a low-fat baking-powder biscuit so quick and easy we could whip up a batch at a moment's notice. As the name suggests, buffins are a cross between drop biscuits and muffins. They're best hot from the oven. Instead of serving them with margarine or butter, we offer jam, jelly or honey.

2	cups all-purpose or unbleached white flour
2	teaspoons baking powder
⅛	teaspoon salt
3	tablespoons nondiet tub-style canola or corn-oil margarine or butter, chilled and cut into small pieces
	About 1 cup buttermilk, divided

Preheat the oven to 450°. Coat 12 standard muffin tin cups with nonstick spray.

In a medium bowl, thoroughly mix the flour, baking powder and salt. Using a pastry blender or forks, cut in the margarine or butter until the mixture resembles coarse meal.

Add ¾ cup of the buttermilk and stir just until mixed. (If the batter seems dry, add a bit more buttermilk. However, be careful not to add too much liquid, as wet batter tends to stick to the muffin cups.)

Divide the batter evenly among the muffin cups. Bake on the center oven rack for 10 to 12 minutes, or until lightly browned. To loosen the buffins, rap the pan sharply against the edge of the counter. If necessary, run a knife around the edges.

Makes 12 buffins.

Per buffin: 109 calories, 3.2 g. total fat (27% of calories), 0.6 g. saturated fat, 1 mg. cholesterol

Mixed-Grain Pancakes

Cornmeal and rolled oats give these pancakes a wonderfully different flavor and texture. Serve them with maple syrup, fruit syrup or applesauce. If you prefer, use one large egg white instead of the egg substitute.

1	cup all-purpose or unbleached white flour
½	cup quick-cooking rolled oats
½	cup white or yellow cornmeal
2	teaspoons granulated sugar (optional)
1	teaspoon baking powder
½	teaspoon baking soda
⅛	teaspoon salt
	Generous 1½ cups buttermilk
¼	cup egg substitute
2	tablespoons canola or safflower oil

Lightly coat a 12" nonstick griddle with nonstick spray. Place over medium heat and let stand for 3 to 4 minutes, or until hot.

Meanwhile, in a large bowl combine the flour, oats, cornmeal, sugar (if using), baking powder, baking soda and salt. Mix well. Add the buttermilk, egg substitute and oil. Stir until the batter is smooth; it will be fairly thick.

Using a measuring cup or large spoon, spoon about ¼ cup of batter for each pancake onto the griddle. Shake the griddle back and forth several times to spread the batter out into 4" circles. Cook for about 3 minutes, or until browned on the underside. Flip using a wide spatula. Cook about 3 to 4 minutes, or until the undersides are nicely browned and the pancakes are cooked through.

Makes 12 pancakes.

Per pancake: 118 calories, 3.5 g. total fat (26% of calories), 0.4 g. saturated fat, 1 mg. cholesterol

Note: If necessary, between batches lightly wipe the pan with a paper towel coated with oil. If the batter thickens upon standing, stir in some more buttermilk.

Timesaving Mix for Pancakes and Quick Breads

One easy way to make pancakes on a moment's notice is to have a ready-made mix stashed in the refrigerator. Then all you have to do is stir in some liquid. This low-fat, fiber-rich blend can also do double duty as an ingredient in quick breads (see the recipe for Quick-Mix Apple Butter Bread on page 286). Because there is oil in the mix, store it tightly covered in the refrigerator. It will keep for up to a month.

All-Purpose Pancake Mix

1⅓ cups quick-cooking rolled oats
½ cup whole wheat flour
2½ teaspoons baking powder
1 teaspoon baking soda
¾ teaspoon salt
¼ cup canola or safflower oil
2½ cups all-purpose or unbleached white flour

In a food processor, combine the oats, wheat flour, baking powder, baking soda and salt. Process for 1 minute, or until the oats are ground to a powder. With the motor running, add the oil through the feed tube.

Stop the machine. Then process with on/off pulses for 1 minute, or until the oil is evenly incorporated; stop and stir the mixture once or twice if it sticks to the bottom of the bowl.

Add the white flour. Process with on/off pulses until smoothly incorporated. Transfer to a large bowl or other container and stir the mixture to aerate it slightly. Store it tightly covered in the refrigerator.

Makes about 4¼ cups; enough for 35 pancakes.

Per ¼ cup: 154 calories, 4.3 g. total fat (25% of calories), 0.4 g. saturated fat, 0 mg. cholesterol

Quick-Mix Buttermilk Pancakes

Pancakes made from our homemade pancake mix are extremely quick, convenient and fuss-free. The recipe calls for buttermilk because we think it makes the tastiest pancakes.

- 1 cup All-Purpose Pancake Mix (opposite page)
  About 1 cup buttermilk
- 2 tablespoons liquid egg substitute
- ½ cup fresh or partially thawed frozen blueberries (optional)

Lightly coat a 12" nonstick griddle or skillet with nonstick spray. Place over medium-high heat and let stand for 2 to 4 minutes, or until hot.

Meanwhile, in a medium bowl, stir together the pancake mix, buttermilk and egg substitute just until evenly blended. If necessary, add a bit more buttermilk to yield a batter that's fluid but not too runny. Fold in the blueberries (if using).

Using a small measuring cup or large spoon, spoon about 3 tablespoons of batter for each pancake into the pan. Cook for about 1 minute, or until the pancakes have bubbles on the surface and are nicely browned on the underside. Flip using a wide spatula. Cook about 3 minutes longer, or until the pancakes are slightly puffy and cooked through.

Makes 8 pancakes.

Per pancake: 91 calories, 2.5 g. total fat (25% of calories), 0.4 g. saturated fat, 1 mg. cholesterol

Note: You may substitute ¾ cup plain nonfat yogurt combined with ⅓ cup water for the buttermilk. Alternatively, use 1 cup skim milk soured by adding 1 tablespoon lemon juice or apple cider vinegar.

Quick-Mix Apple Butter Bread

Our convenient All-Purpose Pancake Mix makes it easy to prepare not only pancakes in a hurry but also this fuss-free bread. Because we add apple butter, the compact, spicy loaf keeps well even though it is quite low in fat. (By the way, despite its name, apple butter contains no butter—it's cooked-down spiced apple puree.) To store the loaf, wrap it well and keep up to four days.

¾	cup apple butter
⅔	cup skim milk
½	cup packed light brown sugar
¼	cup liquid egg substitute
½	cup chopped pitted dates or dark raisins
2¼	cups All-Purpose Pancake Mix (page 284)

Preheat the oven to 350°. Coat an 8" × 4½" loaf pan with nonstick spray.

In a medium bowl, stir together the apple butter, milk, sugar and egg substitute until well blended. Stir in the dates or raisins.

Add the pancake mix and stir just until the dry ingredients are evenly moistened; do not overmix. Transfer to the prepared pan.

Bake on the center oven rack for 45 to 55 minutes, or until the top is nicely browned and a toothpick inserted in the center comes out clean.

Transfer the pan to a wire rack and let stand for 15 minutes. Run a knife around the loaf to loosen it. Then remove it from the pan and let stand on the rack until thoroughly cooled.

Makes 1 loaf; 12 slices.

Per slice: 211 calories, 3.4 g. total fat (14% of calories), 0.3 g. saturated fat, 0 mg. cholesterol

Easy Honey-Oat Yeast Bread

These loaves are rough-textured and have a pleasing nutty aroma. Instead of being traditionally kneaded, the dough is beaten for several minutes in a mixing bowl. That helps keep both preparation and cleanup simple. It's best to use a stand mixer, although a heavy-duty, hand-held model may be used. If not eating the bread immediately, freeze it for up to two weeks; thaw and rewarm (wrapped in foil) before serving. Otherwise wrap airtight and keep at room temperature for up to 24 hours.

⅓   cup instant nonfat dry milk
¼   cup nondiet tub-style canola or corn-oil margarine or butter
¼   cup package light or dark brown sugar
¼   cup mild honey, such as clover
1   package fast-rising dry yeast
1¾ teaspoons salt
5   cups all-purpose or unbleached white flour, divided
2   cups very hot tap water
1½ cups whole wheat flour
1½ cups + 2 tablespoons quick-cooking rolled oats

In a large mixer bowl, combine the dry milk, margarine or butter, sugar, honey, yeast, salt and 3½ cups of the white flour. Beat with an electric mixer on low speed until well blended.

Beat in the water. Scrape down the sides of the bowl. Raise the speed to high and beat for 8 minutes; the mixture will become slightly rubbery.

Using a large wooden spoon, stir in the whole wheat flour, 1½ cups of the oats and the remaining 1½ cups white flour.

Stir or knead the dough in the bowl until the flour is smoothly incorporated; if necessary to keep the dough from being sticky, add a bit more whole wheat flour. Transfer the dough to a very large, lightly oiled bowl. Lightly coat the top of the dough with oil.

Tightly cover the bowl with plastic wrap and set aside in a warm place for 60 to 70 minutes, or until the dough doubles in bulk.

Coat two 9" × 5" loaf pans with nonstick spray.

Punch down the dough. Divide in half and transfer to the pre-pared loaf pans. Lightly oil your hands, then press and smooth the dough evenly into the pans. Sprinkle each loaf with 1 tablespoon of the remaining oats; pat lightly to embed them just slightly.

Loosely cover with plastic wrap and set aside in a warm place for 25 minutes, or until the dough rises almost to the point of touching the plastic. Carefully remove the plastic so you don't deflate the dough. Let rise a little longer until the dough is about ½" above the pan tops.

Meanwhile, preheat the oven to 375°. Gently transfer the pans to the center oven rack. Bake for 28 to 33 minutes, or until the tops are nicely browned and the bottoms are firm and sound hollow when the loaves are removed and tapped.

Transfer the loaves to wire racks and let stand until cooled.

Makes 2 loaves; 12 slices each.

Per slice: 205 calories, 3 g. total fat (13% of calories), 0.5 g. saturated fat, 0 mg. cholesterol

No-Knead Wheat and Sesame Yeast Bread

Even a novice bread baker can succeed with this easy recipe. The loaves have a crispy crust and a pleasant nutty flavor. The yogurt also lends a slight sourdough tang. If not using the loaves within 24 hours, freeze them.

2	packages fast-rising dry yeast
2	teaspoons salt
3	cups all-purpose or unbleached white flour, divided
1⅓	cups water
1	cup plain nonfat yogurt
3	tablespoons canola or safflower oil
3	tablespoons mild honey, such as clover
2⅓	cups whole wheat flour
4	tablespoons sesame seeds, divided

In a large mixer bowl, combine the yeast, salt and 2¾ cups of the white flour. Mix well.

In a medium saucepan, stir together the water, yogurt, oil and honey. Over medium heat, warm the mixture to 125° to 128°. With the mixer on low speed, beat the yogurt mixture into the flour until blended. Scrape down the sides of the bowl. Raise the speed to high and beat for 7 minutes.

Using a large wooden spoon, stir in the whole wheat flour, 2 tablespoons of the sesame seeds and the remaining ¼ cup white flour until evenly incorporated.

Stir or knead the dough in the bowl until the flour is smoothly incorporated; if necessary to keep the dough from being sticky, add a bit more whole wheat flour. Transfer the dough to a very large, lightly oiled bowl. Lightly coat the top of the dough with oil.

Tightly cover the bowl with plastic wrap and set aside in a warm place for 50 minutes, or until the dough doubles in bulk.

Coat two 1½-quart round casseroles or soufflé dishes with non-stick spray.

Punch down the dough. Divide in half and transfer to the prepared dishes. Lightly oil your hands, then press and smooth the dough evenly into the dishes. Sprinkle each portion with 1 tablespoon of the remaining sesame seeds; pat lightly to embed them just slightly.

Loosely cover with plastic wrap and set aside in a warm place for 20 to 30 minutes, or until the dough rises almost to the point of touching the plastic. Carefully remove the plastic, being careful not to deflate the dough. Let rise a little longer until the dough is about 1" above the pan tops.

Meanwhile, preheat the oven to 375°. Gently transfer the pans to the center oven rack. Bake for 28 to 33 minutes, or until the tops are nicely browned and the loaf bottoms are firm and sound hollow when the loaves are removed from the pans and tapped.

Transfer the loaves to wire racks and let stand until cooled. Cut into wedges or thick slices.

Makes 2 loaves; 10 slices each.

Per slice: 162 calories, 3.4 g. total fat (18% of calories), 0.3 g. saturated fat, 0 mg. cholesterol

Herb Bread

No one would guess that these Italian-style toasted bread slices are made with extra-light margarine (the kind with four grams of fat per tablespoon). That's because we've mixed in a flavorful combination of Parmesan cheese and herbs. We like to offer this herb bread at buffet suppers and dinner parties because it's convenient to make and serve. And it adds very little extra fat to the meal. The slices also make an excellent snack: Keep the herb spread in the refrigerator and prepare individual portions as needed. For variety, you may cut the loaf in half lengthwise and slice the pieces after broiling.

¼	cup extra-light tub-style margarine
1	tablespoon grated Parmesan cheese
½	teaspoon dried oregano leaves
⅛	teaspoon dried marjoram leaves
1	small garlic clove, minced
1	loaf (1 pound) French or baguette-style Italian bread, cut into 10 slices

In a small bowl, mix the margarine, Parmesan, oregano, marjoram and garlic until well blended.

Lay the bread slices in a single layer on a large baking sheet. Broil about 2" from the heat for 2 minutes, or until lightly toasted. Flip the slices and spread each with a generous 2 teaspoons of the herb mixture. Broil for 2 minutes, or until lightly browned. Transfer to a napkin-lined bread basket to serve.

Makes 10 servings.

Per serving: 143 calories, 3.5 g. total fat (22% of calories), 0.9 g. saturated fat, 0 mg. cholesterol

French Toast

One of the early sacrifices we reluctantly made to cut cholesterol from our diets was giving up the pleasures of French toast. Then we tried making our old family favorite with egg substitute and were very pleased with the results. Now this easy but satisfying traditional breakfast dish is a frequent weekend treat. We particularly like to use whole wheat or cracked wheat bread. And we use a relatively large amount of milk because it helps the egg substitute soak into the bread.

½   cup egg substitute
⅓   cup 1% fat milk
¼   teaspoon vanilla extract
     Pinch of ground cinnamon or nutmeg
     Pinch of salt (optional)
4   slices whole wheat or cracked wheat bread
     Confectioners' sugar (optional)

In a large shallow bowl or flat casserole, stir together the egg substitute, milk, vanilla, cinnamon or nutmeg and salt (if using).

Coat a 12" nonstick skillet with nonstick spray. Place over medium heat until hot.

Meanwhile, place 2 slices of the bread in the egg mixture. Soak them for about 30 seconds; gently turn over the pieces and soak for another 30 seconds. Transfer to the hot skillet. Repeat with the remaining 2 slices of bread.

Brown for a total of 5 to 6 minutes, flipping the pieces once during cooking. Sprinkle with sugar (if using).

Makes 2 servings.

Per serving: 194 calories, 4.3 g. total fat (21% of calories), 1.1 g. saturated fat, 2 mg. cholesterol

Spicy Pumpkin Bread (page 312); Mulled Cider (page 96)

Mixed-Grain Pancakes (page 283); Fresh Ginger-Peach Sauce (page 145)

French Toast (page 290); Sautéed Apples (page 160)

Blueberry Muffins (page 279)

Cinnamon Buns (page 308)

Cranberry-Orange Bread (page 310)

Honey-Spice Granola (page 307)

Buffins (page 282)

Brown Sugar Bundt Cake with Caramel Glaze (page 319)

Chocolate Bread Pudding (page 340)

Chewy Brownies (page 322); Chocolate Sauce (page 342)

Peach Kuchen (page 334)

No-Bake Light Pineapple Chiffon Cheesecake (page 315)

Raspberry-Plum Cobbler (page 337)

Strawberry-Banana Sorbet (page 348)

Oatmeal-Raisin Cookies (page 342)

Honey-Spice Granola

Since granola is made primarily of toasted grains (usually oats), it's often assumed to be very wholesome. But many commercial mixes are loaded with fat, not only from vegetable oil but also from coconut and nuts. To enjoy granola's mellow, nutty taste and be sure it's healthful, we prepare our own. This honey-spice mixture is easy to make and very economical. Several members of our families have it for breakfast nearly every day. This recipe makes quite a bit of granola, so store it in an airtight container or plastic bags. It will keep for up to two weeks unrefrigerated and up to a month refrigerated.

7⅓   **cups rolled oats**
1   **tablespoon ground cinnamon**
⅔   **cup mild honey, such as clover**
¼   **cup canola or safflower oil**
¾   **cup dark raisins**

Arrange an oven rack in the lower third of the oven and a second just above the middle. Preheat the oven to 250°. Generously coat 2 large jelly-roll pans with nonstick spray. Set aside.

In a large bowl, stir together the oats and cinnamon until evenly blended.

In a small saucepan, stir together the honey and oil until blended. Place over medium heat until just barely hot. Pour the honey mixture over the oat mixture, stirring until evenly incorporated. Divide between the prepared pans, spreading the granola in an even layer.

Place the pans in the oven, staggering them as well as you can. Bake for 30 minutes. Switch the position of the pans and continue baking, without stirring, for 30 minutes longer. Turn off the oven and let the pans stand for 1½ hours, or until completely cooled. Gently stir to loosen the granola from the pans. Lightly stir in the raisins. Break up any large chunks of granola with a spoon.

Makes 8 cups; 16 servings (½ cup each).

Per serving: 372 calories, 8.4 g. total fat (20% of calories), 1.1 g. saturated fat, 0 mg. cholesterol

Cinnamon Buns

Cinnamon buns are usually high in fat (up to 15 grams apiece), so we devised this tempting slimmed-down version. These will keep at room temperature for a day or two. Freeze them for longer storage.

DOUGH

¼	cup warm water (105° to 115°)
2	packages active dry yeast
¾	cup 1% fat milk (warmed to 105° to 115°)
¼	cup packed light brown sugar
1	teaspoon salt
½	teaspoon ground cinnamon
½	teaspoon grated lemon zest
¼	cup nondiet tub-style canola or corn-oil margarine or butter
	About 3½ cups all-purpose or unbleached white flour, divided

SAUCE

½	cup packed light brown sugar
1½	tablespoons nondiet tub-style canola or corn-oil margarine or butter
¼	cup dark corn syrup
3	tablespoons water
½	teaspoon ground cinnamon
½	cup dried currants or dark raisins

To prepare the dough: Place the water in a large mixer bowl. Sprinkle in the yeast. Stir with a large wooden spoon until the yeast is dissolved. Add the milk, sugar, salt, cinnamon, lemon zest, margarine or butter and 1½ cups more flour.

Using an electric mixer on low speed, beat the mixture until blended. Raise the speed to high and beat for 3 minutes longer. Quickly and vigorously stir in about 1½ cups more flour.

Then, quickly work in enough of the remaining flour to yield a soft, kneadable dough. Cover the bowl with a damp cloth. Set in a warm place for 40 to 45 minutes, or until doubled in bulk.

To prepare the sauce: While the dough is rising, combine the sugar, margarine or butter, corn syrup, water and cinnamon in a small saucepan. Stirring constantly, bring the mixture to a boil over medium-high heat. Reduce the heat and simmer, stirring frequently, for 3 minutes. Set aside.

Coat two 9" or 10" pie plates with nonstick spray. Divide the sauce between the pans, spreading it evenly. Set aside.

Knead the dough in the bowl briefly. Divide it in half. With greased hands, knead ¼ cup of the currants or raisins into each piece. Shape into 2 even logs about 11" long. Using a sharp knife, cut each log crosswise into 11 buns. Transfer to the pie plates; position 2 in the center of each plate and surround them with 9 more. Cover with plastic wrap and set in a warm spot for 20 minutes.

Preheat the oven to 375°. Bake on the center oven rack for 13 to 17 minutes, or until the buns are lightly browned on top and spring back when touched lightly. Remove from the oven and immediately invert the buns onto serving plates and serve warm.

Makes 22 buns.

Per bun: 151 calories, 3.1 g. total fat (18% of calories), 0.6 g. saturated fat, 0 mg. cholesterol

Spicy Cornbread

Chilies, chili powder and red peppers give this cornbread a south-of-the-border flavor. For a more traditional taste, omit the spicy extras.

- 1 cup yellow cornmeal
- ¾ cup all-purpose or unbleached white flour
- 2 tablespoons granulated sugar
- 2 teaspoons baking powder
- ¼ teaspoon chili powder
- ⅛ teaspoon salt
  Pinch of ground red pepper (optional)
- 2 tablespoons nondiet tub-style canola or corn-oil margarine or butter
- ¾ cup 1% fat milk
- 1 large egg white
- 2 tablespoons canned chopped mild green chili peppers, well drained
- 2 tablespoons chopped sweet red peppers or pimientos

Preheat the oven to 400°. Coat an 8" × 8" baking dish with nonstick spray.

In a medium bowl, mix the cornmeal, flour, sugar, baking powder, chili powder, salt and ground red pepper (if using).

Using a pastry blender or forks, cut in the margarine or butter until the mixture resembles coarse meal. Add the milk, egg white, chili peppers and red peppers or pimientos. Stir in with a few swift strokes; do not overmix. Transfer to the prepared pan and spread the batter to the edges with a rubber spatula.

Bake on the center oven rack for 15 to 19 minutes, or until the top is lightly browned and a toothpick inserted in the center comes out clean. Serve warm.

Makes 9 servings.

Per serving: 131 calories, 3.3 g. total fat (23% of calories), 0.6 g. saturated fat, 1 mg. cholesterol

Cranberry-Orange Bread

Since this quick bread is so colorful and festive, we particularly like to prepare it during the Thanksgiving and Christmas holidays. It makes a nice addition to a buffet or tea table. This bread keeps well for up to four days if wrapped airtight and stored in the refrigerator. Also, you can easily freeze it for later use.

	Finely grated zest of 1 medium orange
¼	cup orange juice
¾	cup granulated sugar
¾	cup plain nonfat yogurt
⅓	cup diced dark raisins (optional)
¼	cup canola or safflower oil
¼	cup mild honey, such as clover
2	large egg whites
½	tablespoon ground cinnamon
2	teaspoons vanilla extract
2	cups all-purpose or unbleached white flour
1	cup whole wheat flour
1½	teaspoons baking powder
½	teaspoon baking soda
1	cup coarsely chopped fresh or thawed frozen cranberries

Preheat the oven to 350°. Coat a 9" × 5" loaf pan with nonstick spray.

In a medium bowl, thoroughly mix the orange zest, orange juice, sugar, yogurt, raisins (if using), oil, honey, egg whites, cinnamon and vanilla.

In a large bowl, thoroughly stir together the white and wheat flours, baking powder and baking soda until well blended. Using a large wooden spoon, stir in the orange mixture just until the dry ingredients are moistened; do not overmix. Stir in the cranberries. Transfer to the prepared pan.

Bake on the center oven rack for 50 to 60 minutes, or until the top is nicely browned and springs back when touched lightly, and a toothpick inserted in the thickest part comes out clean. Transfer the pan to a wire rack and let stand for 15 minutes. Run a knife around the loaf to loosen it. Then remove it from the pan and let stand on the rack until thoroughly cooled.

Makes 1 loaf; 12 slices.

Per slice: 254 calories, 5 g. total fat (17% of calories), 0.5 g. saturated fat, 0 mg. cholesterol

Spiced Fruit Bread

This loaf is dark, moist and spicy. What's more, it keeps well in the refrigerator or freezer. It is particularly nice served with tea.

1¼	cups diced pitted prunes
⅓	cup dark raisins
1	cup orange juice, divided
¾	cup packed light brown sugar
¼	cup canola or safflower oil
1	teaspoon vanilla extract
2	teaspoons ground cinnamon
½	teaspoon ground allspice
½	teaspoon ground ginger
¾	teaspoon finely grated orange zest
2	large egg whites
1	cup all-purpose or unbleached white flour
1	cup whole wheat flour
1½	teaspoons baking powder
¾	teaspoon baking soda
½	teaspoon salt

Preheat the oven to 375°. Coat a 9" × 5" loaf pan with nonstick spray.

In a medium saucepan, combine the prunes, raisins and ½ cup of the orange juice. Bring to a boil over medium heat, then adjust the heat so the mixture simmers gently. Cook, stirring occasionally, for 4 minutes, or until the fruit is soft and all but about 1 tablespoon of the juice has been absorbed. Transfer to a medium bowl.

Stir in the sugar, oil, vanilla, cinnamon, allspice, ginger, orange zest and the remaining ½ cup orange juice. Set aside for 5 minutes to cool. Using a wooden spoon, beat in the egg whites.

In a large bowl, thoroughly stir together the white and wheat flours, baking powder, baking soda and salt. Add the fruit mixture. Fold just until the dry ingredients are moistened; do not overmix. Transfer to the prepared pan. Spread the batter to the edges.

Bake on the center oven rack for 30 minutes. Reduce the heat to 350° and bake for 10 to 15 minutes longer, or until the top is golden brown and a toothpick inserted in the center comes out clean.

Transfer the pan to a wire rack and let stand for 15 minutes. Run a knife around the loaf to loosen it. Then remove it from the pan and let stand on the rack until thoroughly cooled.

Makes 1 loaf; 12 slices.

Per slice: 229 calories, 4.9 g. total fat (19% of calories), 0.4 g. saturated fat, 0 mg. cholesterol

Spicy Pumpkin Bread

Although very low in fat, this bread tastes rich, moist and flavorful. It slices best when cold. Store well wrapped in the refrigerator for three to four days. Be sure to use plain canned pumpkin rather than pie filling, which contains spices.

1⅔ cups all-purpose or unbleached white flour
1 teaspoon baking powder
1 teaspoon baking soda
1 teaspoon ground cinnamon
½ teaspoon ground nutmeg
½ teaspoon ground allspice
⅛ teaspoon salt
1 cup canned solid-pack pumpkin
¾ cup granulated sugar
½ cup liquid egg substitute
2½ tablespoons canola or safflower oil
1 teaspoon vanilla extract
⅔ cup dark raisins

Preheat the oven to 350°. Coat an 8" × 4½" loaf pan with nonstick spray. Cut a piece of wax paper to fit the bottom of the pan and press it into place. Set aside.

In a medium bowl, thoroughly stir together the flour, baking powder, baking soda, cinnamon, nutmeg, allspice and salt. Set aside.

In a large bowl, mix the pumpkin, sugar, egg substitute, oil and vanilla until well blended.

Gradually stir in the dry ingredients until evenly moistened; do not overmix. Fold in the raisins. Spoon the batter into the prepared pan.

Bake on the center oven rack for 45 to 50 minutes, or until a toothpick inserted in the center comes out clean.

Transfer the pan to a wire rack and let stand for 10 minutes. Run a knife around the loaf to loosen it. Then remove it from the pan and peel off the wax paper. Let stand on the rack until thoroughly cooled.

Makes 1 loaf; 9 slices.

Per slice: 233 calories, 4.6 g. total fat (17% of calories), 0.5 g. saturated fat, 0 mg. cholesterol

Banana-Orange Bread

Grated orange zest and bananas lend a wonderfully rich taste but not much fat to this simple quick bread. For best flavor, use overripe bananas—ones that are too ripe for eating.

⅓	cup skim milk
2	large overripe bananas, cut into chunks
	Grated zest of 1 orange
⅓	cup liquid egg substitute
3	tablespoons canola or safflower oil
1	teaspoon vanilla extract
1¼	cups all-purpose or unbleached white flour
1	cup whole wheat pastry flour or whole wheat flour
½	cup granulated sugar
1¾	teaspoons baking powder
½	teaspoon baking soda
¼	teaspoon salt

Preheat the oven to 375°. Coat an 8" × 4½" loaf pan with nonstick spray. Set aside.

In a blender, combine the milk, bananas and orange zest. Blend on high speed for 2 minutes, or until the mixture is very smooth. Transfer to a 4-cup glass measure. If there is less than 1¼ cups, blend a bit more banana and add it.

Using a fork, stir in the egg substitute, oil and vanilla until well mixed.

In a large bowl, thoroughly stir together the white and wheat flours, sugar, baking powder, baking soda and salt.

Add the banana mixture and stir gently just until the dry ingredients are evenly moistened; do not overmix. Transfer to the prepared pan.

Bake on the center oven rack for 30 to 35 minutes, or until the top is nicely browned and springs back when touched lightly.

Transfer the pan to a wire rack and let stand for 15 minutes. Run a knife around the loaf to loosen it. Then remove it from the pan and let stand on the rack until thoroughly cooled.

Makes 1 loaf; 10 slices.

Per slice: 203 calories, 4.9 g. total fat (21% of calories), 0.5 g. saturated fat, 0 mg. cholesterol

Chapter 21

D E L E C T A B L E
D E S S E R T S

For all those who think that eating low-fat means going dessertless, think again! We've lightened up a wide variety of recipes and made this chapter a large one to give you a wealth of choices. How about Chocolate Layer Cake with Chocolate Fudge Frosting? Creamy Cheesecake with Raspberry Glaze? Banana Cream Pie? Moreover, these selections deliver every bit of the pleasure you expect from dessert.

The best part is that all the recipes are nutritionally improved to reduce fat and cholesterol, so you can enjoy them without guilt. Even our most "decadent" desserts fit quite comfortably into an eating plan that gets 30 percent or less of its calories from fat. Besides being leaner than traditional recipes, many of our desserts incorporate significant amounts of healthful fruits and grain products as well as calcium-rich (low-fat) dairy products.

No-Bake Light Pineapple Chiffon Cheesecake

A surprisingly small amount of reduced-fat cream cheese lends rich taste and smooth texture to this very airy chiffon cheesecake. It makes a tempting ending to a festive summer dinner—especially when topped with Quick Pineapple Glaze for Cheesecake. Note: *Although the cheesecake filling isn't baked, the crust is.*

CRUST

1	cup graham cracker crumbs
1	tablespoon nondiet tub-style canola or corn-oil margarine or butter
1	tablespoon light corn syrup
½	tablespoon water

FILLING

¼	cup cold water
¼	cup instant nonfat dry milk
1	can (20 ounces) juice-packed crushed pineapple, with juice
1	package + 1 teaspoon unflavored gelatin
¾	cup + 2 tablespoons granulated sugar
3	tablespoons lemon juice
1½	teaspoons vanilla extract
¾	teaspoon finely grated lemon zest
6	ounces reduced-fat cream cheese, cubed and at room temperature
¾	cup plain nonfat yogurt
	Berries or other fresh fruit (optional)

To prepare the crust: Preheat the oven to 350°. Generously coat a 9" springform pan with nonstick spray.

In a food processor, combine the crumbs and margarine or butter. Mix lightly with on/off pulses.

In a small cup, stir together the corn syrup and water until well blended. Pour over the crumbs. Process with on/off pulses until the mixture is well blended and begins to hold together. Add a few more drops of water if the mixture is too dry.

Press the crumbs evenly into the bottom of the prepared pan. Bake for 7 to 10 minutes, or until the crust is firm to the touch and lightly tinged with brown. Remove from the oven and place on a wire rack to cool.

To prepare the filling: In a small bowl, gradually whisk the water into the dry milk until completely smooth. Chill in the freezer for 40 to 50 minutes, or until frozen but not completely hard. (If the mixture freezes hard, break it up with a spoon and set aside until softened just slightly.)

Drain the liquid from the pineapple into a small saucepan,

reserving the pineapple. Sprinkle the gelatin over the juice. Let stand for 5 minutes, or until softened. Place over medium heat and stir constantly until the mixture is hot and the gelatin dissolves. Set aside, stirring occasionally to prevent mixture from setting.

Combine the sugar, lemon juice, vanilla and lemon zest in a blender or food processor. Process until well mixed. With the machine running, drop in the cream cheese and process until smooth. Stir in the reserved pineapple. Set aside.

Transfer the frozen milk to a large mixer bowl. Beat with an electric mixer at the highest speed for 5 to 7 minutes, or until the mixture whips into soft peaks. (Be patient, this is a slow process.)

Stir the yogurt into the gelatin mixture until smoothly incorporated. Immediately add the gelatin mixture to the whipped milk and continue beating for 2 minutes longer. Beat in the cream cheese mixture just until well blended and smooth.

Pour the mixture into the springform pan and smooth the surface with a rubber spatula.

Refrigerate for at least 1 hour. Garnish with the berries or other fruit (if using).

Makes 12 servings.

Per serving: 160 calories, 4.3 g. total fat (20% of calories), 2.3 g. saturated fat, 11 mg. cholesterol

Quick Pineapple Glaze for Cheesecake

Use this fat-free glaze to dress up No-Bake Light Pineapple Chiffon Cheesecake or instead of the glaze on our Creamy Cheesecake with Raspberry Glaze.

- 3   tablespoons granulated sugar
- 1   tablespoon cornstarch
- 1   can (15 ounces) juice-packed crushed pineapple, with juice
- ½   cup orange juice
- 2   teaspoons lemon juice
- ¼   teaspoon vanilla extract
- ⅛   teaspoon finely grated lemon zest

In a small nonreactive saucepan, stir together the sugar and cornstarch until thoroughly blended. Drain ¼ cup of the juice from the pineapple and add to the pan; stir well. Stir in the orange juice.

Bring the mixture to a boil over medium-high heat, stirring constantly. Cook, stirring, for 1½ minutes, or until the mixture thickens slightly and turns clear. Remove the pan from the heat.

Drain the remaining juice from the pineapple and discard it or reserve it for another use. Stir the crushed pineapple, lemon juice, vanilla and lemon zest into the pan. Refrigerate until well chilled. Stir before using.

Makes enough for a 9" cheesecake; 12 servings.

Per serving: 38 calories, <0.1 g. total fat (1% of calories), 0 g. saturated fat, 0 mg. cholesterol

Creamy Cheesecake with Raspberry Glaze

This creamy cheesecake looks spectacular with its raspberry glaze. If you wish, you may omit the glaze and serve the cheesecake with a fat-free fruit sauce such as Sour Cherry Topping or with lightly sweetened fresh fruit. You'll notice that the cheesecake bakes in a water bath and at a low temperature. This ensures that the filling bakes evenly. The cheesecake keeps in the refrigerator up to three days.

CRUST

1	cup graham cracker crumbs
2	teaspoons nondiet tub-style canola or corn-oil margarine or butter
¼	teaspoon finely grated lemon zest
2½	teaspoons light corn syrup
2	teaspoons water

FILLING

1	cup plain nonfat yogurt (see note on page 319)
1¼	cups granulated sugar
	Finely grated zest of ½ small lemon
12	ounces 1% fat cottage cheese
½	cup nonfat tub-style cream cheese
1	tablespoon vanilla extract
1	teaspoon lemon juice
1	cup liquid egg substitute, divided
12	ounces reduced-fat cream cheese, cubed and at room temperature
¼	cup all-purpose or unbleached white flour

GLAZE

1	package (10 ounces) frozen red raspberries in syrup, thawed
1	teaspoon lemon juice
½	teaspoon unflavored gelatin

To prepare the crust: Preheat the oven to 375°.

Generously coat the bottom of a 9" springform pan with nonstick spray. To make the pan watertight for the water bath, wrap the bottom in a sheet of heavy-duty foil large enough to extend up the pan sides at least 3" all around. Set aside.

In a food processor, combine the crumbs, margarine or butter and lemon zest. Mix lightly with on/off pulses.

In a small cup, stir together the corn syrup and water until well blended. Pour over the crumbs. Process with on/off pulses until the mixture is well blended and begins to hold together. Add a few more drops of water if the mixture is too dry.

Press the crumbs evenly into the bottom of the prepared pan. Bake for 5 to 8 minutes, or until the crust is firm to the touch and lightly tinged with brown. Remove from the oven and set aside.

Lower the oven temperature to 325°.

To prepare the filling: Line a colander with a clean tea towel (smooth weave, not terry cloth) folded in half; place the colander over a bowl. Spoon the yogurt into the colander and set aside to drain until needed.

Wash and dry the food processor bowl. Add the sugar and lemon zest. Process for 1½ minutes, or until the zest is very fine. Add the cottage cheese, nonfat cream cheese, vanilla, lemon juice and ½ cup of the egg substitute. Process for 2 minutes, or until very smooth.

With the machine running, drop the reduced-fat cream cheese through the feed tube until all the cubes are incorporated and the mixture is well blended. Add the flour and process until smoothly incorporated.

Gather up the tea towel around the yogurt to form a bag. Carefully twist the top closed. Squeeze gently to remove as much liquid as possible. Add the yogurt to the food processor. Add the remaining ½ cup egg substitute. Process just until blended (depending on the size of your food processor, it may be almost full).

Pour the mixture into the prepared pan. Rap the pan on the counter a few times to release any air bubbles; let stand for several minutes, then rap again.

Place the pan in a baking dish large enough to hold it. Set on the center oven rack. Add enough hot tap water to the baking dish to come 1" up the sides of the springform pan. Bake for 40 minutes.

Lower the heat to 300°. Bake for 1 hour longer. Turn off the oven; let the cheesecake stand in the closed oven for 30 minutes. Remove the springform pan from the water bath and transfer it to a wire rack. Let stand until cooled to room temperature.

To prepare the glaze: Press the raspberries through a fine sieve into a small saucepan. Stir in the lemon juice and gelatin. Let the mixture stand for 5 minutes to allow the gelatin to soften.

Place over medium heat and stir constantly until the mixture is hot and the gelatin dissolves. Set aside for a few minutes until the mixture is cooled and just slightly thickened but not set. Carefully pour the glaze over the center of the cheesecake. Then gently tip the pan from side to side to cover the entire top.

Refrigerate for at least 6 hours.

Makes 12 servings.

Per serving: 284 calories, 9 g. total fat (29% of calories), 4.7 g. saturated fat, 25 mg. cholesterol

Note: Be sure to use yogurt that is free of vegetable gums, modified vegetable starch or gelatin. Such stabilizers prevent yogurt from releasing excess moisture (whey), which would make the crust soggy.

Variation: To make Grand Marnier Cheesecake, prepare the crust as directed but substitute orange zest for the lemon zest. Prepare the filling as directed but substitute 2 tablespoons Grand Marnier liqueur for the lemon juice; add a pinch of finely grated orange zest. Omit the raspberry glaze and serve the cheesecake with fresh orange slices that you've tossed with a little Grand Marnier.

Brown Sugar Bundt Cake with Caramel Glaze

Good old-fashioned flavor and aroma make this homey cake a winner. For best texture, be sure to use cake flour and don't sift it before measuring. The cake keeps, covered, for about three days. For longer storage, wrap it airtight and freeze for up to two weeks.

CAKE

3	cups cake flour
1	tablespoon baking powder
½	teaspoon salt
2	cups packed light brown sugar
¼	cup nondiet tub-style canola or corn-oil margarine or butter
¼	cup canola or safflower oil
⅓	cup liquid egg substitute
⅔	cup plain nonfat yogurt
⅓	cup water
¼	cup evaporated milk
1	tablespoon vanilla extract

GLAZE

¼	cup evaporated milk
1	teaspoon nondiet tub-style canola or corn-oil margarine or butter
½	cup packed light brown sugar
1½	tablespoons light corn syrup
1	teaspoon vanilla extract

To prepare the cake: Preheat the oven to 350°. Generously grease a 12-cup Bundt pan. Dust the pan with flour, tapping out the excess. Set aside.

Sift the flour, baking powder and salt onto a sheet of wax paper or into a bowl.

Place the sugar, margarine or butter, oil and egg substitute in a large mixer bowl. Beat with an electric mixer at medium speed for 4 minutes, or until very light and well blended. Reduce the speed to low and beat in half of the flour mixture until just incorporated. Beat in the yogurt, water, milk and vanilla. Then beat in the remaining flour mixture just until smoothly incorporated; do not overbeat.

Transfer the batter to the prepared pan. Spread it evenly with a rubber spatula.

Bake on the center oven rack for 50 to 60 minutes, or until a toothpick inserted in the thickest part comes out clean and the top springs back when lightly pressed. Transfer the pan to a wire rack and let stand for 2 hours, or until the cake is completely cooled.

Loosen the cake from the pan using a table knife. Rap the pan sharply against the counter several times to loosen the cake completely. Then invert the cake onto a serving plate.

To prepare the glaze: In a 2-cup glass measure or similar microwave-safe bowl, combine the milk and margarine or butter. Microwave on high power for 30 to 40 seconds, or until the margarine or butter melts and the mixture is very hot but not boiling. Set aside.

Place the sugar and corn syrup in a heavy medium saucepan. Cook over high heat, stirring carefully with a long-handled wooden spoon, just until the sugar melts and the mixture liquefies. Remove the pan from the heat.

Working carefully and standing back to avoid any steam or spattering, add the hot milk mixture to the pan. Stir until the ingredients are well blended and any large lumps of sugar have dissolved. Stir in the vanilla. If any small lumps of sugar remain, strain the glaze through a fine sieve to remove them.

Drizzle the glaze decoratively over the cake top. Let the cake stand for at least 20 minutes to allow the glaze to cool before serving.

Makes 14 servings.

Per serving: 331 calories, 8.5 g. total fat (23% of calories), 1.4 g. saturated fat, 3 mg. cholesterol

Cinnamon Coffee Cake

This easy coffee cake is one of our old favorites, updated to remove a great deal of the fat. The nonfat sour cream is an important flavor component.

CAKE

1¾	cups all-purpose or unbleached white flour
1	teaspoon baking powder
½	teaspoon baking soda
¼	teaspoon ground cinnamon
1	cup nonfat sour cream
⅔	cup granulated sugar
¼	cup liquid egg substitute
3	tablespoons canola or safflower oil
1	teaspoon vanilla extract

TOPPING

1½	tablespoons granulated sugar
¼	teaspoon ground cinnamon

To prepare the cake: Preheat the oven to 350°. Coat an 8" × 8" baking pan with nonstick spray. Set aside.

In a medium bowl, combine the flour, baking powder, baking soda and cinnamon. Stir to mix well.

In a large bowl, combine the sour cream, sugar, egg substitute, oil and vanilla. Stir vigorously until well blended. Stir in the flour mixture until thoroughly combined. Pour the batter into the prepared pan and spread evenly with a rubber spatula.

To prepare the topping: In a small cup, stir together the sugar and cinnamon. Sprinkle the mixture evenly over the batter.

Bake on the center oven rack for 20 to 25 minutes, or until a toothpick inserted in the center comes out clean. Cool on a wire rack for 10 to 15 minutes before serving.

Makes 9 servings.

Per serving: 224 calories, 5 g. total fat (20% of calories), 0.4 g. saturated fat, 0 mg. cholesterol

Molasses-Honey Gingerbread

Dark, robust and spicy, this easy gingerbread makes a great snack or dessert. The combination of molasses and honey helps keep the cake moist and enhances the blend of spices. To dress up individual portions, dust them lightly with powdered sugar just before serving.

2⅓	cups all-purpose or unbleached white flour
	Generous 1 teaspoon ground ginger
1	teaspoon ground cinnamon
¾	teaspoon baking soda
¼	teaspoon ground cloves
⅛	teaspoon salt (optional)
¼	cup granulated sugar
⅓	cup nondiet tub-style canola or corn-oil margarine or butter
2	large egg whites
¾	cup light molasses
¼	cup mild honey, such as clover
⅔	cup hot water

Preheat the oven to 325°. Coat an 11" × 7" baking dish with nonstick spray. Set aside.

In a medium bowl, combine the flour, ginger, cinnamon, baking soda, cloves and salt (if using). Stir to mix well. Set aside.

In a large mixer bowl, combine the sugar and margarine or butter. Beat with an electric mixer on low speed until smooth and light in color. Add the egg whites, molasses and honey. Beat well.

Add the water. Beat until the mixture is smooth. Gradually add the flour mixture and beat just until all of the flour is incorporated.

Pour the batter into the prepared pan. Bake on the center oven rack for 33 to 37 minutes, or until a toothpick inserted in the center comes out clean.

Cool on a wire rack.

Makes 10 servings.

Per serving: 259 calories, 6.3 g. total fat (22% of calories), 1.1 g. saturated fat, 0 mg. cholesterol

Chewy Brownies

It's hard to believe that brownies this chocolatey and moist can be low in fat. The secret to their chewy texture and tempting taste is the combination of cocoa powder (which is very lean), chocolate and corn syrup. Stored airtight, these will keep for two to three days.

1	cup all-purpose or unbleached white flour
1	cup powdered sugar
¼	cup + ½ tablespoon unsweetened cocoa powder
¾	teaspoon baking powder
1½	ounces semisweet chocolate, coarsely broken or chopped
3	tablespoons nondiet tub-style canola or corn-oil margarine or butter
½	cup packed light or dark brown sugar
2	tablespoons light corn syrup
1	tablespoon water
2	teaspoons vanilla extract
2	large egg whites

Preheat the oven to 350°. Line an 8" × 8" baking pan with foil, making sure the foil overlaps the dish by about 1½" at 2 ends. (The easiest way to shape the foil is to invert the pan and mold the foil around the bottom; then insert the shaped foil in the pan.) Coat the foil with nonstick spray. Set aside.

Sift the flour, powdered sugar, cocoa and baking powder onto a sheet of wax paper or into a bowl.

Place the chocolate and margarine or butter in a heavy medium saucepan. Stir over the *lowest* heat until the chocolate is just melted and smooth; be very careful not to scorch the chocolate. Remove the pan from the heat and stir in the brown sugar, corn syrup, water and vanilla until well blended.

Using a wooden spoon, beat the egg whites into the chocolate mixture. Gently stir in the flour mixture just until well blended and smooth. Transfer the batter to the prepared pan, spreading it evenly with a rubber spatula.

Bake on the middle oven rack for 24 to 28 minutes, or until the center of the top is almost firm when tapped. Transfer the pan to a wire rack and let stand for 15 minutes. Then, using the overhanging foil as handles, carefully lift the brownies from the pan and place the foil on the wire rack.

Let stand until completely cooled. Peel off the foil. Set the brownies, right side up, on a cutting board. Trim off any dry edges. Using a large sharp knife, mark and cut into individual brownies; wipe the knife blade with a damp paper towel between cuts.

Makes 12 brownies.

Per brownie: 167 calories, 4.3 g. total fat (23% of calories), 0.5 g. saturated fat, 0 mg. cholesterol

Chocolate Layer Cake

This moist chocolate cake is remarkably low in fat. Ice it with either our Chocolate Fudge Frosting or our White Mountain Frosting. For a special finishing touch, top it with fresh raspberries and chocolate shavings. Store the cake in an airtight container. It will keep for two to three days. For longer storage, tightly wrap the unfrosted layers and freeze. Bring to room temperature before icing.

1½	ounces unsweetened chocolate, coarsely chopped
1⅔	cups cake flour
7	tablespoons unsweetened cocoa powder
1¼	teaspoons baking powder
¾	teaspoon baking soda
⅛	teaspoon salt
¼	cup nondiet tub-style canola or corn-oil margarine or butter
1½	cups granulated sugar, divided
5	large egg whites, at room temperature, divided
½	cup plain nonfat yogurt
1	cup skim milk, divided
2½	teaspoons vanilla extract

Preheat the oven to 350°. Coat two 8" round cake pans with nonstick spray. Line the pans with wax paper cut to fit the bottoms. Coat the paper with nonstick spray and dust with cocoa powder, tapping out the excess. Set aside.

Place the chocolate in the top of a double boiler. Set over a larger pan containing 1" of almost-simmering water. Heat, stirring occasionally, until melted. Remove the pan from the heat and set it aside.

Sift the flour, cocoa, baking powder, baking soda and salt onto a piece of wax paper or into a bowl.

In a large mixer bowl, combine the margarine or butter, 1¼ cups of the sugar and 2 of the egg whites. Beat with an electric mixer on medium speed for 2 minutes, or until light in color and well blended. Beat in the melted chocolate.

Beat in the yogurt, 2 tablespoons at a time. Add about one-third of the flour mixture and beat just until evenly incorporated; do not overbeat. Beat in ½ cup of the milk.

Beat in the remaining flour mixture, then the vanilla and the remaining ½ cup milk. Mix until smoothly incorporated but do not overmix.

In a clean large mixer bowl with clean beaters, beat the remaining 3 egg whites on medium speed until opaque. Raise the speed to high and beat until soft peaks begin to form. Gradually beat in the remaining ¼ cup sugar. Continue beating until firm but no dry or stiff peaks form.

Using a rubber spatula, scoop out about 1 cup of the beaten whites and fold into the chocolate mixture to lighten it. Then gently pour the chocolate mixture into the bowl with the remaining beaten whites. Fold until thoroughly incorporated but not overmixed.

Divide the batter evenly between the prepared pans. Spread it to the edges with a rubber spatula. Bake on the middle oven rack for 25 to 30 minutes, or until a toothpick inserted in the center comes out clean and the tops spring back when lightly touched.

Transfer the pans to wire racks and let cool completely. Working carefully, run a knife around the edge of each pan to loosen the cake. Invert onto wire racks and peel off the wax paper.

Makes 2 layers; 12 servings.

Per serving: 227 calories, 6.3 g. total fat (24% of calories), 0.7 g. saturated fat, 1 mg. cholesterol

Chocolate Fudge Frosting

This dark, shiny frosting tastes like old-fashioned fudge and goes perfectly with our Chocolate Layer Cake. The frosting isn't really hard to make, but you must follow the directions carefully. Like fudge, it's boiled, cooled at room temperature and then beaten. Don't be tempted to skip the cooling period, as it helps ensure that the frosting will be smooth. Using a candy thermometer will help guarantee excellent results.

2	cups granulated sugar
⅔	cup water
3	tablespoons dark corn syrup
1½	teaspoons nondiet tub-style canola or corn-oil margarine or butter
1½	ounces unsweetened chocolate, finely chopped
⅓	cup powdered sugar
3	tablespoons unsweetened cocoa powder
1½	teaspoons vanilla extract

In a heavy medium saucepan, stir together the granulated sugar, water, corn syrup and margarine or butter. Using a damp paper towel, wipe down the sides of the pan so that no sugar crystals remain on them.

Bring the mixture to a boil over medium-high heat. Cover and boil for 2 minutes. Remove the cover and clip a candy thermometer to the side of the pan, adjusting it so the tip is submerged in the mixture but does not touch the bottom of the pan. Boil, *without stirring*, until the thermometer registers 230°, 4 to 6 minutes.

Immediately remove the pan from the heat and set it on a wire rack. Do not remove the thermometer and do not stir or jar the pan. Sprinkle the chocolate over the sugar mixture but *do not stir*. Allow the mixture to cool at room temperature until it reaches 120°, 25 to 30 minutes. At this point, the mixture should be just slightly hot to the touch. Don't let the mixture get cold.

Transfer the sugar mixture to a large mixer bowl. Begin beating with an electric mixer on medium speed. Add the powdered sugar, cocoa and vanilla. Continue beating, stopping once to scrape down the sides of the bowl, for 4 minutes. With a large spoon, stir the mixture until it begins to set. (The texture will not change for a minute or two. Then the mixture will begin to stiffen. Test by holding up the spoon. If the frosting runs freely back into the bowl, the frosting is not stiff enough for spreading.)

Makes enough to frost two 8" round cake layers or a 13" × 9" cake; 12 servings.

Per serving: 173 calories, 2.5 g. total fat (12% of calories), 0.1 g. saturated fat, 0 mg. cholesterol

Note: For best results, use this procedure to ice your cake: First make sure your cake is ready when the icing is at the proper consistency. Place the bottom layer on a cake plate and have the second layer handy. Using a long-bladed spatula or spreading knife, begin frosting the cake as soon as the frosting is just stiff enough to spread evenly. Spread a generous one-quarter of the mixture over the bottom layer. The frosting will continue to stiffen as you work with it. Center the top cake layer over the first. Working quickly, spread the remaining frosting over the top and sides of the cake. Don't overwork the mixture or it may become dull. The frosting will firm up as it stands. Let stand at least 15 minutes before cutting the cake.

White Mountain Frosting

This shiny white frosting has virtually no fat because it's made with egg whites and sugar. Food handling guidelines recommend that egg whites always be cooked. We accomplish that by beating boiling sugar syrup into them. For perfect results, it's important to warm the whites first as directed in the recipe and to be sure the syrup has reached 243° before beating it in. Be careful not to cook the syrup to a higher temperature, as the whites may not fluff up properly if it's too hot. As is always the case when beating egg whites, make sure to use a very clean bowl and beaters. And be sure there are no bits of yolk mixed in with the whites or they won't beat up properly. This frosting will stay fluffy and soft for two days.

2	large egg whites
½	cup granulated sugar
¼	cup light corn syrup
2	tablespoons water
1	teaspoon vanilla extract

Place the egg whites in a small bowl. Set the bowl in a larger pan containing warm (about 100°) water. Let stand while you prepare the syrup; stir the whites occasionally.

In a small heavy saucepan, combine the sugar, corn syrup and water. Stir over low heat until the sugar dissolves. Increase the heat to medium and bring the mixture to a boil. Cover and boil for 2 minutes. Boil rapidly until a candy thermometer dipped into the mixture registers 241°. Remove the syrup from the heat and set aside temporarily.

Transfer the egg whites to a large mixer bowl. Beat with an electric mixer on high speed until soft peaks form.

Return the syrup to the stove and boil until the mixture reaches 243°. Immediately remove the pan from the heat.

Begin to beat the egg whites again on high speed. Pour the hot syrup in a thin stream down the side of the bowl, taking about 15 seconds to incorporate all of it. Add the vanilla. Continue to beat until stiff peaks form. Use immediately.

Makes enough to frost a 13" × 9" sheet cake or two 8" round cake layers; 20 servings.

Per serving: 32 calories, 0 g. total fat (0% of calories), 0 g. saturated fat, 0 mg. cholesterol

No-Cholesterol Pastry

There is really no way to make a good tender-crisp pastry crust without a considerable amount of fat. Still, it's possible to trim away some fat without compromising texture or taste. In the following recipe, we use vegetable oil for tenderness and margarine or butter for both crispness and flavor. To keep the total amount of fat per serving moderate, we prepare only enough pastry for a single crust.

1½ cups all-purpose or unbleached white flour
½ teaspoon salt
¼ cup + 2 teaspoons canola or safflower oil
1 tablespoon nondiet tub-style canola or corn-oil margarine or butter, well-chilled and cut into small pieces
3½ tablespoons ice water
1 tablespoon lemon juice

Combine the flour and salt in a food processor. Process for 10 seconds. Sprinkle the oil and margarine or butter over the flour. Process just until the mixture is the consistency of coarse crumbs; don't overprocess. If necessary, stop and scrape the bowl bottom and sides once or twice. Transfer the mixture to a large bowl. (Alternatively, place the flour and salt in a large bowl. Use a pastry blender or forks to cut in the oil and margarine or butter.)

In a cup, mix the water and lemon juice. Sprinkle 2 tablespoons plus 2 teaspoons of the lemon water over the flour. Mix gently with a fork until the flour is moistened and holds together. If necessary, add a bit more lemon water until the mixture is evenly moistened but not wet.

Knead the dough briefly with your hands until the flour particles are smoothly incorporated. Shape the pastry into a smooth disk. Lay the dough between 2 sheets of wax paper.

Using a rolling pin and working with a pressing motion, roll the pastry into a circle. (For a 9" pie plate, form a 12" circle. For a 9½" deep-dish pie plate or a 10" pie plate, form a 12½" circle.) As you work, check the underside of the dough and smooth out any wrinkles that form. Patch tears as necessary.

Peel off the top sheet of wax paper. Center the dough, paper side up, in a pie plate that you've coated with nonstick spray. Gently press the dough into place. Peel off the other sheet of wax paper. If any tears develop in the pastry, patch them.

If the dough feels soft or warm at this point, refrigerate it for about 10 minutes. Trim the dough so the edge is even and overhangs the plate by ½" all around. Fold the overhang back into the plate to form a plump edge. Decoratively crimp the edge with your fingers or the tines of a fork.

Cover the pastry with plastic wrap. Refrigerate for at least 30 minutes and up to 8 hours. Bake as directed in individual recipes.

Makes 1 pastry shell; 8 servings.

Per serving: 165 calories, 9.1 g. total fat (50% of calories), 0.8 g. saturated fat, 0 mg. cholesterol

Graham Cracker Pie Shell

This updated graham crust tastes very much like traditional versions, but it is much leaner. Usually the crumbs are held together with lots of margarine or butter. We use just a little margarine or butter and oil combined with corn syrup and water. The corn syrup makes the crust crisp, but it also makes the mixture a bit sticky, so be sure to generously coat the pie plate with nonstick spray. Incidentally, all graham crackers look and taste fairly similar, but their fat content varies, so check labels and choose the leanest crackers.

1⅓ cups graham cracker crumbs
1 tablespoon nondiet tub-style canola or corn-oil margarine or butter, chilled and cut into small pieces
2 teaspoons canola or safflower oil
1 tablespoon + 1 teaspoon light corn syrup
1½ tablespoons water

Preheat the oven to 375°. Very generously coat a 9", 9½" deep dish or 10" pie plate with nonstick spray. Set aside.

In a food processor, combine the crumbs, margarine or butter and oil. Process with on/off pulses until well blended.

In a small cup, stir together the corn syrup and water until well blended. Add to the food processor. Process with on/off pulses until the mixture is well blended and begins to hold together. If the mixture seems dry, blend in a little more water, a few drops at a time.

Transfer the crumbs to the prepared pie plate. Press them evenly into the bottom and up the sides. If the crumbs stick to your hands, cover them with a sheet of wax paper and press through the paper.

Bake on the center oven rack for 5 to 8 minutes, or until the crust is lightly tinged with brown. Let cool on a wire rack. Use the shell immediately or cover it well and store at room temperature for several days.

Makes 1 pie shell; 8 servings.

Per serving: 138 calories, 4.3 g. total fat (29% of calories), 0.7 g. saturated fat, 0 mg. cholesterol

Banana Cream Pie

Here's a healthier version of an old-fashioned dessert. Since there is considerable variation in the fat content of graham crackers from brand to brand, check the label to make sure the ones you buy have only one gram or less of fat per half-ounce serving.

2	cups 1% fat milk
½	cup liquid egg substitute
⅓	cup granulated sugar
¼	cup cornstarch
⅛	teaspoon salt (optional)
2	teaspoons nondiet tub-style canola or corn-oil margarine or butter
1	teaspoon vanilla extract
4	ripe bananas, divided
1	9" Graham Cracker Pie Shell (page 329), baked
1	teaspoon lemon juice

In a 4-cup glass measure, thoroughly mix the milk and egg substitute. Microwave on high power for 2½ to 3½ minutes, stopping and stirring several times, until the mixture is hot but not boiling.

In the top of a double boiler, mix the sugar, cornstarch and salt (if using). Gradually beat in the milk mixture, stirring vigorously and scraping the bottom of the pan until smooth. Cook over 1" of boiling water, stirring vigorously, for 6 to 7 minutes, or until the mixture thickens. Remove the pan from the heat.

Stir in the margarine or butter and vanilla until well blended. Cover and place in the refrigerator for about 30 minutes, or until the custard is lukewarm; stir occasionally.

Slice 2 of the bananas and arrange the slices concentrically in the bottom of the pie shell. Spoon the custard mixture over the bananas. Cover the pie tightly and refrigerate.

Shortly before serving, thinly slice the remaining 2 bananas. Sprinkle with the lemon juice to prevent the slices from discoloring. Arrange the slices attractively on top of the pie and serve.

Makes 8 servings.

Per serving: 285 calories, 6.7 g. total fat (21% of calories), 1.5 g. saturated fat, 3 mg. cholesterol

Variation: For an even easier, lower-fat treat, make Banana Pudding. Instead of the graham cracker crust, line a 1½-quart square glass baking dish with graham crackers. Arrange the banana slices on top of them in rows. Top with the custard mixture. Add the remaining banana slices just before serving.

Pumpkin Pie

We've lightened this American favorite in several ways. First, we used a no-cholesterol, reduced-fat pie dough. Then we replaced the usual whole eggs and whole milk in the filling with egg substitute and evaporated skim milk. What we didn't do is remove any of the traditional flavor and creamy texture! The pie will keep, covered and refrigerated, for up to three days.

1	recipe No-Cholesterol Pastry (page 328)
¾	cup packed light or dark brown sugar
1½	tablespoons granulated sugar
¾	teaspoon ground cinnamon
½	teaspoon ground ginger
½	teaspoon ground nutmeg
¼	teaspoon ground allspice
2	cups canned solid-pack pumpkin
1¼	cups evaporated skim milk
¾	cup liquid egg substitute
2½	teaspoons vanilla extract

Preheat the oven to 375°.

Roll out the pastry and fit it into a 9½" deep-dish pie plate. Prick it all over with a fork. Set aside.

In a large bowl, combine the sugars, cinnamon, ginger, nutmeg and allspice. Mix well. Add the pumpkin, milk, egg substitute and vanilla. Stir until well blended. Pour into the prepared pastry.

Bake on the center oven rack for 50 to 60 minutes, or until the crust is nicely browned and the filling is set in the center when the dish is jiggled. Transfer to a wire rack. Let stand until completely cooled. Chill lightly before serving.

Makes 8 servings.

Per serving: 326 calories, 10.2 g. total fat (28% of calories), 1.2 g. saturated fat, 2 mg. cholesterol

Lemon Meringue Pie

We've updated this zesty classic to reduce the fat by about half. We've modified the meringue topping so that the egg whites are fully cooked. This pie keeps well in the refrigerator for up to two days.

PIE

1	recipe No-Cholesterol Pastry (page 328)
1¼	cups granulated sugar
⅓	cup cornstarch
1	tablespoon very finely grated lemon zest
1	large egg yolk
7	tablespoons lemon juice
⅓	cup orange juice
1⅓	cups boiling water

MERINGUE

4	large egg whites, at room temperature
½	teaspoon cream of tartar
	Pinch of salt
½	cup granulated sugar
½	teaspoon vanilla extract

To prepare the pie: Preheat the oven to 425°.

Roll out the pastry and fit it into a 9½" deep-dish pie plate. Prick it all over with a fork. Cover the pastry with a large sheet of heavy-duty foil and firmly smooth the foil over the pastry. Fold down the edges to completely encase the dough. Fill the plate with dry beans, uncooked rice or pie weights to weigh down the crust.

Bake on the center oven rack for 18 minutes. Remove the foil. Bake for 6 to 9 minutes longer, or until the crust is nicely browned. Let cool on a wire rack.

Reduce the oven temperature to 350°.

In a medium saucepan, thoroughly combine the sugar, cornstarch and lemon zest. Add the egg yolk, lemon juice and orange juice. Whisk until smooth. Whisk in the water in a thin stream.

Place the pan over medium-high heat. Cook, whisking constantly, until the mixture comes to a boil. Continue to whisk, scraping the bottom of the pan, for 3 minutes. Immediately remove the pan from the heat. Pour the mixture into the prepared crust.

To prepare the meringue: Place the egg whites, cream of tartar and salt in large mixer bowl. Beat with an electric mixer on medium-low speed until frothy. Raise the mixer speed to medium and continue beating just until very soft peaks begin forming. Beat in the sugar, 1 tablespoon at a time. Then add the vanilla and continue beating until the mixture is smooth and stands in soft peaks. Spread and swirl the meringue over the filling, being sure to seal the edges all the way around.

Bake in the lower third of the oven for 15 to 18 minutes, or until the meringue is nicely browned all over. Transfer to a wire rack. Let stand until cool. Refrigerate until chilled, at least 1 hour.

Makes 8 servings.

Per serving: 364 calories, 9.8 g. total fat (24% of calories), 1.1 g. saturated fat, 26 mg. cholesterol

Apple Crisp

One of our all-time favorites, apple crisp, is much lower in fat than apple pie. We leave the apples unpeeled; you can peel them if desired.

FILLING

8	cups thinly sliced tart apples
2	tablespoons granulated sugar
½	teaspoon ground cinnamon
3	tablespoons water

TOPPING

¾	cup quick-cooking or old-fashioned rolled oats
½	cup all-purpose or unbleached white flour
½	cup packed light brown sugar
1	teaspoon ground cinnamon
¼	cup diet tub-style canola or corn-oil margarine, chilled and cut into small pieces
	Nonfat vanilla frozen yogurt or ice milk (optional)

To prepare the filling: Preheat the oven to 375°.

Spread the apples in a 2-quart rectangular baking dish. In a cup, mix the sugar and cinnamon. Sprinkle over the apples, then stir to coat them well. Sprinkle with the water.

To prepare the topping: In a medium bowl, combine the oats, flour, sugar and cinnamon. Stir to mix well. Using a pastry blender or forks, cut in the margarine until the mixture resembles coarse meal. Sprinkle evenly over the apples.

Bake on the center oven rack for 35 to 40 minutes, or until the topping begins to brown and the apples are tender.

Spoon into bowls. If desired, garnish each serving with a small scoop of frozen yogurt or ice milk.

Makes 6 servings.

Per serving: 336 calories, 6.1 g. total fat (16% of calories), 1 g. saturated fat, 0 mg. cholesterol

Peach Kuchen

No one would ever guess this homey, fragrant peach cake is low in fat; it seems too rich and satisfying. For fullest flavor, use top-quality summer peaches. The kuchen is best served warm and fresh, but it will keep for 24 hours. Reheat it before serving.

CRUMB MIXTURE

⅓	cup all-purpose or unbleached white flour
⅓	cup packed light brown sugar
2	tablespoons granulated sugar
¼	teaspoon ground cinnamon
1½	tablespoons nondiet tub-style canola or corn-oil margarine or butter, chilled and cut into small pieces

BATTER AND PEACHES

1¼	cups all-purpose or unbleached white flour
1	teaspoon baking powder
½	teaspoon baking soda
¼	teaspoon salt
¼	teaspoon ground ginger
¼	teaspoon ground cinnamon
6½	tablespoons granulated sugar
2	tablespoons nondiet tub-style canola or corn-oil margarine or butter
1	large egg or 3 tablespoons liquid egg substitute
2	teaspoons vanilla extract
⅛	teaspoon almond extract
½	cup plain nonfat yogurt
6	large ripe peaches, peeled, pitted and coarsely sliced

To prepare the crumb mixture: Preheat the oven to 375°. Coat an 11" × 7" baking dish with nonstick spray. Set aside.

In a food processor, combine the flour, sugars, cinnamon and margarine or butter. Process the mixture for about 1 minute, or until the ingredients are well blended.

To prepare the batter and peaches: In a medium bowl, thoroughly stir together the flour, baking powder, baking soda, salt, ginger and cinnamon.

In a mixer bowl, combine the sugar and margarine or butter. Beat with an electric mixer on medium speed until very well blended. Beat in the egg or egg substitute, vanilla and almond extract until well blended. Beat in the yogurt.

Add the flour mixture and stir just until evenly incorporated; do not overmix. Transfer the batter to the prepared dish, spreading it evenly with a rubber spatula.

Sprinkle about one-third of the crumb mixture over the batter.

Spread the peaches evenly over the batter. Pat the slices down to embed them slightly. Sprinkle the remaining crumb mixture evenly over the peaches.

Bake on the center oven rack for 28 to 33 minutes, or until the top is bubbly and browned, and a toothpick inserted in the center comes out clean. Transfer to a wire rack and let stand for 10 to 15 minutes before cutting.

Makes 8 servings.

Per serving: 261 calories, 5.9 g. total fat (20% of calories), 0.8 g. saturated fat, 27 mg. cholesterol

Fresh Cherry Compote

We often serve this compote of dark sweet cherries over our Vanilla Custard Pudding. We also enjoy it with a dollop of low-fat frozen vanilla yogurt or ice milk.

3	cups pitted dark sweet red cherries (about 1 pound unpitted)
1	tablespoon granulated sugar
½	teaspoon lemon juice
	Pinch of ground cinnamon
1	cup cranberry juice, divided
½	tablespoon cornstarch
¼	teaspoon vanilla extract

In a medium saucepan, combine the cherries, sugar, lemon juice, cinnamon and ¾ cup of the cranberry juice. Mix well. Bring to a boil over medium-high heat. Cover, reduce the heat and simmer, stirring occasionally, for 5 minutes.

Stir together the cornstarch and the remaining ¼ cup cranberry juice.

Raise the heat so that the liquid in the pan begins to boil. Add the cornstarch mixture and stir for 1 minute, or until the liquid thickens and becomes clear. Transfer to a serving bowl and add the vanilla.

Cover and refrigerate for at least 4 hours.

Makes 4 servings.

Per serving: 134 calories, 1.1 g. total fat (7% of calories), 0.2 g. saturated fat, 0 mg. cholesterol

Sour Cherry Slump

A slump is a cobblerlike dessert featuring a juicy fruit filling with simple drop biscuit dumplings on top. In this zesty sour cherry version, we enhanced the fruit with a little cranberry juice concentrate to brighten its color and bring out the flavor of the cherries. This is a very gratifying, full-bodied dessert—yet only 16 percent of its calories come from fat.

FILLING

2	cans (16 ounces each) pitted tart red cherries, with juice
⅔	cup granulated sugar
2½	tablespoons cornstarch
⅛	teaspoon ground cinnamon
¼	cup cranberry juice cocktail concentrate

DOUGH

1¼	cups all-purpose or unbleached white flour
2	tablespoons granulated sugar
¾	teaspoon baking powder
¼	teaspoon salt
3	tablespoons nondiet tub-style canola or corn-oil margarine or butter, chilled and cut into small pieces
½	cup skim milk
1	tablespoon lemon juice
	Nonfat frozen vanilla yogurt or ice milk (optional)

To prepare the filling: Preheat the oven to 375°.

Drain the juice from the cherries into a Dutch oven or a large heavy stove-top and ovenproof casserole. Bring to a boil over high heat. Boil for 3 minutes.

In a 2-cup glass measure, stir together the sugar, cornstarch and cinnamon. Slowly stir in the juice concentrate and mix until well blended and smooth. Whisk into the boiling cherry juice. Continue boiling, whisking vigorously, for 2 minutes, or until the mixture thickens and clears. Add the cherries and set aside.

To prepare the dough: In a medium bowl, thoroughly stir together the flour, sugar, baking powder and salt. Using a pastry blender or forks, cut in the margarine or butter until the mixture resembles coarse meal.

In a cup, stir together the milk and lemon juice. Add to the flour mixture and toss it with a fork just until the liquid is evenly incorporated.

Using large spoons, drop tablespoonfuls of the dough over the cherry mixture, separating them as much as possible.

Bake on the center oven rack for 25 to 30 minutes, or until the top is nicely browned and a toothpick inserted in a center dumpling comes out clean. Transfer to a wire rack and let cool for at least 10 minutes.

Spoon into bowls. If desired, garnish each serving with a small scoop of frozen yogurt or ice milk.

Makes 6 servings.

Per serving: 340 calories, 6.2 g. total fat (16% of calories), 1.1 g. saturated fat, 0 mg. cholesterol

Raspberry-Plum Cobbler

Satisfying and delicious, this brightly colored cobbler features a succulent combination of fruit. For best results, choose tart, very flavorful plums, as these lend appealing zestiness and help bring out the taste of the berries. The cobbler will keep, covered and refrigerated, for up to three days. Reheat it in a 300° oven just before serving.

FILLING

- ¾ cup granulated sugar
- 2 tablespoons all-purpose or unbleached white flour
- ⅛ teaspoon ground cinnamon
- 2⅔ cups pitted and diced red or black plums
- 2½ cups fresh or unsweetened frozen raspberries (see note on page 338)

DOUGH

- 1½ cups all-purpose or unbleached white flour
- 1½ tablespoons granulated sugar
- ¾ teaspoon baking powder
- ¼ teaspoon salt
- 1½ tablespoons nondiet tub-style canola or corn-oil margarine or butter, chilled and cut into small pieces
- 1½ tablespoons canola or safflower oil
- ¼ cup + 1 tablespoon skim milk
  Low-fat vanilla ice cream or ice milk (optional)

To prepare the filling: Preheat the oven to 375°.

In a 1½-quart or slightly larger round casserole, thoroughly stir together the sugar, flour and cinnamon. Add the plums and raspberries; stir to coat well with the sugar mixture.

To prepare the dough: In a medium bowl, thoroughly stir together the flour, sugar, baking powder and salt. Using a pastry blender or forks, cut in the margarine or butter and oil until the mixture resembles coarse meal.

Add the milk and toss the mixture with a fork just until the milk is evenly incorporated. Pat the mixture into a ball. Place between sheets of wax paper and press into a round large enough to fit the casserole used.

Peel off the top sheet of wax paper. Turn over the dough and center it over the fruit mixture. Peel off and discard the second sheet of wax paper. Make several 1½" long decorative slashes in the dough, radiating them from the center.

Bake on the center oven rack for 35 to 45 minutes, or until the top is nicely browned, the edges are bubbly and a toothpick inserted in the center of the dough comes out clean. Transfer to a wire rack and let cool for at least 10 minutes before serving.

Spoon into bowls. If desired, garnish each serving with a small scoop of the ice cream or ice milk.

Makes 5 servings.

Per serving: 411 calories, 6.6 g. total fat (14% of calories), 0.7 g. saturated fat, 0 mg. cholesterol

Note: If using frozen berries, rinse and drain them well after measuring.

Meringues

Meringues seem sinful but are virtually fat free. For a very light dessert, serve them with fresh strawberries or our Sour Cherry Topping spooned over them. For a slightly more substantial treat, add a small scoop of low-fat vanilla ice cream or frozen yogurt before you spoon on the fruit. As always, when beating egg whites, make sure your mixing bowl and beaters are completely clean. And be very careful that no bits of yolk are mixed in with the whites. Fat of any sort will keep the whites from whipping properly. Store meringues in an airtight container or plastic bag in a cool place for up to a week. Or wrap them well and freeze for up to a month.

½   **cup egg whites, at room temperature**
¼   **teaspoon cream of tartar**
1   **cup granulated sugar**
1   **teaspoon vanilla extract**

Preheat the oven to 225°. Line 2 jelly-roll pans or large baking sheets with parchment or foil. If you use foil, coat it with nonstick spray. Set aside.

In a large mixer bowl, beat the egg whites with an electric mixer on low speed for 30 seconds. Gradually raise the speed to high and continue beating until the whites are frothy and opaque. Add the cream of tartar. Continue beating until the whites just begin to form soft peaks.

Beat in the sugar, 2 tablespoons at a time, until it is all incorporated. Beat in the vanilla. Continue to beat for 1½ minutes, or until the meringue mixture stands in glossy peaks that are firm but not dry or stiff.

Transfer the meringue to a large pastry bag fitted with a ½" diameter plain or open star tip. Pipe the mixture onto the prepared pans, forming it into 8 rings measuring approximately 4½"; leave about 2" between rings. Build up the sides of the rings by piping a second layer on top of the first. If any meringue is left, continue to build the rings. (Alternatively, form simple meringue shells by spooning dollops of the mixture onto the sheets. Hollow out the center of the mounds using the back of a spoon.)

Stagger the pans on separate racks in the center portion of the oven. Bake for 1 hour. Switch the position of the pans. Bake for 1 hour longer, or until the meringues are firm, dry and faintly tinged with beige. Transfer the parchment or foil (with the meringues still attached) to wire racks. Let cool thoroughly.

Gently peel off the paper or foil. (If the meringues stick, they're not done. Return them to a preheated 225° oven and bake for 20 to 30 minutes longer. Let cool completely before serving or storing.)

Makes 8 servings.

Per serving: 100 calories, 0 g. total fat (0% of calories), 0 g. saturated fat, 0 mg. cholesterol

English Berry Trifle

Our version of this traditional English dessert features layers of cake, raspberries, strawberries and custard. It always draws rave reviews when we serve it, yet it's really very simple to prepare. To show off the layers to best advantage, serve the trifle in a large footed glass bowl, preferably one with straight sides.

1	package (10 ounces) frozen raspberries in syrup, thawed
1	package (10 ounces) frozen strawberries in syrup, thawed
	Cranberry juice cocktail or cranapple juice (optional)
1	tablespoon cornstarch
2	tablespoons raspberry or blackberry brandy or rum (optional)
1	recipe Vanilla Custard Pudding (page 348)
1	angel food cake (about 10 ounces)
¼	cup fresh raspberries or strawberries (garnish)

Place the thawed raspberries and strawberries in a large sieve and drain over a bowl. Place the fruit in a medium bowl and set it aside. Measure the syrup. You should have 1 cup; if necessary, add enough cranberry juice to bring up the level.

Transfer ¼ cup of the syrup to a small saucepan. Add the cornstarch and stir to mix well. Stir in the remaining syrup and mix well. Bring to a boil over medium-high heat. Cook, stirring, until the juice thickens and turns clear. Stir in the brandy or rum (if using). Pour over the fruit. Stir well, cover and refrigerate until well chilled. Measure out and reserve ½ cup of the fruit for a garnish.

Meanwhile, prepare the custard, cover and chill.

Cut the cake into bite-size pieces using a serrated knife. Place half of the pieces in a large straight-sided glass bowl. Spoon half of the fruit over the cake. Cover with half of the custard. Repeat to use all the cake, fruit and custard.

Garnish the top with the reserved fruit and the fresh raspberries or strawberries. Cover and refrigerate for at least 2 hours and up to 6 hours before serving.

Makes 6 servings.

Per serving: 341 calories, 3.1 g. total fat (8% of calories), 0.9 g. saturated fat, 3 mg. cholesterol

Chocolate Bread Pudding

Like most old-fashioned bread puddings, this one is an unpretentious dessert. However, it does seem mellower and richer than many traditional recipes because the custard is enlivened with chocolate, spices and rum-soaked raisins. Store covered and refrigerated for up to two days; reheat before serving.

⅓	cup dark raisins
¼	cup rum or orange juice
¾	cup packed light or dark brown sugar
2½	tablespoons unsweetened cocoa powder
2¾	cups 1% fat milk
⅛	teaspoon ground nutmeg
	Pinch of ground cinnamon
	Pinch of salt
1	ounce unsweetened chocolate, chopped
⅔	cup liquid egg substitute
2	teaspoons vanilla extract
3½	cups finely diced fresh French, Italian or sourdough bread, crusts removed
1	tablespoon powdered sugar (garnish)

Preheat the oven to 375°. Coat a 1½-quart or slightly larger round baking dish with nonstick spray. Set aside.

In a small bowl, mix the raisins and rum or orange juice. Set aside.

In a medium saucepan, thoroughly stir together the sugar and cocoa. Slowly stir in the milk, nutmeg, cinnamon and salt. Bring just to a simmer over medium-high heat. Remove from the heat.

Place the chocolate in a small bowl. Pour about ¼ cup of the hot milk mixture over the chocolate and stir until the chocolate partially melts. Gradually add ½ cup more milk; stir until the chocolate is completely melted and smooth. Stir the chocolate mixture into the saucepan. Set aside until just barely hot.

In a medium bowl, mix the egg substitute and vanilla. Gradually beat in about 1 cup of the milk mixture. Then slowly stir the egg mixture into the saucepan. Drain any unabsorbed rum or orange juice from the raisins and add to the pan, reserving the raisins.

Pour one-third of the milk mixture into the prepared baking dish. Add half of the bread and half of the raisins. Top with another third of the milk mixture and the remaining bread and raisins. Add the remaining milk mixture.

Lay a piece of wax paper over the top and press down slightly to be sure all the bread is moistened; discard the paper. Let stand for 10 minutes to allow the bread to absorb the liquid.

Set the baking dish in a larger pan. Place in the upper third of the oven. Add enough hot water to the larger pan to come 1½" up the sides of the smaller dish. Bake for 15 minutes.

Reduce the oven temperature to 350°. Continue baking for 20 to 30 minutes, or just until the top is browned and the pudding appears to be set when the dish is jiggled. Transfer to a wire rack and let cool for 10 minutes. Just before serving, dust the top of the bread pudding with the powdered sugar.

Makes 5 servings.

Per serving: 358 calories, 6.7 g. total fat (16% of calories), 1.3 g. saturated fat, 6 mg. cholesterol

Chocolate Sauce

This is a very chocolatey, glossy, bittersweet sauce that's good drizzled over brownies, ice milk, cake or other desserts. The cocoa powder—which is low in fat—provides most of the chocolate taste. We add only a small amount of regular chocolate to round out the flavor and add richness. Store the sauce in the refrigerator for up to two weeks. Although you can serve it chilled, it will become more fluid and flavorful if you allow it to warm to room temperature.

- ½   cup unsweetened cocoa powder
- ½   cup packed light brown sugar
- ½   cup hot water
- ½   cup light corn syrup
- 1½ ounces unsweetened chocolate, chopped into ¼" pieces
- 2   teaspoons vanilla extract

In a heavy medium saucepan, stir together the cocoa and sugar until well combined. Stir in the water, then the corn syrup until very smooth and well blended. Bring to a boil, stirring constantly, over medium heat. Boil, stirring and scraping the pan bottom, for 1 minute. Immediately remove the pan from the heat.

Place the chocolate pieces in a small deep bowl. Add about ¼ cup of the hot cocoa mixture and stir until well blended and the chocolate partially melts. Add about ¼ cup more of the cocoa mixture and stir until smoothly incorporated.

Pour into the saucepan and stir until the sauce is completely smooth. Stir in the vanilla.

Let cool to room temperature before serving.

Makes 1½ cups; 8 servings (3 tablespoons each).

Per serving: 157 calories, 3.5 g. total fat (19% of calories), 0 g. saturated fat, 0 mg. cholesterol

Oatmeal-Raisin Cookies

No one ever guesses that these chewy-crispy drop cookies are low in fat. They are great for lunchboxes and after-school snacks. Store the cookies in an airtight container for up to a week. To prevent them from sticking together, place the cookies flat in the container and put wax paper between the layers. For longer storage, freeze the cookies; they'll keep for up to a month.

½   cup dark raisins
¼   cup dark corn syrup
2   tablespoons skim milk
2½   cups old-fashioned rolled oats, divided
1   cup all-purpose or unbleached white flour
¾   teaspoon baking powder
¾   teaspoon ground cinnamon
¼   teaspoon ground nutmeg
¾   teaspoon baking soda
¼   teaspoon salt
⅓   cup nondiet tub-style canola or corn-oil margarine or butter
⅔   cup packed dark brown sugar
⅓   cup granulated sugar
1   large egg white
2   teaspoons vanilla extract

Preheat the oven to 375°. Lightly coat several large baking sheets with nonstick spray. Set aside.

In a medium bowl, combine the raisins, corn syrup and milk. Set aside for 15 minutes. Add 1¼ cups of the oats.

Meanwhile, place the remaining 1¼ cups oats in a food processor or blender. Grind to a powder. (If using a blender, stop several times to stir and redistribute the oats.) Transfer to a large bowl.

Thoroughly stir the flour, baking powder, cinnamon, nutmeg, baking soda and salt into the oats.

In a large mixer bowl, combine the margarine or butter and the sugars. Beat with an electric mixer on medium speed until light and smooth. Add the egg white and vanilla. Beat until well blended.

Reduce the mixer speed to low. Beat in about half of the flour mixture. Using a large wooden spoon, stir in the remaining flour mixture and the raisin mixture just until evenly incorporated.

Form the cookies by dropping rounded heaping teaspoonfuls of dough on the prepared baking sheets, leaving about 2" between cookies. Oil your fingertips and lightly pat down each cookie just slightly.

Bake 1 sheet at a time in the center of the oven for 7 to 10 minutes, or until the cookies are just tinged with brown at the edges (they will be soft and seem slightly underdone). Transfer the sheet to a wire rack and let cool for 2 minutes. Using a spatula, transfer the cookies to wire racks. Let stand until completely cooled.

Makes 45 cookies.

Per cookie: 85 calories, 2 g. total fat (21% of calories), 0.3 g. saturated fat, 0 mg. cholesterol

Gingerbread People

Gingerbread people are always a favorite, even of those who aren't concerned about lowering dietary fat. Still, for dedicated fat watchers, it's nice to know that you can enjoy these tasty cookies without guilt. The icing adds a festive touch to the cookies. Have it ready when you remove the cookies from the oven, so you can decorate them immediately and then return them to the oven. This final baking both cooks and sets the icing. Stored airtight, the cookies will keep for about two weeks. Freeze them for longer storage.

COOKIES

3	cups all-purpose or unbleached white flour
1½	teaspoons ground ginger
1¼	teaspoons baking powder
1¼	teaspoons ground cinnamon
¾	teaspoon baking soda
⅛	teaspoon ground cloves
⅛	teaspoon salt
⅔	cup packed light or dark brown sugar
⅓	cup nondiet tub-style canola or corn-oil margarine or butter
1	large egg white
⅓	cup light molasses
3	tablespoons light corn syrup
1	teaspoon vanilla extract
	Dark raisins
	Cinnamon red-hot candies (optional)

ICING

1	large egg white, at room temperature
½	teaspoon lemon juice
¼	teaspoon vanilla extract
½	cup powdered sugar, sifted

To prepare the cookies: Preheat the oven to 375°. Lightly coat several large baking sheets with nonstick spray. Set aside.

In a large bowl, thoroughly stir together the flour, ginger, baking powder, cinnamon, baking soda, cloves and salt. Set aside.

In a large mixer bowl, combine the sugar and margarine or butter. Beat with an electric mixer on medium speed until well blended. Add the egg white, molasses and corn syrup. Continue beating until thoroughly blended and smooth. Beat in the vanilla.

Gradually beat in about half of the dry ingredients. Using a large wooden spoon, stir in the rest of the dry ingredients until well mixed.

Divide the dough in half. Wrap each portion in plastic wrap.

Refrigerate for at least 1 hour, or until the dough is firm.

Remove 1 portion of dough from the refrigerator. Unwrap and place on a lightly floured work surface. Dust the surface of the dough and the rolling pin with flour. Roll out the dough until it's about ³⁄₁₆" thick. As you roll, lift the dough frequently by running a metal spatula under it and add a bit more flour to the work surface and rolling pin if necessary to prevent the dough from sticking.

Cut out the cookies using a 4" or 5" cutter. Use a wide spatula to transfer the cookies to the baking sheets; leave about 1½" between cookies. Save any dough scraps.

Repeat the rolling and cutting process with the second portion of dough. Combine the dough scraps and chill until firm. Roll and cut until all the dough is used. Decorate the cookies using the raisins for eyes and the cinnamon candies (if using) for buttons.

Bake 1 sheet at a time in the upper third of the oven for 7 to 9 minutes, or until the edges are just barely tinged with brown; be careful not to overbake.

To prepare the icing: While the cookies are baking, place the egg white in a small bowl and whisk with a fork until smooth. Measure out 1 tablespoon of egg white and place in a small mixer bowl; discard the remaining egg white or reserve it for another purpose.

Add the lemon juice. Beat with an electric mixer on low speed until frothy. Add the vanilla and then the sugar, gradually raising the mixer speed and beating for about 2 minutes, or until the icing is glossy and stiffened. (As you beat, scrape the down the sides of the bowl as needed.) If the icing seems too thick to pipe or drizzle, gradually beat in a few drops of water until the desired consistency is reached. Cover the icing with a damp towel to prevent it from drying out until needed.

Spoon the icing into a piping cone or a small pastry bag fitted with a plain tip. Pipe decorative trim, such as the outlines of mittens, collars, boots, belts and so forth, on the cookies as they come from the oven. Return them to the oven for 3 minutes longer.

Transfer the baking sheets to wire racks; let cool for several minutes. Using a wide spatula, transfer the cookies to wire racks and let stand until the cookies are cooled and the icing is completely set.

Makes 18 cookies.

Per cookie: 175 calories, 3.6 g. total fat (18% of calories), 0.6 g. saturated fat, 0 mg. cholesterol

Note: If not icing the cookies, remove them from the oven after 7 to 9 minutes and let stand for several minutes. Transfer the cookies to wire racks to cool.

Brown-Sugar-and-Date Cookies

Rich in fiber and extremely low in fat, these chewy, spicy cookies can be stored in an airtight container for up to ten days. (The dates and honey help keep them moist.) For longer storage, wrap well and freeze for up to a month.

1⅓	cups all-purpose or unbleached white flour
⅔	cup whole wheat flour
1	tablespoon ground cinnamon
1½	teaspoons ground allspice
1¼	teaspoons baking soda
¾	teaspoon baking powder
½	teaspoon ground ginger
⅛	teaspoon ground cloves
¼	teaspoon salt
¾	cup diced pitted dates
⅔	cup packed light brown sugar
1	large egg white
¼	cup mild honey, such as clover
3	tablespoons light corn syrup
3	tablespoons canola or safflower oil
2	tablespoons skim milk
2	teaspoons vanilla extract

Lightly coat several baking sheets with no-stick spray. Preheat the oven to 375°.

In a medium bowl, thoroughly stir together the flours, cinnamon, allspice, baking soda, baking powder, ginger, cloves and salt until well mixed. Stir in the dates.

In a large bowl, whisk together the sugar, egg white, honey, corn syrup, oil, milk and vanilla until well blended. With a large spoon, stir in the dry ingredients just until evenly incorporated.

Form the cookies by dropping rounded heaping teaspoonfuls of dough on the prepared baking sheets, leaving about 2" between cookies.

Bake 1 sheet at a time in the center of the oven for 9 to 11 minutes, or until the cookies are just tinged with brown at the edges. (They will be soft and seem underdone but will firm up as they cool.) Using a spatula, transfer the cookies to wire racks. Let them stand until completely cooled.

Makes 35 cookies.

Per cookie: 77 calories, 1.2 g. total fat (14% of calories), 0.1 g. saturated fat, 0 mg. cholesterol

Apricot Bars

These low-fat bars make a great snack or simple dessert. If stored tightly covered, they will keep for four to five days at room temperature.

FILLING

1¼ cups coarsely chopped dried apricots
1 large apple, peeled, cored and shredded or grated
1 cup water
½ cup mild honey, such as clover
⅛ teaspoon ground cinnamon

CRUST

1 cup all-purpose or unbleached white flour
⅔ cup graham cracker crumbs
2 tablespoons packed dark brown sugar
⅛ teaspoon salt (optional)
2 tablespoons nondiet tub-style canola or corn-oil margarine or butter, chilled and cut into small pieces

To prepare the filling: Preheat the oven to 400°. Coat a 13" × 9" baking dish with nonstick spray. Set aside.

In a medium saucepan, combine the apricots, apples, water, honey and cinnamon. Cook over medium heat, stirring occasionally, for 10 minutes, or until the mixture thickens; reduce the heat slightly if the mixture starts to stick to the bottom of the pan. Set aside.

To prepare the crust: In a medium bowl, combine the flour, crumbs, sugar and salt (if using). Mix well. With a pastry blender or forks, cut in the margarine or butter until the mixture resembles coarse meal.

Evenly press half of the crumbs into the prepared pan. Gently spoon the filling over the crumbs and spread it evenly with the back of the spoon. Top with the remaining crumbs, spreading them out evenly and lightly pressing them into place over the filling.

Bake in the center of the oven for 22 to 26 minutes, or until the top is lightly browned. Place on a wire rack and cool slightly. Cut into bars while still warm.

Makes 36 bars.

Per bar: 55 calories, 0.8 g. total fat (13% of calories), 0.1 g. saturated fat, 0 mg. cholesterol

Vanilla Custard Pudding

It's hard to believe this creamy custard is so low in fat and cholesterol. We serve the custard with our Fresh Cherry Compote or with fresh raspberries or peaches. We also use it in the English Berry Trifle. Store the custard in the refrigerator, where it will keep for two to three days.

    2   cups 1% fat milk
    ½   cup liquid egg substitute
    ⅓   cup granulated sugar
    2   tablespoons cornstarch
    ⅛   teaspoon salt (optional)
    2   teaspoons nondiet tub-style canola or corn-oil margarine or butter
    1   teaspoon vanilla extract

In a 4-cup glass measure, mix the milk and egg substitute. Microwave on high power 2½ to 3½ minutes, stirring after each minute, until the mixture is just hot, but not boiling.

In the top of a double boiler, mix together the sugar, cornstarch and salt (if using). Gradually stir in the milk mixture until smooth.

Cook over 1" of boiling water, stirring vigorously, for 5 to 7 minutes, or until the custard thickens. Remove from the heat. Stir in the margarine or butter and vanilla. Cover and place in the refrigerator. Let cool, stirring occasionally, for about 30 minutes.

Makes 4 servings.

Per serving: 173 calories, 4.2 g. total fat (22% of calories), 1.3 g. saturated fat, 5 mg. cholesterol

Strawberry-Banana Sorbet

We use a food processor rather than an ice-cream maker to quickly create this cool, fresh sorbet. It is pretty and virtually fat free. Although this is best served soon after preparing it, you may store unused portions in the freezer for up to a week; let soften for a few minutes before serving.

    1   medium fully ripe, but not overripe, banana
    3   cups unsweetened frozen strawberries, cut into equal-size pieces
    ½   cup frozen cranberry juice cocktail concentrate
    1-2   tablespoons light corn syrup or mild honey, such as clover

Peel the banana and wrap it in plastic. Freeze for at least 1½ hours, or until solid.

Place the strawberries in a food processor. Process with on/off pulses until finely chopped; stop several times to scrape down the sides of the container. Then process the mixture for about 1½ minutes, or until very smooth. Scrape down the sides of the container.

With the machine running, add the juice concentrate. Process for 1 minute, or until completely smooth.

Slice the frozen banana. With the machine running, slowly add the slices. Process for at least 1 minute, or until the mixture is completely smooth and creamy. Sweeten to taste with the corn syrup or honey; process briefly.

Serve immediately or transfer to a chilled storage container and freeze for 30 minutes.

Makes 6 servings.

Per serving: 164 calories, 0.3 g. total fat (2% of calories), 0 g. saturated fat, 0 mg. cholesterol

Sour Cherry Topping

Use this zesty, fat-free topping to dress up cheesecake or to spoon over meringues filled with scoops of ice milk. The topping keeps in the refrigerator for two to three days. Stir well before serving.

1	can (16 ounces) pitted tart red cherries, with juice
¼	cup thawed frozen cranberry juice cocktail concentrate
¼	cup granulated sugar, or to taste
1	tablespoon water
1	tablespoon cornstarch
½	teaspoon lemon juice

Drain the juice from the cherries to a medium saucepan; reserve the cherries. Stir in the juice concentrate. Boil over high heat for about 5 minutes, or until the juice is reduced to ¼ cup; as most of it evaporates, watch carefully to avoid scorching. Remove from the heat.

In a small bowl, thoroughly stir together the sugar, water, cornstarch and lemon juice. Add to the saucepan. Stir in the cherries.

Return the pan to the stove and bring to a boil over medium heat. Boil, stirring constantly, for 2 minutes, or until the mixture thickens slightly and clears. Remove from the heat and cool to room temperature before serving.

Makes 5 servings.

Per serving: 96 calories, 0.1 g. total fat (1% of calories), 0 g. saturated fat, 0 mg. cholesterol

Chapter 22

NUTRITION
AT A GLANCE

Because cutting fat is a high priority in our kitchens, we often use tables such as the ones that follow to compare the fat content of various types of foods, like dairy products, or to help us choose the most healthful cuts of meat or poultry and the leanest seafoods.

The tables aren't meant to be all-inclusive. With dairy foods in particular, new low-fat products are being developed every day. Use the table to get an idea of what some full-fat and low-fat products are. Then read labels at your supermarket to make the best choices for your needs.

Note that the meats listed have had as much fat as possible trimmed from them. And the poultry has had its fatty skin removed. Be aware that if you don't trim meats or if you consume poultry skin, you will be getting much higher amounts of fat and calories.

Fat Content of Selected Dairy Products

Food	Quantity	Calories	Fat (g.)	% of Calories from Fat
Butter	1 teaspoon	33	3.8	100
Buttermilk	1 cup			
low-fat		99	2.2	20
nonfat		80	0	0
Cream	1 cup			
half-and-half		315	27.8	78
heavy		821	88.1	95
Cream cheese	1 ounce			
whole-fat		100	10.0	88
reduced-fat, package		70	7.0	81
reduced-fat, tub-style		60	5.0	69
nonfat		25	0	0
whipped		100	10.0	90
Hard and semi-soft cheeses	1 ounce			
American		106	8.8	75
blue		100	8.1	73
Cheddar, whole-fat		114	9.4	74
Cheddar, reduced-fat		80	5.0	56
Cheddar, nonfat		40	<0.5	<1
feta		75	6.0	72
Monterey Jack, whole-fat		106	8.6	73
Monterey Jack, reduced-fat		80	5.0	56
mozzarella, whole-milk		80	6.1	69
mozzarella, part-skim		72	4.5	57
mozzarella, low-fat		60	2.0	29
muenster, whole-fat		104	8.5	73
muenster, low-fat		80	5.0	58
Parmesan		129	8.5	60
Swiss, whole-fat		107	7.8	66
Swiss, low-fat		90	5.0	53
Margarine	1 teaspoon			
corn, regular, stick		34	3.8	100
corn, regular, tub-style		34	3.8	100
diet (light)		17	1.9	100
ultra-light		12	1.3	92
liquid soy, regular		34	3.8	100

(continued)

Fat Content of Selected Dairy Products—Continued

Food	Quantity	Calories	Fat (g.)	% of Calories from Fat
Mayonnaise	1 tablespoon			
regular		100	11.1	100
light		40	4.0	90
nonfat		12	0	0
soy		99	11.0	98
Milk	1 cup			
whole (3.3% fat)		150	8.1	49
low-fat (2% fat)		121	4.7	35
low-fat (1% fat)		102	2.6	23
nonfat/skim		86	0.4	5
evaporated, regular		339	19.1	51
evaporated, skim		199	0.5	2
Soft cheeses	1 cup			
cottage cheese, whole-milk (4% fat)		232	10.1	40
cottage cheese, reduced-fat (1% fat)		164	2.3	13
cottage cheese, nonfat		160	<1	5
ricotta cheese, whole-milk		428	31.9	67
ricotta cheese, part-skim		340	19.5	52
ricotta cheese, nonfat		160	0	0
Sour cream	1 ounce			
cultured		61	5.9	86
imitation		59	5.5	83
light		35	2.0	51
nonfat		30	0	0
Yogurt, plain	1 cup			
whole-fat		139	7.4	47
low-fat		144	3.5	22
nonfat		127	0.4	3

Fat Content of Selected Beef Cuts

Cut	Calories	Fat (g.)	% of Calories from Fat
Ground beef			
extra-lean, broiled	225	13.4	55
ground chuck, broiled	282	20.2	66
ground round, broiled	177	7.4	39
lean, broiled	238	15.0	58
regular, broiled	248	16.5	62
Roasts and steaks			
bottom round, braised	181	7.4	38
chuck arm, braised	187	7.4	37
chuck roast, blade, braised	225	12.5	52
eye of round, roasted	149	4.8	31
flank, broiled	176	8.6	46
rib roast, large end, roasted	215	12.8	55
sirloin, top, broiled	170	6.6	37
tenderloin, broiled	180	8.6	45
top round, braised	176	4.9	27

Note: Values are for 3 ounces cooked choice grade, trimmed before cooking.

Fat Content of Selected Pork Cuts

Cut	Calories	Fat (g.)	% of Calories from Fat
Bacon	490	41.9	77
Bacon, Canadian	157	7.2	41
Center loin, roasted	204	11.1	51
Ham, country, roasted	134	4.7	33
Ham, cured butt, cooked	136	3.9	26
Ham, cured shank, cooked	151	5.4	32
Ham, fresh	190	5.4	26
Loin chop, broiled	218	13.0	55
Shoulder, roasted	208	12.7	57
Sirloin, roasted	169	6.1	32
Tenderloin, roasted	141	4.1	27

Note: Values are for 3 ounces cooked, trimmed before cooking.

Fat Content of Selected Seafood

Seafood	Calories	Fat (g.)	% of Calories from Fat
Catfish, channel	127	4.6	33
Clams	126	1.7	12
Cod, Atlantic	64	0.5	7
Cod, Pacific	62	0.5	7
Crab, blue	87	1.5	16
Flounder	99	1.3	12
Grouper	100	1.1	10
Haddock	96	0.8	8
Halibut	119	2.5	19
Lobster	83	0.5	5
Mackerel	223	15.1	61
Mussels, blue	147	3.8	23
Orange roughy	137	7.6	50
Oysters	117	4.2	32
Perch	100	1.0	9
Pompano	179	10.4	52
Red snapper	109	1.5	13
Salmon, Atlantic	151	6.7	40
Salmon, chinook	99	3.7	34
Salmon, smoked	99	3.7	34
Salmon, sockeye	183	9.3	46
Sea bass	105	2.2	19
Shrimp	84	0.9	10
Sole	87	1.1	11
Trout, rainbow	128	3.7	26
Tuna, bluefin	156	5.3	31
Tuna, canned in oil	168	7.0	38
Tuna, canned in water	111	0.5	4
Tuna, skipjack	113	1.1	9
Tuna, yellowfin	118	1.0	8

Note: Values are for 3 ounces cooked (without added fat).

Fat Content of Selected Cuts of Poultry

Cut	Calories	Fat (g.)	% of Calories from Fat
Chicken			
breast, roasted	140	3.0	21
breast, stewed	129	2.6	19
leg, roasted	162	7.2	40
leg, stewed	157	6.8	41
thigh, roasted	178	9.3	49
thigh, stewed	165	8.3	47
wing, roasted	174	6.9	38
wing, stewed	152	6.1	37
Turkey			
breast, roasted	115	0.6	5
ground, cooked	195	11.7	56
ground breast, cooked	107	2.9	26
thigh, roasted	159	6.1	36

Note: Values are for 3 ounces cooked, skin removed before cooking.

Note: <u>Underscored</u> page references indicate boxed text. **Boldface** references indicate photographs. *Italic* references indicate tables.